PRAISE FOR *ACTIVATE BRAND*

We're living in a world that requires leaders to think differently and create a new playbook for operating. There's never been a more important time to lead with purpose and learn from experts like Scott Goodson and Chip Walker.
Hans Vestberg, Chairman and CEO, Verizon

Don't just babysit your brand. Honour and activate your brand to fit the environment.
Steve Wozniak, Co-founder, Apple

This book identifies a fundamental problem facing companies today: How to not merely talk about purpose but actually do it.
Ranjay Gulati, Professor, Harvard Business School

The purpose economy is upon us. This book puts forth a new competitive advantage, 'Movement Thinking', as a way to activate purpose for the people who matter inside and outside your company.
Anand Mahindra, Chairman, Mahindra Group

Purpose unlocks the power of marketing to drive business growth. This book is a blueprint for its execution.
Susan Johnson, CMO, Prudential

Chip Walker and Scott Goodson tackle the toughest part of any purpose journey, which is also the most important one: How to convert wonderful words of a purpose statement into actual behaviour. A must-read for anyone wanting to make sure their purpose work truly connects and drives enduring change.
Amy Fuller, Global Chief Marketing and Communications Officer, Accenture

We can only solve the problems confronting society today – inequality, social injustice, sustainability, polarization – if businesses play a key role. And businesses can only play a role when they lead with purpose. To activate your credible purpose, read this book.
Susan Fournier, Dean, Boston University Questrom School of Business

With a pandemic raging and widespread calls to address societal systemic racism, it's no wonder business leaders in 2020 drew their focus to how company purpose can play a larger role in their organization. They see that creating value for all stakeholders and society at large – not just financial gain for shareholders – means doing more. Done well, many are finding that doing good can also add to the bottom line, and the recommendations within this book share insight on how to activate on this now.

Matthew Lieberman, Chief Marketing Officer, PwC

Activate Brand Purpose

*How to harness the power of movements
to transform your company*

Scott Goodson and Chip Walker

KoganPage

Publisher's note

Every possible effort has been made to ensure that the information contained in this book is accurate at the time of going to press, and the publishers and authors cannot accept responsibility for any errors or omissions, however caused. No responsibility for loss or damage occasioned to any person acting, or refraining from action, as a result of the material in this publication can be accepted by the editor, the publisher or the author.

First published in Great Britain and the United States in 2021 by Kogan Page Limited

2nd Floor, 45 Gee Street	122 W 27th St, 10th Floor	4737/23 Ansari Road
London	New York, NY 10001	Daryaganj
EC1V 3RS	USA	New Delhi 110002
United Kingdom		India

www.koganpage.com

Kogan Page books are printed on paper from sustainable forests.

ISBNs

Hardback	978 1 78966 826 1
Paperback	978 1 78966 824 7
Ebook	978 1 78966 825 4

British Library Cataloguing-in-Publication Data

A CIP record for this book is available from the British Library.

Library of Congress Cataloging-in-Publication Data

Names: Goodson, Scott, author. | Walker, Chip (Brand strategist), author.
Title: Activate brand purpose: how to harness the power of movements to
    transform your company / Scott Goodson and Chip Walker.
Description: London, United Kingdom; New York, NY: Kogan Page Limited,
    2021. | Includes bibliographical references and index.
Identifiers: LCCN 2020054350 (print) | LCCN 2020054351 (ebook) | ISBN
    9781789668261 (hardback) | ISBN 9781789668247 (paperback) | ISBN
    9781789668254 (ebook)
Subjects: LCSH: Social responsibility of business. | Industries–Social
    aspects. | Branding (Marketing)–Social aspects.
Classification: LCC HD60 .G6628 2021 (print) | LCC HD60 (ebook) | DDC 658.4/08–dc23
LC record available at https://lccn.loc.gov/2020054350
LC ebook record available at https://lccn.loc.gov/2020054351

Typeset by Integra Software Services Pondicherry
Print production managed by Jellyfish
Printed and bound by CPI Group (UK) Ltd, Croydon CR0 4YY

CONTENTS

LIST OF FIGURES

ABOUT THE AUTHORS

Scott Goodson, based in New York, is the founder and CEO of Strawberry-Frog. For the last 25 years, he has worked with some of the world's most iconic companies including Google, Emirates Airlines, Heineken, Coca-Cola, Jim Beam, Mercedes, Mahindra and Walmart. He invented the concept of *Movement Thinking*, an approach that uses the principles of societal movements to solve marketing and leadership challenges. Scott has lectured on the subject at Harvard Business School, Columbia, Cambridge, TEDx, on BBC World Service, NPR, CNN, and has appeared in *The New York Times*, *Financial Times*, *The Wall Street Journal*, *The Economist*, *Harvard Business Review*, *Fast Company, Inc.* and *Forbes*.

Chip Walker, based in New York, is the head of strategy and a partner at StrawberryFrog. He's recognized for his expertise in brand creation and re-invention, and has led the charge in transforming brands such as Goldman Sachs, Lexus, Bank of America, Jim Beam, and Heineken. Chip is a frequent speaker at some of the branding world's major events, including the Cannes Lions Festival, the Advertising Research Foundation, Sustainable Brands and the Conference Board. His writing and opinions have appeared widely in places like *Adweek*, *The New York Times*, *Chicago Tribune* and CNBC.

ACKNOWLEDGEMENTS

This book is based principally on the personal experiences and projects that Scott Goodson and Chip Walker have stewarded with leaders. For this book, we interviewed dozens of people including the CEOs, CMOs, CHROs, CSOs, and other leaders of some of the most admired companies in the world. The interviews were conducted on an attribution basis, meaning that we could interview the executives and publish their interviews verbatim. They were an indispensable resource. Journalist Rae Ann Fera provided a tremendous service to the authors with her research and guidance. Elizabeth Scordato provided an incredibly useful management of our process, working closely with Madisen Anderson, who provided a valuable timeline, and each of them steeped themselves in our vision of Movement Thinking. We are particularly grateful for the extraordinary work of these three talented people.

As for books on purpose, we inhaled the especially vast contemporary literature but would like to thank Adam Morgan, Jim Stengel and Afdhel Aziz for their works. Our thanks also to the invaluable partnership with Kylie Wright-Ford and her team at RepTrak on the Purpose Power Index.

In 2020, anyone in the world would understand that as COVID-19 expanded across the globe, it has been an unprecedented time to write and publish a new book. We would like to take this opportunity to thank those who joined us on this extraordinary journey. During the publishing of Scott Goodson's *Uprising* in 2011, we thanked all those who helped in the publishing of the book, but now we wish to thank those who run the printing presses, who are physically present in the warehouses, the truck drivers. With this in mind, we want to also thank all those who have kept our lives moving forward during difficult and often unprecedented times presented by the COVID-19 pandemic: grocery store clerks, shelf stockers, shipping delivery drivers, as well as the post office and mail carriers, and of course all the healthcare professionals who have dealt with the virus despite the setbacks and surges. These are modern heroes and we wish to salute them.

And we want to also thank all those in proximity to our quarantined homes who made this new book possible. At StrawberryFrog, we would like to thank David Orton for his stylish figure designs. We wish to thank the extraordinarily supportive Nicola Conneally, as well as Sarah Landsberg,

Ali Demos and Maeve Doherty. At Kogan Page, we have had the good fortune to work with excellent editors, Stephen Dunnell and Heather Wood, and Amanda Picken, our copy editor, who were able to bring this publication to market during incredibly difficult circumstances, and we are very grateful to the entire team and board at Kogan Page, who believed in the book and its global appeal.

We remain grateful to our remarkable and committed colleagues at StrawberryFrog without whom our day-to-day work would not be possible. We are incredibly grateful to our loved ones who have supported us throughout this book and lived with us night and day during the pandemic: Karin Drakenberg Goodson, Jacoby and Ellis Goodson, and Vera the Nova Scotia Duck Toller, who was a most helpful support during the quarantine. Chip would like to thank Stan, Veli, Elissa, Eleanor, and Nick for putting up with him during the quarantine and beyond.

Scott Goodson and Chip Walker
StrawberryFrog (not in our offices in the
Empire State Building due to COVID-19)

ABBREVIATIONS

ACS	Affiliated Computer Services Inc.
Amex	American Express
ANA	Association of National Advertisers
B2B	Business-to-business
BHAG	Big hairy audacious goal
BLM	Black Lives Matter
BS	Bullshit
CEO	Chief executive officer
CFO	Chief financial officer
CHRO	Chief human resources officer
CMO	Chief marketing officer
CSR	Corporate social responsibility
CV	Curriculum vitae
DNA	Deoxyribonucleic acid
ESG	Environmental, social and corporate governance
EVP	Executive vice president
EY	Ernst & Young
FAB	First Abu Dhabi Bank
FGB	First Gulf Bank
GPTW	Great Places to Work
HBR	*Harvard Business Review*
HR	Human resources
IBM	International Business Machines
IT	Information technology
LBH	LifeBridge Health
LGTBQ	Lesbian, gay, bisexual, transgender and queer
M&A	Mergers and acquisitions
MAT	Medically assisted treatment
MD	Maryland
NAACP	National Association for the Advancement of Colored People
NBAD	National Bank of Abu Dhabi
NBFC	Non-banking finance company
OECD	Organisation for Economic Co-operation and Development

PPI	Purpose Power Index
PR	Public relations
PTSD	Post-traumatic stress disorder
PwC	PricewaterhouseCoopers
REI	Recreational Equipment, Inc.
SUV	Sport utility vehicle
SVP	Senior vice president
TED	Ted Conferences
TP	Toilet paper
UAE	United Arab Emirates
UK	United Kingdom
US	United States
USAA	United Services Automobile Association
VP	Vice president
VUCA	Volatility, uncertainty, complexity and ambiguity
VW	Volkswagen
WEF	World Economic Forum

Introduction

Movement Thinking: How to lead a revolution at work

We started writing this book just as COVID-19 descended on New York City. We sat on the 48th floor of the Empire State Building in early 2020 and mapped out what we felt was an important advancement in helping leaders create a competitive advantage. On that day, we coined the idea of Movement Thinking™. Just as Design Thinking gave designers a human-centric approach to creating things, Movement Thinking is a human-centric approach to changing things in a peer-to-peer world and the purpose economy. It uses the principles of societal movements to mobilize the people that matter to your brand inside and out. Many great entrepreneurs, as well as innovators in literature, art, music, science, engineering and business, have practised it. The premise of Movement Thinking is that the processes that create great social movements can help us systematically apply a human-centred approach to solve problems in a creative and innovative way – in our lives, in our businesses, in our communities and countries.

As we brainstormed that day, we had no way of knowing just how relevant our work would become to purpose-driven companies. Because of the results of our Purpose Power Index (PPI) – the world's first empirical measure of purpose-driven brands – we had unequivocal evidence that brands that activated their purpose inside and outside their organization fared better than those that did not. But the COVID-19 crisis made this even clearer. Companies that had a purpose and actualized it were avoiding panic, shifting into recovery, and thriving better than those that did not.

We introduced the marketing world to movements over 20 years ago with the launch of the Smart Car, developed and brought to the world by Swatch and Mercedes Benz. Back then the Movement Marketing idea was 'to reinvent the urban environment'. In those days the problems at the heart of cities, like unending traffic jams, automotive sprawl, lack of parking, pollution, rental car parking lots full of cars on weekends, made no sense. In fact, it caused people to feel unhealthy both emotionally and physically. Our idea was to launch the new B-segment automobile, not with ads talking about unique features and facilities of the car, but rather by positioning it as the mobility solution to the enemy of us all: *urban congestion*. This was a breakthrough. On a collective level, the stakes were high. We knew that we lived in complex times with complex thoughts and needs. We knew that we were having more complex conversations about the urban problems we all faced as a collective and that together we could overcome them. Together we could rethink old orthodoxies and create new solutions. The movement to reinvent the urban environment provided limitless connectivity to people and organizations with the same goal of righting a common wrong and fixing a common problem. In effect, we brought to bear what Josh Newman, a former client at Walmart, describes as 'the power of people to push ideas into action'.

We continued to spark external marketing movements around the globe for brands ranging from Emirates Airlines to Google, Jim Beam, LG in Korea, Pampers, Northwell Health, and the Government of Dubai (many of these cases were presented in Scott Goodson's first bestselling book, *Uprising: How to build a brand and change the world by sparking cultural movements*, 2011). But over the years, we've come to realize that the principles of societal movements can solve even broader problems.

Today, we are applying Movement Thinking not just in marketing to grow brands, but to internal employee engagement, culture and habit change, to organizational transformation and leadership advisory for clients like Coca-Cola, LifeBridge Health and Walmart. Based on our combined experience, and hundreds of movements behind us, we've learned a thing or two about defining purpose and making it sticky by activating it with Movement Thinking. We've expanded our company and today it lives at the intersection of creative, funky agencies with rebel attitude, and purpose experts, change management consultancies and innovations companies.

This book is about how to think about purpose today, how to activate and actualize it with a movement inside your organization and outside among different stakeholders. Movement Thinking is designed for this new time, the time of Instagram, Facebook and Snapchat, to capitalize on our natural human desire to belong to a bigger idea that galvanizes us to do something. In this book, we'll be illustrating several movements that will serve to inspire you to think bigger.

We are movement-makers and problem-solvers. Many of the ideas in this book formed over years of working through business problems and arguing the importance of purpose and designing a movement to activate that purpose, sometimes with leaders who didn't see the point. We can't help but ask a question: how can we simply do business transformation and more marketing/advertising when the world faces great problems? Thus, our purpose strategies and movements drive positive change around environmental and social issues in a time when a greater number of consumers demand it, not to mention the CEO participants of the Business Roundtable.

One thing we've noticed about movement culture is that it can be contagious. When you spend time with others around an idea you feel passionate about, you invariably start to pay close attention to the things that matter in this new shared reality. In modern life, where our attention spans are briefer than a goldfish's, a movement helps you notice and engage with things and also avoid engaging with things. These aspects suggest to us that Movement Thinking is a revolutionary management change and marketing idea in revolutionary times.

01

A call to arms

How to activate purpose with Movement Thinking

The tag on the back of the new pair of pants bought for Scott's 90-year-old mother had a secret. When you flipped the size tag on the back of the waistband, it read 'Vote the a**holes out'. Patagonia is a purpose-driven brand unafraid to mince words. The company and its followers believe in saving the great outdoors and they live their purpose every day, sometimes to the extreme – to great effect for the planet but also for the business. That's why, with 40 days to go before the US election, people like Scott and his mother were finding covert messages in their clothing. Patagonia knew that sewing this message in its clothing would generate headlines and stoke its base, its fans, its consumers to vote.

This is exactly the kind of move you'd expect from Patagonia; its leadership is known for their stances regarding protecting nature and their direct forms of political activism. In fact, CEO Yvon Chouinard has been saying 'Vote the a**holes out' for several years, referring to politicians from any party who deny or disregard the climate crisis and ignore science, not because they aren't aware of it, but because their pockets are lined with money from oil and gas interests (Walk-Morris, 2020).

But the action didn't stop there: Patagonia implemented measures to help employees and customers to vote, such as closing its California headquarters, distribution centre and all retail stores on 3 November, election day; it encouraged its employees to volunteer as poll workers by providing up to four days of paid time off and provided access to a photocopier in areas where voters needed to produce copies of their ID for their mail-in ballots. The company also worked with non-profit partnerships to give grants, paid ads and other resources to organizations working to ensure November's elections were accessible – particularly for groups working with communities whose voting rights historically have been suppressed (Walk-Morris, 2020).

While marketing around areas like sustainability and environmentalism is growing mainstream, few brands had directly challenged the president of the United States in this way, given the obvious threat of backlash and other repercussions. But if brands like Patagonia know their employees and audience well and operate in a tight enough niche, they may be able to ignite passions, generate significant online engagement, and reinforce their core customer base, as Patagonia appeared to have done with its latest tag action.

When we talk about activating brand purpose, as we will throughout this book, this is a highly provocative example of what we mean. Not every example is as stark, as you will see in the following pages. This one serves to illustrate the activation of purpose in a highly dramatic way. With its clothing tags, Patagonia transformed its purpose of being in business to *save our home planet* into an active political statement (though as the stories that follow in these pages will show, not every business purpose success story needs to be activated in a political manner; most of the examples that follow do not). It didn't let its purpose lay dormant; its provocation gave additional fuel to its movement that has been burning bright for many years – to address the climate crisis with action and urgency.

Patagonia's actions also demonstrate one of the core tenets of brand purpose activation: it's much more than marketing; it's at the core of strategy, part of everything a company does. As Patagonia European Marketing Director Alex Weller told *Marketing Week* in 2018:

> You can't reverse into a mission and values through marketing. The organizations that are struggling with this are probably the ones that are thinking about marketing first. The role of marketing is to authentically elevate that mission and purpose and engage people in it, but the purpose needs to be the business. (Rogers, 2018)

That's what this book is about: activating the purpose that already exists within the brand or company in a way that puts all of the tools at a company's disposal to work with the same goal. Marketing is just one of those tools. A movement is a new leadership tool, a business operations process that uses creativity and emotion to rally everyone within a company to work in concert. Many organizations have defined a brand purpose. The important dynamics of business success are increasingly becoming related to doing something tangible with that purpose such as mobilizing people. Movement Thinking as a new management science, or more accurately an art, is emerging and for the first time, the concept of managing human minds through Movement Thinking is being taken seriously by the new business leaders.

This book is a call to arms for those leaders and business pioneers whose experiences have led them to the same conclusion as the authors: that Movement Thinking, igniting purpose with creativity and innovation, will differentiate your brand in a way that gives it a sustainable business advantage.

In a world where leaders and companies have access to the same data and talent, leaders who realize the critical importance of galvanizing employees will have a competitive advantage. In an increasingly competitive environment, we believe that sparking a movement is the key to success. Movement Thinking is about company change and growth, creating momentum and motivation. We're living in a purpose economy, where business will increasingly be driven by human movements as the predominant marketplace factor and leadership skill. For you and those you lead, you should note that it will not be easy to operate this way. But making yourself reject the familiar in favour of an alternative approach, making movement momentum real, will be the surest path to success. It's time to be brave and take responsibility for driving change. Here's to a more proactive, positive and empowering approach to leadership. Welcome to the revolution.

We should note, this book is not about finding purpose – there are entire shelves lined with books and *Harvard Business Review* articles on this topic. Here, we will focus on purpose activation and what holds purpose back. That said, allow us this exception: we'd like to tell you how StrawberryFrog discovered its own purpose of helping other brands activate theirs. It starts with another story.

Designing, then activating brand purpose

When PepsiCo CEO Indra Nooyi stood on the field at Yankee Stadium in 2008, she wasn't there to make a political speech or even throw a ceremonial pitch. She was showing off PepsiCo's new product to the company's shareholders who filled the stands. What she held in her hand, however, wasn't a new chip flavour; it wasn't a new soda brand. It was TrueNorth, a health-conscious nut snack from Frito-Lay (a division of PepsiCo) – and PepsiCo's first consumer brand that had a purpose – that Nooyi declared was to be a model for the company's future.

At the time, the concept of a snack brand having a purpose was a bit out of left field – the purpose conversation that we now hear so much of had yet to fill the halls of power. But Nooyi saw how the sands were shifting, that people were coming to expect more of brands and corporations, they were losing patience with companies that were profiting on the backs of the people. She saw how the cultural moment was just right for a product like True North. People were wising up to how unhealthy snacks were contributing to the runaway obesity problem in the United States and around the world. Although the bans on extra-large sodas that New York City mayor Michael Bloomberg would eventually put forth were a couple of years away, there was a rising tide of consumers seeking better and healthier food choices.

That's why Nooyi was receptive to an idea StrawberryFrog presented to her about a better-for-you nut snack aimed chiefly at Boomers with the purpose of helping them find their passion in life. At the time, we sat down with bags of delicious but nameless nut clusters and began to imagine what this brand of snacks could be. We were guided by the insight that women between the ages of 35 and 50 were cutting way back on eating traditional snacks. So, if they weren't interested in the concept of traditional snacks, what about this brand-to-be would appeal to them?

As we delved into cultural research, we noticed something interesting: this demographic was entering a point in their lives at which our cultural research found people began thinking about their legacy. This presented an opportunity to create a purpose-driven brand that helped people connect with their own purpose. Named True North, the brand was launched in 2008 with a movement in which we encouraged people to share their own stories about finding their calling – their own *true north*. We received 2,300 entries (well above our goal) of people finding their passion. The winning story was that of Lisa Nigro, creator of Chicago's Inspiration Café, which fed the homeless with respect and dignity. The winner was announced at the Oscars with a commercial directed by Hollywood star Helen Hunt. More than just a campaign, True North Stories became a movement that activated True North's brand purpose of helping people search for their own true passion.

At the time, Regan Ebert was vice president/GM of Warehouse Direct Business Unit at Frito-Lay (she's now senior vice president of Danone North America) and worked to help bring TrueNorth to market. Reflecting on the launch in a conversation with us, she said that for companies like PepsiCo, business growth was typically achieved by buying existing brands. Her task with TrueNorth was to build the brand from scratch:

> We broke new ground by designing a new good-for-you nut snack brand
> around a purpose, and then we activated it among consumers with Movement

Marketing. With the TrueNorth movement, we were able to exceed our Year 1 expectations, and proved that this model of marketing and brand building was genuinely effective at a time when traditional advertising was in decline and seeing limitations.

This was not the first time StrawberryFrog had developed a purpose-based brand and activated that strategy with a movement. Years earlier, back in the early 1990s, Scott owned an agency in Stockholm, Sweden. At that time, Nordic consumers were demanding more from their brands. They wanted companies to reduce packaging and waste, they wanted more women on boards, and they wanted fewer toxins in their household products and in food. From this consumer awakening, Swedish brands that Scott worked with sought purpose strategies to help showcase how brands and companies were committed to solving these bigger issues with creativity. Brands like IKEA democratized style so not only the rich could have a beautiful home, but everyone could. Stockholm-based Pharmacia took a stand for improving quality of life and against simply manufacturing medicines for profit – Pharmacia ignited the 'To Life' movement.

As we referenced in the introduction to this book, our first experience with Movement Marketing came when StrawberryFrog – at the time a nascent agency started by Scott and Karin Drakenberg – launched the Smart Car for the Switzerland-based Micro Car Company. Rather than devise an advertising campaign, StrawberryFrog created a purpose for the start-up B-segment car brand and then activated it with a movement against congestion. It was a movement for small, for sustainability; it was an idea that people could relate to and join called 'Reduce to the Max'. It was about tackling urban issues and reinventing the city environment for the better, bringing together consumers, city officials, parking authorities and rental car companies all to drive positive change. This launch was a shoe-drop moment for us. We realized that this was the way we wanted to work, that we wanted to drive positive change, and from there we wrote our own purpose for StrawberryFrog: *Use creativity for good.*

Fast forward to 2008 and this search for purpose was on the rise in the United States, which we saw when working on TrueNorth. People were getting fatter, the planet was becoming more polluted, the climate was in crisis and yet businesses continued to make money at the expense of stakeholders. It was still the era of a shareholder-takes-all mentality of business. When Chip and Scott sat down in their office at StrawberryFrog with that silver pouch of nut clusters they realized that world-renowned economist

Milton Friedman had it wrong. His view that a business's chief priority was to create shareholder value didn't feel right. It seemed like there was a better way, that as communicators we had an opportunity to change the message. That companies can make a difference in people's lives by tackling the bigger issues, and that it is in their interest to do so. That business should serve all the stakeholders – employees, the community, society, consumers – as well as shareholders.

At that point, we transformed StrawberryFrog's business from a creative-driven advertising agency pioneering movement marketing to a company that uses Movement marketing to help leaders activate higher purpose. Which in turn leads to transformation and growth for their companies, inside and out. We operate under the belief that businesses have the ability to drive social and human progress in ways that governments can't always do. We believe that a company's purpose should extend to how it engages with its employees. Not only that, we believe that companies should drive positive change in the world, not simply because they have the global reach that's not confined by borders or nationhood. Rather, they should do it because it's ultimately in the best interests of companies for their customers to live longer, for the health of the planet to be sustained, and for their employees to be treated equitably and to prosper.

In the chapters to come, we'll talk to business leaders from around the world to find out how they've activated purpose and used Movement Thinking to do things like uniting a multifaceted conglomerate or radically transforming corporate culture. We'll talk to those who use movements to engage, evaluate and reward employees, and those who have helped the lives of their customers with movements that inform, educate and inspire. And we'll hear from a visionary leader on why the future of business hinges on understanding purpose as something far greater than a do-gooder exercise, but as something that is essential to remain successful in the purpose economy.

But before we do that, read on to understand what we actually mean by purpose, why everyone seems so enthusiastic about purpose in the first place, how to avoid common missteps along the purpose journey, and how to start getting yourself in the Movement Thinking mindset.

The purpose craze

While we've been at this purpose game for a while at StrawberryFrog, we've seen a profound shift as of late. Purpose has moved from a nice to have to a house-on-fire necessity. You could say there's a purpose craze going on in the world right now. How do we know? There are several indicators.

Oxford University and Ernst & Young found that discourse about corporate purpose has increased fivefold since 1994 and is trending at a rate that surpasses conversations around sustainability (*Harvard Business Review*, 2015). Evidence of that trend bore out in marketing circles when, in 2018, 'brand purpose' was the Association of National Advertisers' marketing word of the year, its buzz-worthiness fuelled by interest among ANA members who were shifting focus from selling to consumers to engaging them (Duggan, 2018).

The more high-profile indicator that brand purpose is reaching a tipping point is the fact that the chief executives of the World Economic Forum (WEF) have made it a priority at their annual meeting in Davos for the last few years. Virgin CEO Richard Branson provided leadership on the issue when at the 2016 meeting he said, 'It's always been my objective to create businesses with a defined purpose beyond just making money' (Branson, 2016).

That sentiment has grown to the point that the theme for its 2020 meeting was 'Stakeholders for a Cohesive and Sustainable World', during which WEF executives issued a manifesto (Schwab, 2019) on purpose. In part, that manifesto declares the purpose of a company is to engage not just shareholders but all its stakeholders – employees, customers, suppliers, local communities and society at large – in shared value creation. But perhaps the most surprising part of the manifesto is the assertion that a company's performance should be measured based on how it achieves its environmental, social and governance objectives (ESG), not just generating profit.

This is an incredible evolution in thinking that, to us, signals an understanding that purpose is neither simply a feel-good CSR activity, nor relegated to a single issue like environmental causes; it shows us that business leaders are coming to the realization that a company's purpose must exist in a larger societal context.

What is purpose?

Before we go any further we want to take a moment to contemplate a core question: what is purpose? This might seem obvious, but there are a few ways to think about it, so it's worth defining how we view purpose at StrawberryFrog.

The simplest definition is the underlying fundamental reason a business exists. Any brand that's met with any level of success has got to have somewhere in its DNA a good reason for being; otherwise, it wouldn't be very successful. This kind of purpose tends to be more functional. Google's purpose is to *organize the world's information* and make it universally accessible, for example.

Then there's higher brand purpose. In other words, the reason a brand exists beyond making money, a reason that is noble and beneficial to society, a reason that reflects the aspirations of the company. Afdhel Aziz, co-founder of global purpose consultancy Conspiracy of Love, and author of *Good is the New Cool* and the forthcoming book *The Principles of Purpose*, which is co-authored by Bobby Jones, put it eloquently in a conversation we had about purpose:

> Purpose is the soul of a company. It should reflect the aspirations of a company and it should be a common dream that people have when they join a company. That dream helps define what the company can be and the world that its people can create together.

Through that lens, higher purpose is rooted in the story of the brand and helps guide everything from internal communications and policies to brand communication, social activism and innovation. Patagonia is in business to help save the planet; SunTrust (now Truist) exists to eliminate financial stress and enable financial confidence for all.

Both of these views of purpose – functional and societal – can successfully define why a brand exists. But to us, the most successful brands for the future will be those whose purpose contributes to the greater societal good. Brands that are self-aware enough and take the time and effort to do so will gain the support of *all* stakeholders – not just customers or shareholders, but employees and the broader communities the company serves.

A guide in times of crisis

Purpose also provides companies guidance in times of change and turmoil. In his telling of how higher purpose helped revive *This Old House*, the PBS show he executive-produced from 2004 to 2016, Scott Omelianuk, now editor-in-chief of *Inc.* magazine, wrote that brand purpose isn't a slogan or a mission. It's not about copying companies like Patagonia through corporate social responsibility (CSR) initiatives. Instead, he said, a strong brand purpose is the starting point for a dialogue with consumers:

> When it's internal (like a sense of direction), not external (like someone else's map), brand purpose helps you understand why you matter to people. In a changing business landscape, brand purpose helps you continually reorient your core capabilities to remain relevant, even as market and methods change, sometimes drastically. (Omelianuk, 2019)

Indeed, throughout 2020 we saw companies around the world struggling to adapt following the emergence of COVID-19, which turned into a global pandemic. Companies grasped for ways to do right by their employees and customers. In our opinion, the ones driven by a higher purpose found their footing faster.

Maryam Banikarim, chief marketing officer at Nextdoor, a hyperlocal social networking service for neighbourhoods, told us that in uncertain times purpose is a grounding force. She saw that play out at Nextdoor, whose purpose is to *cultivate a kinder world where everyone has a neighbourhood they can rely on*, during the pandemic:

> As COVID-19 hit, our employees were galvanized. We quickly turned to enabling neighbours to help each other – offering to run groceries for each other, support their local businesses, and care for essential workers. It was a reminder that when we all have neighbours we can rely on, the world is a better, kinder place.

In conversation with us for this book, T-Mobile President and CEO Mike Sievert (who we speak with again in Chapter 8's discussion on purpose and mergers) said that purpose has been a driving force in the telecom company's response to the pandemic. Fuelled by its 'Un-carrier' movement, which positions T-Mobile as a customer-centric antithesis to its competitors, the company quickly pivoted to increase its network capacity to meet demand and it launched Project 10Million with the goal of ensuring unconnected schoolkids had internet access. In an op-ed on the pandemic, he called on the business community to prepare for the next set of societal challenges that will inevitably arise by tackling big issues with solutions that deliver long-term impacts. As he wrote, COVID-19 has laid bare the need for society to step up and make rapid changes. 'We *all* have a role to play in bringing about changes when called upon. The truth is, we have no other choice! Because whether big business or individual citizen – we have only one collective future' (Sievert, 2020).

Actions like these, says Suzanne Tosolini, growth consultant at purpose consultancy the Jim Stengel Company, are what set purpose-driven companies apart. The pandemic, she said to us, revealed that to be relevant and meaningful in times of crisis, brands must prove their worth. While many brands showed empathy, she said that more than anything, purpose-driven brands need to be useful. 'As always, actions speak louder than words and brands with a defined purpose are more clearly able to determine what they care about and where they should act in times of crisis.'

How stakeholders eclipsed shareholders

The stories of Nextdoor and T-Mobile above show that in the purpose economy, all stakeholders matter, and that perspective has been gaining support from business power players. As the 2020 agenda at Davos showed, our current global reality is shaping how companies, corporations and brands behave. This stance was cemented in late 2019 when Larry Fink, CEO of BlackRock, which is the single largest corporate investor in the world, said in his annual letter to CEOs that he would only invest in those companies that have a strategy for climate change:

> A pharmaceutical company that hikes prices ruthlessly, a mining company that shortchanges safety, a bank that fails to respect its clients – these companies may maximize returns in the short term. But, as we have seen, again and again, these actions that damage society will catch up with a company and destroy shareholder value. (Fink, 2019)

It was earth-shattering stuff from the world's most influential investor. And it had a near-instant impact. Mere weeks after Fink's announcement, the Business Roundtable, which consists of CEOs from the 182 largest corporations in America, issued their 'Statement on the Purpose of a Corporation', which, they said, was to supersede any previous statements by the group. 'While each of our individual companies serves its own corporate purpose, we share a fundamental commitment to all of our stakeholders,' the letter said (Business Roundtable, 2019). Those commitments include: delivering value to customers; investing in employees; dealing fairly and ethically with suppliers; supporting the communities in which they work by embracing sustainable practices; and generating long-term value for shareholders.

So why is this happening now? In short: uncertainty and fear. These days, the news media trades on sensationalized click-bait headlines to draw in readers, leaving us with a constant barrage of scary news. We're inundated with the multitude of problems facing our existence on the planet, whether technological or climate-oriented or nuclear or military or, as we saw throughout 2020, viral. It all leaves us searching for something more – for purpose.

Who do we trust to help fix these problems? Not the government it seems, since the OECD and others have shown that in 2019 most citizens globally don't trust their own governments (OECD, 2020). As a result, we're turning to the business world for answers. Consumers, particularly younger ones, are pushing for companies to be more socially conscious; they expect their employers to take a stand on important issues (Glassdoor, 2017); they want the brands they support to actually develop strategies that help society in addition to stakeholders.

A paper from Brian Tayan, a researcher with the Corporate Governance Research Initiative at Stanford Graduate School of Business, found that 64 per cent of global consumers believe CEOs 'should take the lead on change rather than waiting for the government to impose it'. As well, 56 per cent said they have 'no respect for CEOs that remain silent on important issues'. Another thing to consider is that as Millennials age into middle and senior management, their world view begins to shape corporate policy, and potential recruits look to employers to have a higher purpose (Larcker *et al*, 2018).

Purpose has a *big* problem

With so much evidence that consumers expect companies to have a higher purpose and take a stand on societal issues, all of these corporations and brands trying to do so must be succeeding, right? Wrong.

'The Business Case for Purpose', a global survey of 474 executives from Harvard Business Review Analytic Services and the EY Beacon Institute, found that while 90 per cent of executives surveyed said their company understands the importance of purpose, less than half said purpose informs their strategic and operational decision-making. In fact, only 37 per cent of executives say their purpose is well articulated and understood by their employees (*Harvard Business Review*, 2015). This is what we refer to as the Purpose Gap (see box below), the chasm between intentions and actions.

It's also true that consumers generally fail to give companies and brands credit for having a higher purpose. We know this because we recently launched the Purpose Power Index (purposepowerindex.com) working with RepTrak (formerly Reputation Institute), a renowned consumer research firm, to create the first empirical study of purpose-based brands. The first wave of the research received over 17,000 responses in the US and was conducted in September 2019.

We'll go into the method and findings of the study in much more depth in Chapter 7, but the results undeniably show that most consumers think the vast majority of companies and brands are *not* purpose-driven but, more importantly, those that are purpose-driven rise to the top only when they've effectively activated purpose inside and outside their organizations. Across the 200-plus companies and brands included in the survey, a majority (54 per cent) received a 'Weak' or 'Poor' score. Only 3 per cent of the brands we evaluated were seen by consumers as highly purpose-driven. The top 10 purpose brands are: Seventh Generation, TOMS Shoes, Method, REI, Wegmans, Stonyfield Organic, USAA, allbirds, Chick-fil-A and Ben & Jerry's.

This focus on how people perceive brand purpose is particularly important since we found that consumers reward brands they perceive as having a higher purpose. They're more likely to recommend and buy from the company or brand, as well as to advocate for it and give it the benefit of the doubt in a crisis.

It's also worth noting that the purpose problem isn't limited to consumer companies and brands; it also happens in the B2B world. A 2020 report called the 'B2B Purpose Paradox', a collaborative effort conducted by the ANA, Carol Cone ON PURPOSE and the Harris Poll, revealed that 86 per cent of B2B companies embrace purpose as important to growth, but only 24 per cent said purpose is embedded in their business to the point of influencing innovation, operations and their engagement with society (Cone, 2020). This is what the authors call the 'B2B Purpose Paradox'.

Why asking 'why' is not enough

So, if there's so much interest in brand purpose, why are so few companies succeeding? Why are the brands that you might expect to be purpose-driven failing to connect with and be rewarded by consumers? What are leaders getting wrong?

A big part of the problem is that business leaders become so focused on finding and articulating their purpose – their 'why' – that they neglect to actually do something with it. Their higher purpose never gets activated and just lies there dormant.

By now most of us are familiar with the notion of a brand's 'why', which was popularized by Simon Sinek in 2009 in his book *Start With Why*. During his TED Talk on the topic, Sinek outlined how most companies start with their 'what', which is the indisputable thing that they do (Sinek, 2009). Better ones get to their how, or their unique selling proposition. Very few organizations know their 'why', which is how Sinek describes a higher purpose.

To borrow from Sinek's TED Talk, here's how he articulates the difference between starting with why versus starting with what (TED, 2009). He uses Apple, since it's an easy-to-understand example.

If Apple started with 'what', its marketing might sound like this, he says: 'We make great computers. They're beautifully designed, simple to use, and user friendly. Want to buy one?' By contrast, he says, a brand that starts with its 'why', Apple actually markets like this: 'Everything we do, we believe in challenging the status quo, we believe in thinking differently. The way we challenge the status quo is by making our products beautifully designed, simple to use, and user friendly. We just happen to make great computers. Want to buy one?'

'People don't buy what you do, people buy why you do it,' he says. We couldn't agree more. But we go one step further: to be truly considered a purpose-driven brand, getting to your 'why' is not enough – that 'why' needs activation.

This book is designed to take you beyond why to deal with the number one issue facing purpose brands: the need for actualization.

INTRODUCING THE PURPOSE GAP
How to measure purpose

There's great agreement among company leaders that purpose is important, but there are still many questions about how to measure success. In its April 2020 report titled 'Purpose: Shifting from why to how', global management consulting firm McKinsey found that of 1,000 US participants surveyed, 82 per cent agreed that purpose was important. Unfortunately, only 42 per cent said their company's stated purpose had much effect (Gast *et al*, 2020).

What's the Purpose Gap? The way we help clients measure this gap when launching a movement is by assessing whether or not the movement is still being adopted and used by front-line staff 18 months after it launches. We measure the Purpose Gap by surveying employees on key questions, such as:

- understanding of the company purpose and movement;
- feeling like they are living the purpose;
- degree of participation in the movement;
- level of energy and enthusiasm they have for the purpose.

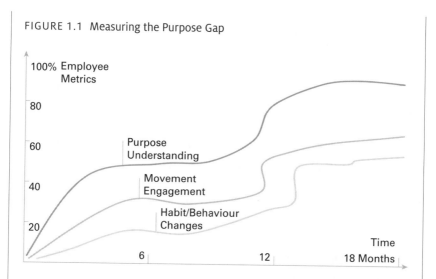

FIGURE 1.1 Measuring the Purpose Gap

SOURCE StrawberryFrog

So, the test of a purpose is, obviously, not whether it is met rapturously when it is unveiled by the leadership team, but whether it is still being used as a rudder in the water by the staff a year and a half later. The gap between those two events is the Purpose Gap, or as Adam Morgan, founder of UK-based brand consultancy eatbigfish calls it, the purpose distance. If, after time, it's vibrant and alive, that's the sign of a healthy movement. If not, then it's a sign that something didn't connect and requires a fresh look.

Why activate your 'why'?

Why is purpose alone not enough? Why does it need to be activated? We asked purpose expert Suzanne Tosolini these exact questions. She said that in today's world, where brands are expected to have a point of view on everything from government policy to pop culture to social issues, operating from purpose guides a brand's reaction to these things. 'A great purpose articulation is ideally supported by a set of values that translate into and guide what a brand chooses to care about in the world,' she said.

In wondering why you should activate your 'why', we've found in our experience there are four major reasons.

1. An activated brand purpose ensures that all internal stakeholders are on the same page strategically

This sounds like basic table stakes of business, but we're frequently surprised by the degree to which we go into a company and the employees are either unaware of or don't know what to do with the brand's higher purpose. This is especially true of companies with a lot of front-line, public-facing employees.

One leader who understands this is our client SunTrust (now Truist), a bank with over 22,000 employees across 1,400 branches. Working in close collaboration with the leadership, we sought to unify all of the bank's stakeholders around a single higher idea. We discovered that many Americans were still living in the shadow of the recession. Despite the supposed economic recovery, our research found that in 2015, 75 per cent of Americans were still financially stressed. That led to a powerful way of framing SunTrust's purpose in the form of a movement: *a stand against financial stress for financial confidence*. This resonated with the bank's leaders and galvanized front-line team mates, and it also struck a chord with the consumers, many of whom were experiencing financial stress. Through the 'onUp' movement, SunTrust was able to change the company culture and employee behaviour and, in the process, drive positive change. This approach was highly relevant and engaging to people outside the bank but also inside the company, from the ground–up, versus top–down. We'll share more details about how we did this in the coming chapters.

2. An activated purpose can create a more engaged employee base

Research from Gallup and others has consistently shown that employee engagement is generally terrible (Harter, 2020). This is particularly true in large corporations, where often the majority of employees are *actively* unengaged. Having a clear purpose that is easy to understand and act upon can give employees a reason to get up and go to work every day. In the SunTrust example mentioned above, the notion of taking people out of financial stress and into financial confidence made the bank's associates feel like the work they were doing was important and meaningful, certainly more so than only facilitating transactions. Employee engagement scores increased dramatically. An activated purpose can also improve collaboration inside corporations between divisions and leaders, which typically are not good at working together.

3. An activated purpose can create a more engaged consumer base

As our Purpose Power Index research found, when consumers see a brand as purpose-driven, they are significantly more likely to want to buy the brand, recommend it, work for the company and give it the benefit of the doubt in a crisis.

4. An activated purpose can provide big financial payoffs

There have been many articles and studies published attempting to link higher purpose to financial rewards for companies. One of the most compelling is a 2018 article from *Harvard Business Review* called 'The type of purpose that makes companies more profitable'. Written by Harvard Business School professor George Serafeim and Wharton professor Claudine Gartenberg, the article outlines the authors' in-depth empirical research into the topic. We'll go into more depth about this ground-breaking work in Chapter 2, but their major finding was that higher purpose is indeed linked to superior accounting and stock market performance if – *and only if* – the higher purpose is clearly understood throughout the company's layers of management (Gartenberg *et al*, 2016).

When purpose fails

As we mentioned earlier, 90 per cent of executives understand the importance of purpose but only 37 per cent say their purpose is well articulated and understood by their employees. On one hand, it's easy to give credit to those trying to articulate their purpose. It's better to try than to do nothing at all, right?

Not quite. The challenge with a poorly articulated purpose, or one that's not universally understood by all internal stakeholders, is that it can lead to purpose activation fails. What do we mean by that? Well, it's when a company's purpose does not come to life in the intended way. Activation failure can take many forms, from the banal and benign to the damaging and offensive. Here are some examples of how purpose activation can fail.

It's office décor

This is the most common form of activation fail. This is what we talked about when we said getting to your brand's 'why' is not enough. When purpose – which is the core value of a company – is esoteric and theoretical, it has no meaning.

This kind of purpose sits dormant as a slogan on the CEO's door, posters around the company, coffee mugs or plaques, but is never acted upon. It's the result of purpose consultants who plan and host off-site meetings to help the team develop lofty statements like *inspiring lives* or *making the world a better place*. Everyone wants an inspired life or a better world but purpose statements like that inspire no action. Instead, a company-wide memo goes out, a section is added to the website and everyone returns to business as usual.

We've seen this play out over and over, where companies have been through two or three rounds of consultants and purpose statements, but have still been unable to turn it into anything actionable throughout the company.

It's purpose-washing

It's hard to fault a company or brand for wanting to champion some good in the world. However, if done in a way that's inauthentic, it will always come off as purpose-washing – or, in the words of more pointed critics, 'woke-washing' (Iqbal, 2019). Rather than being true to a brand's purpose, it comes off as something that's done to gain public-opinion points but is not followed up on in any meaningful way.

Gillette's stance on toxic masculinity comes to mind. We know it might raise a few eyebrows to call this purpose-washing, but here's why we think it is.

Gillette has always been about *the best a man can get*. It's also been a hyper-macho brand that's been about blade performance. Then the landscape began to change. Conversations around toxic masculinity dominated, especially following the rise of the #MeToo movement. So, Gillette released an ad reframing what it means to be a man, offering a more modern and progressive view of masculinity. On the face of it, it seems like a great move. *The best a man can get* should certainly be more than having a smooth face that the ladies like. It means being respectful, aware and a good role model. Who could argue with that?

The problem is that anyone following Gillette knows that its business is in crisis. Not only are sector disruptors like Dollar Shave Club, with their more cost-effective subscription service, redefining the men's grooming sector, but there are also larger cultural forces cutting into profits: men aren't shaving as much because beards are, well, everywhere.

With that background, it's hard not to question the motivation. Is Gillette a real champion for a better form of masculinity, or is it a ploy to get people to buy more razors? Is it making substantial efforts to be a values-driven company, or is it in it for the PR (Patel, 2019)? Of course, it's no problem for a brand to want to sell more of what it sells or generate good press, and Gillette could actually have a meaningful role in discussing masculinity, but where the activation truly falls is that there is no move or action on behalf of the brand to support its new claims. There are no internal policies that would support this kind of stance, there's no foundation aligned with this new mission. It comes across as just an ad aping the cultural zeitgeist with a woke stance to sell more razors. The fact that Gillette seemed to promptly re-embrace conventional masculinity in its ads following intense backlash from men who didn't much like being told they weren't very nice didn't help convince people its stance was meaningful (Kay, 2019).

It's tone deaf

If purpose-washing is detrimental to a brand's reputation, being tone-deaf is way worse. Where Gillette was well in tune with the conversations stemming from #MeToo, Pepsi was completely oblivious to the fact that making allusions to Black Lives Matter (BLM), one of the most significant racial movements in a generation, in an ad featuring one of the wealthiest socialites in the world was more than a tad off base.

The ad featured a group of people protesting as a line of police encroached. From a distance, Kendall Jenner of the Kardashian empire looks on. Dismayed by all this discord, she decides to break past the crowd, confront the police who are holding riot shields and hand them a Pepsi. Everyone cheers. Kendall saved the day!

The issue here is that a multinational conglomerate was seen to be co-opting and thereby trivializing a very real, very heated protest movement (Victor, 2017). Jenner breaking through to confront police was seen as an allusion to a brave young woman who did the same in a real protest. Black Lives Matter grew in response to police brutality and death. Pepsi had no business trying to profit from it.

It has little/no connection to what the company or brand does

Then, there are the head-scratcher fails. This variety of purpose fail occurs when a brand perhaps has good intentions, but the resulting effort has no connection to the cause it's championing.

The earlier Pepsi example fits this category. Why is a brand that sells sugar water saving the day amid racially fuelled protests? The brand's connection to what's going on in the spot is a mystery.

Another puzzler is Planters NUTrition's campaign around National Equal Pay Day that aimed to raise awareness around the gender pay gap. To highlight how unfair it is that women get paid less than men for the same work, it created a hidden-camera spot where customers were sold gender-specific bags of nuts. Men were only allowed to buy male-branded bags. The catch was that they had 20 per cent less product but cost the same. The difference in the product was meant to represent the disparity in wages between men and women.

So, what's the connection between the brand and the pay equality issue? According to NUTrition, *the pay gap is nuts*. Again, no one is going to argue that raising awareness around income inequality is not a worthy cause. And here, purchases of a special 'equal pay pack' benefited women's rights non-profit Equal Rights Advocates, which demonstrated the brand's commitment to the cause.

What's the issue, then? To us, the connection between brand and cause is too loose. Rather than activating a thoughtfully developed higher purpose, the brand attached itself to a controversial issue. Instead of making it look noble and worthy, we think activations like this make a brand look opportunistic. The missed opportunity here is that since this is Planters' health-conscious line, NUTrition had so many areas it could have made a meaningful contribution. It's in its name!! Had NUTrition chosen to raise awareness around issues like nutrition, obesity or food scarcity, it could have had relevant and compelling things to say that people could rally around.

This is something that successful purpose-driven brands like outdoor sports retailer REI understand well. REI's #OptOutside movement – in which the company gave employees Black Friday off work so they could enjoy the great outdoors – caused a considerable stir among business leaders and marketers in the year after it launched. The company's VP of public affairs, Alex Thompson, cautioned against poorly executed brand activism. He told *PR Week* at the time it was enormously risky if done for the wrong reasons, noting that the top 2,000 organizations in the world account for $35 trillion of revenue annually, half the global GDP (Bradly, 2016).

'It puts jobs at risk, and we should be cautious about that as an industry,' he said. 'As counsellors to CEOs, we need to help them understand why they want to take a particular move on a particular issue and be strong in that counsel and not be drawn to the light like moths,' said Thompson.

The antidote to purpose fail: Movement Thinking

Throughout this chapter we've been talking about brand purpose, why it matters, and how purpose needs to be activated in order to become meaningful and not just some vague, lofty statement in the 'about' section of your corporate website.

So how then do you activate a brand's purpose? By sparking a movement. That's how REI took its brand purpose of 'awakening a lifelong love of the outdoors for all' and grew it into a cause that is working to better both people's wellbeing and the planet (which you'll read more about in Chapter 2). It's how SunTrust inspired 6 million people to achieve greater financial confidence.

Movement Thinking in effect reframes your company or brand's purpose in a way that people can understand and want to participate in. Because people don't join a purpose. They join a movement inspired by purpose. In fact, one way to define a movement is that it is 'purpose, activated'.

As Suzanne Tosolini said to us:

> What Movement Thinking does is create a way of internally activating a purpose that inspires action. It turns strategic choices involved in creating a company or brand's vision, purpose, promise and values into something that every employee can understand and see their place in. It makes strategy relevant and actionable as well as more inspiring.

While the rest of this book is dedicated to how Movement Thinking can transform companies from the inside out (note: Movement Thinking is not a top–down approach), there are movement building blocks we'd like to introduce now – building blocks that invite people into a cause they care about.

1 **Dissatisfaction**

   Identify your dissatisfaction in the world. All movements start with a grievance. What's the wrong that urgently needs to be made right? For the 'Against Dumb' movement StrawberryFrog launched for Smart Car, the dissatisfaction was the fact that a large number of people were against overconsumption and waste, especially big, unnecessary cars, minivans and SUVs.

2 **Desired change**

   Name the change you want to see in the world. What do you want to see made different in the future? In the Smart Car example, it was a desire to restore the urban landscape.

3 Nemesis

Name your enemy. What are you against? You need to identify it/them and pick a fight. Note that it is often the 'villain' that's causing the grievance above. In the case of Smart Car, the enemy was stupidly over-consuming, which we shorthanded as 'dumb'. (There's one caveat when identifying the enemy: don't simply be *against* your competition. You may hate your competitor's guts, but nobody else cares; the outside world is looking for you to take on something more meaningful and interesting.)

4 Stand

What will you stand for in the quest to overcome your nemesis and achieve the desired change? In the case of Smart Car, it was a stand for a more conscious form of consuming, which we shorthanded as 'smart'.

5 Action

What will you do to get people to care and participate? This is often a form of communication or expression, as many movements first get traction via strong symbols (eg pink ribbon, yellow bracelet), posters, ads, or even a song (eg 'We Shall Overcome').

Taking Movement Thinking further

A common misconception is that higher purpose and Movement Thinking are the domain of marketing and branding within a company – and thus matter only to the chief marketing officer. We hear this often in our meetings with clients, which is why Scott can often be heard saying that company leaders can change company culture and employee mindsets and behaviour more effectively with a movement than with old-fashioned mandates. A movement ignites trust, engagement, ownership, creativity and passion, whereas the mandate pushes for compliance, and typically pushes the best employees out the door.

Too often, CEOs end up issuing a mandate around their company's purpose, when they should be leading a movement. Movement Thinking, we've seen, can help CEOs to introduce a new purpose for their organization in a way that is connected to its employees, that's cross-company and not top–down because, in today's environment, the power to change corporate culture is with employees, not leadership alone. You can read more about how CEOs can embrace Movement Thinking for corporate transformation in Chapter 4.

Movement Thinking can also help CHROs engage, support and attract talent in a way that benefits employees, not simply the corporation. This is becoming increasingly important as more and more of today's employees are motivated to work at companies that stand for something greater than profit. You'll hear more about Movement Thinking as an internal tool in Chapter 5.

And, of course, it goes without saying that Movement Thinking helps CMOs move away from traditional 'advertising think' and create a grass-roots groundswell for their brands. We cover how Movement Marketing helps marketers in Chapter 6.

KEY TAKEAWAYS

It's become accepted wisdom that today we're living in a VUCA world – volatile, uncertain, complex and ambiguous. Even as we are writing this book, the team at StrawberryFrog is collaborating digitally as everyone shelters in place amid the outbreak of COVID-19. When we started this project, no one could have predicted the swiftness and the degree to which the COVID-19 outbreak would change daily life. Businesses of all types are wondering how, if at all, they'll weather this crisis. In a time of incredible change like this, the only thing that's going to keep an organization focused and on track is purpose. It's the only compass to guide when things change rapidly in our VUCA world.

So, if purpose is why you exist in the world beyond making money, the challenge is how do you actually take a theoretical idea and use it to activate your employees, drive your organization and grow your business? Here are some key points to remember:

1 Purpose is no longer a nice-to-have. Consumers and employees, leaders and shareholders are demanding it from the companies they choose to do business with or work for.

2 The problem with purpose is that, in most cases, consumers don't view companies as being purpose-driven.

3 You have to activate your purpose, your 'why'. Movement is the proven business tool for leaders to make it happen.

4 Without clarity, purpose is prone to failure. Not designing in a stickiness factor will decrease your chances of success.

5 Movement building blocks are the basis of Movement Thinking and invite people into a cause they care about. They are dissatisfaction, change, nemesis, stand and action.

6 Movement Thinking can be transformative for all parts of a business, from leadership to human resources to marketing. Movement Thinking engages the entire business and everyone it touches. It is the framework within which leaders can change the culture, and employee habits, and grow consumers.

References

Bradly, D (2016) REI's Alex Thompson: Embrace activism only for right reasons, *PR Week*, 22 September. https://www.prweek.com/article/1409832/reis-alex-thompson-embrace-activism-right-reasons (archived at https://perma.cc/8CZH-CCSE)

Branson, R (2016) How to manifest purpose in business, [Blog] Virgin.com. https://www.virgin.com/richard-branson/how-to-manifest-purpose-in-business (archived at https://perma.cc/P5GF-LCB2)

Business Roundtable (2019) Statement on the purpose of a corporation, businessroundtable.org. https://opportunity.businessroundtable.org/ourcommitment/ (archived at https://perma.cc/5B8S-Q3EH)

Cone, C (2020) The B2B business paradox, 11 February, Carol Cone ON PURPOSE. https://www.carolconeonpurpose.com/b2b-purpose-paradox (archived at https://perma.cc/EQ3N-JJE6)

Duggan, B (2018) Brand purpose: ANA 2018 marketing word of the year, ANA. net, 7 December. https://www.ana.net/blogs/show/id/mm-blog-2018-12-brand-purpose-marketing-word-of-the-year (archived at https://perma.cc/YRS9-82U6)

Fink, B (2019) A fundamental reshaping of finance, Blackrock.com). https://www.blackrock.com/corporate/investor-relations/larry-fink-ceo-letter (archived at https://perma.cc/9JCT-AG82)

Gartenberg, C, Prat, A and Serafeim, G (2016) Corporate purpose and financial performance, Harvard Business School Working Paper, No. 17-023, September 2016. https://dash.harvard.edu/handle/1/30903237 (archived at https://perma.cc/A46G-LYTY)

Gast, A, Illanes, P, Probst, N, Schaninger, B and Simpson, B (2020) Purpose: Shifting from why to how, *McKinsey Quarterly*, 22 April. https://www.mckinsey.com/business-functions/organization/our-insights/purpose-shifting-from-why-to-how (archived at https://perma.cc/6KGY-YQNH)

Glassdoor (2017) Glassdoor survey finds 75% of Americans believe employers should take a political stand, Glassdoor.com), 26 September. https://www.glassdoor.com/employers/blog/glassdoor-survey-finds-75-of-americans-believe-employers-should-take-a-political-stand/ (archived at https://perma.cc/UVW3-AAWV)

Harter, J (2020) Historic drop in employee engagement follows record rise, Gallup, 2 July. https://www.gallup.com/workplace/313313/historic-drop-employee-engagement-follows-record-rise.aspx (archived at https://perma.cc/QB84-4XDU)

Harvard Business Review (2015) The business case for purpose, *Harvard Business Review*. https://hbr.org/resources/pdfs/comm/ey/19392HBRReportEY.pdf (archived at https://perma.cc/N83Y-2GXS)

Iqbal, N (2019) Woke washing? How brands like Gillette turn profits by creating a conscience, *The Guardian*, 19 January. https://www.theguardian.com/media/2019/jan/19/gillette-ad-campaign-woke-advertising-salving-consciences (archived at https://perma.cc/8GJK-8QGV)

Kay, B (2019) After going woke and losing $8 billion, Gillette embraces masculinity again, *The Post Millennial*, 22 August. https://thepostmillennial.com/after-losing-8-billion-gillette-embraces-masculinity-again (archived at https://perma.cc/2LMT-C3FD)

Larcker, D, Miles, S, Tayan, B and Wright-Violich, K (2018) *The Double-Edged Sword of CEO Activism*. Rock Center for Corporate Governance at Stanford University Closer Look Series: Topics, Issues and Controversies in Corporate Governance No. CGRP-74; Stanford University Graduate School of Business Research Paper No. 19-5. https://ssrn.com/abstract=3283297 (archived at https://perma.cc/SD6C-2JKQ)

OECD (2020) *Trust in Government*, OECD.org. https://www.oecd.org/gov/trust-in-government.htm (archived at https://perma.cc/YWC6-GDYZ)

Omelianuk, S (2019) Everyone's obsessed with brand purpose. Too bad no one understands it, *Fast Company*, 17 November. https://www.fastcompany.com/90431315/everyones-obsessed-with-brand-purpose-too-bad-no-one-understands-it (archived at https://perma.cc/43UL-TK3E)

Patel, S (2019) Brands: Stop saying you've got a purpose. Put your money where your mouth is, Warc.com), 14 February. https://www.warc.com/newsandopinion/opinion/brands_stop_saying_youve_got_a_purpose_put_your_money_where_your_mouth_is/2975 (archived at https://perma.cc/MU5U-DV2Z)

Rogers, C (2018) Patagonia on why brands 'can't reverse into purpose' through marketing, *Marketing Week*, 18 July. https://www.marketingweek.com/patagonia-you-cant-reverse-into-values-through-marketing/ (archived at https://perma.cc/ZF9Q-ES5D)

Schwab, K (2019) *Davos Manifesto 2020: The universal purpose of a company in the fourth industrial revolution*, World Economic Forum, 2 December. https://www.weforum.org/agenda/2019/12/davos-manifesto-2020-the-universal-purpose-of-a-company-in-the-fourth-industrial-revolution/ (archived at https://perma.cc/92GH-4AH2)

Sievert, M (2020) In a crisis, businesses large and small can be rapid force for positive change [LinkedIn], 17 September. https://www.linkedin.com/pulse/crisis-businesses-large-small-can-rapid-force-positive-mike-sievert/ (archived at https://perma.cc/6G9A-N8ZD)

Sinek, S (2009) *Start With Why*, Portfolio, New York

TED (2009) How great leaders inspire action [Online video] https://www.ted.com/talks/simon_sinek_how_great_leaders_inspire_action (archived at https://perma.cc/E283-P4BB)

Victor, D (2017) Pepsi pulls ad accused of trivializing Black Lives Matter, *The New York Times*, 5 April. https://www.nytimes.com/2017/04/05/business/kendall-jenner-pepsi-ad.html (archived at https://perma.cc/YKV7-XCPD)

Walk-Morris, T (2020) Patagonia escalates activism with voting rights push before elections, RetailDive.com). https://www.retaildive.com/news/patagonia-escalates-activism-with-voting-rights-push-before-elections/585520/ (archived at https://perma.cc/RA59-ZGAU)

02

The business case for activating purpose

When Jason Orr woke up on Black Friday, he basked in the morning calm. As a 20-year retail employee, the morning after Thanksgiving usually meant hustling out of the house extra early to sell more stuff to the deal-seeking customers who streamed into his REI (the outdoors sports retailer) store in Fort Collins, Colorado. Instead, the store manager savoured his coffee and contemplated what fun his family was going to get up to that day. Following a ski day, turkey dinner with family and now another day off, Jason declared on social media that he was having the best Thanksgiving week he'd ever had (Orr, 2015).

That's because a few weeks before the holiday, the CEO of REI did something that shocked Jason and his colleagues: he said no. No one was going to work Black Friday. No one would have to deal with crowds and sales and the frantic spending that Black Friday is famous for. There would be no online sales, thus no orders to fulfil. There would be no sales before or after Black Friday, either. Instead, REI was completely opting out of this peak moment of American consumerism and was paying its employees to take the day off and go outside. They called it '#OptOutside' and it was meant to demonstrate the company's indelible commitment to their core values. For Jason and 13,000 other REI colleagues, it was a day to go skiing, hiking, horseback riding, stargazing, or whatever outdoor activity struck their fancy.

No, REI doesn't exist on some foreign planet where the bottom line doesn't matter. But it does operate in such a way that the bottom line isn't the only thing that matters. For REI, employee wellbeing, environmental sustainability and promoting conscious consumerism versus mindless, rabid consumption all matter to the company. So much so that paying people to go outside rather than staff its physical and online stores is more important than raking in Black Friday cash.

Like the example from Patagonia in the last chapter, a move like this may seem completely counter to growing the bottom line. But the action, while much less political than Patagonia's, still led to mass engagement by the masses and, moreover, business results that speak for themselves. In April 2019, REI Co-op published its annual stewardship report announcing a record $3.12 billion in revenue, growth of 8 per cent and the addition of more than 1 million new members, bringing the co-op's total membership to more than 19 million. That allowed REI to return $210.8 million to members through dividends and credit card rewards, and give $78.5 million to employees through profit-sharing and retirement (REI, 2019). And this was just the most recent in a slew of record-breaking years for REI business performance.

So, let this sink in for a minute: by living its purpose and closing on the world's busiest shopping day, Black Friday, REI actually made its sales go up!

When the '#OptOutside' initiative was announced in 2015, Jerry Stritzke, then-president and CEO of REI, said, 'Black Friday is the perfect time to remind ourselves of the essential truth that life is richer, more connected and complete when you choose to spend it outside' (REI, 2015). It sounds wonderful, inspirational and totally in line with a brand that is about living your best life outdoors. But its success extends beyond the many feel-good press headlines REI received. With '#OptOutside', REI took ownership of a large portion of the anti-consumerism narrative related to the largest shopping day, engaged employees in a way that mattered to them, and showed leadership from the C-suite. It demonstrated that REI is a brand with purpose. More importantly, one that has successfully activated its brand purpose through the '#OptOutside' movement. Since then, the movement has grown and evolved, even as the company's leadership has changed. Over 700 other companies followed suit, millions have taken part, and the National Parks Department also announced plans to participate in the '#OptOutside' movement, with many states waiving their entrance fees into the parks (REI, 2019).

In announcing those record-breaking 2019 financial results, then acting REI CEO Eric Artz said:

Today's results show that doing good is good business. We have a strong foundation, but we must do more. As a community, we must confront the serious problems facing society. Spending time outside isn't only good for people's health. It connects people to something bigger – a desire to fight for the future of life outside. (Artz and Hooper, 2019)

The REI case demonstrates something we've seen over and over again: that what might be seen as counterintuitive business moves – like closing on the biggest shopping day of the year and focusing on the greater good – can do great things for the overall performance of a company. In the remainder of this chapter, we'll take a closer look at five of the underlying business benefits to higher purpose that explain *why* it contributes to the bottom line. We'll show how activating purpose:

1 drives financial performance;

2 aligns stakeholders;

3 creates motivated employees;

4 transforms company culture;

5 engages customers and consumers.

Activated purpose drives financial performance

One of the big questions when it comes to prioritizing purpose within an organization is that of financial performance. Does focusing on purpose help the bottom line? Is purpose good business or merely a feel-good endeavour? It worked for REI, but does it work for others?

As you might expect, there are a number of conflicting opinions on this question. For example, EY found in its 2018 report, 'Purpose-driven leadership' (Canwell and Cotton, 2018), that purposeful companies outperform the market by 42 per cent. Great news. But there will be naysayers, of which marketing consultant and former business school professor Mark Ritson is one. He frequently argues that purpose sacrifices rather than grows profits (Ritson, 2019).

But, in fact, that question has received a clear answer. In a 2016 study, Harvard Business School professor George Serafeim, Wharton professor

Claudine Gartenberg and Columbia professor Andrea Prat sought to systematically measure the relationship between purpose and performance. What did they find? That higher purpose does indeed drive superior financial performance if – *and only if* – it's clearly activated among employees.

The research paper, titled 'Corporate purpose and financial performance' (Gartenberg *et al*, 2016), constructed a measure of purpose using a sample of 429 US companies and more than 450,000 survey responses of workers' perceptions about their companies. The data came from a survey from the Great Places to Work (GPTW) Institute that regularly surveys employees from hundreds of companies. It was a breakthrough because it was based on actual employee beliefs about their employers and workplaces, such as whether they felt a sense of pride, whether they felt as though their work had meaning, or whether their company contributed to the betterment of their community.

The analysis identified two kinds of companies with purpose. There are high *purpose-camaraderie* organizations, ones where people feel a sense of belonging and get along with their co-workers. Then there are high *purpose-clarity* organizations, which are ones where people have an understanding of what's expected of them and a clear view of where their organization is going and how it's going to achieve that goal. The authors found that only the high *purpose-clarity* organizations performed well when it came to stock market performance. 'A portfolio of high *purpose-clarity* firms earns significant positive seven risk-adjusted stock returns in the future, up to 7.6 per cent annually,' they wrote. Their analysis suggests that high *purpose-clarity* organizations performed better financially because their purpose was well understood by those in the middle ranks.

This means middle managers and professional workers are key to a company's success (Serafeim and Gartenberg, 2016). 'This last finding underscores the absolute importance of fostering an effective middle manager layer within firms: managers who buy into the vision of the company and can make daily decisions that guide the firm in the right direction,' they wrote in *Harvard Business Review*. The conclusion, in the authors' words: 'An organization's purpose is not a formal announcement, but depends on the employees believing in and acting to promote that purpose.'

This gives us proof that there's a strong relationship between higher purpose and financial performance if the purpose is properly activated.

Activating purpose aligns all stakeholders

Yes, purpose can drive financial performance and that is no doubt a powerful motivator for many business leaders. However, in our experience working with dozens of companies big and small, profit is rarely the main reason they pursue a purpose agenda. More often, activating purpose is the lynchpin in addressing the number one business challenge facing the leadership of most organizations: *rallying all stakeholders around a shared mission.*

When we introduced the concept of activating purpose via movements in the first chapter, we made a point of saying it's not a top–down strategy. This is important because when a directive comes from on high, the meaning and the message frequently get lost as it filters through the organization. If that happens with purpose, it will fail to become activated.

For example, you may have encountered a scenario like the following: senior management goes to an off-site with the goal of setting a strategic North Star for the company. They come back with a new purpose statement in hand, memos go out and then they assume everyone is informed and on board. In reality, it typically doesn't trickle its way down all the way to the front lines. Maybe the first couple of layers of the organization know what's going on, but for the vast majority of the company, if you were to ask them what the purpose was, they would just give you a blank stare. When it comes to purpose, this is the worst thing that can happen. It's how good intentions die on the vine.

By contrast, when an organization is aligned to a purpose, all aspects of the organization end up marching in the same direction with the same strategic thrust. When a company lacks a clearly articulated purpose that is known and shared and understood throughout the organization and across the public, people within an organization tend to work at odds with each other. So, all the arrows aren't going in the same direction (see Figure 2.1).

Afdhel Aziz of Conspiracy of Love, who shared his views on purpose in the last chapter, put it another way when we spoke to him about the importance of purpose. He says purpose is like a rope that weaves together all of the strands a company or brand might be holding. Whereas companies typically have dealt with issues of sustainability, cause marketing (purposeful marketing's predecessor), corporate social responsibility, diversity and inclusion, employee engagement and so on in different silos, purpose is a way to bring them all together into something bigger. 'That's really the key to being a

FIGURE 2.1 With and without an activated purpose

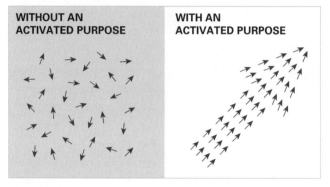

SOURCE StrawberryFrog

purpose-driven company – you put it at the centre of your growth strategy,' he said to us. 'So that way it's not just in marketing, it's not just in HR, it's not just in something else; it means the core reason for your business to exist is to make more money by doing more good.'

Purpose isn't simply an advertising, branding or marketing idea, nor is it a CSR move or an HR strategy. It's all of those things working together in an integrated, synchronized manner. Purpose has the potential to move people inside the organization, to help establish or crystallize a culture that already exists within the organization. It can also connect with the external stakeholders, like the community, consumers and shareholders. But not unless purpose is released by Movement Thinking.

In our experience of helping companies activate their purpose, this is where Movement Thinking becomes critical. Just as design thinking gave designers a human-centric approach to creating things over a decade ago, Movement Thinking is a human-centric approach to changing things in the new peer-to-peer world and the coming purpose economy. It uses the principles of social movements to mobilize employees and consumers alike towards the same goal. Activated properly, purpose can provide a strategic North Star that guides everything a business does.

Activating purpose creates motivated employees

It's no secret that employee engagement is abysmal. Simply put, the average employee is not happy at work. A 2016 PricewaterhouseCoopers (PwC) study found this was particularly true among employees at larger companies. In the research, 43 per cent of workers at small US companies reported being happy at work, while just 27 per cent of workers at large (1,000+ employees) organizations felt that way (PwC, 2016a). You can see why those kinds of *purpose-camaraderie* organizations we mentioned earlier from that *Harvard Business Review* study might not fare as well in terms of financial performance. Camaraderie doesn't immediately equate to happiness, and people are just as likely to feel bonded with their colleagues over their bad work experiences as their good ones – perhaps even more so.

Dissatisfaction with pay and/or benefits is usually the first thing employers point to as a source of disengagement. But there is significant research proving that if we want engaged employees, money is not the answer. A meta-analysis in the *Journal of Vocational Behavior* reviewed 92 quantitative studies and found the association between salary and job satisfaction was very weak (Judge *et al*, 2010). The authors wrote: 'One might argue that pay level is weakly related to overall job satisfaction because, of the facets of job satisfaction, pay is not as important as other facets such as work satisfaction.'

This is consistent with Gallup's engagement research. Based on 1.4 million employees from 192 organizations across 49 industries and 34 nations, the report found that how much someone makes does not significantly affect their engagement at work. And its survey results, published in the article 'Majority of American workers not engaged in their jobs', show that those with incomes over $90,000 are just as disengaged as those with salaries under $36,000. For both groups, only 30 per cent reported being engaged, whereas only 28 per cent of those with incomes in the middle reported being engaged at work (Blacksmith and Harter, 2011). Simply put: money does not buy employee motivation.

So, what does motivate people, then? There's a growing consensus that the real culprit in employee disengagement is the fact that most employees lack a sense of meaning and purpose in their work. If you asked the average employee why they get up and go to work every day, you'd undoubtedly hear things like 'to keep a roof over my head, pay my bills, feed my family'. Yet, other evidence suggests that having a sense of purpose is the factor that gets and keeps employees engaged. Keying off the SunTrust example, which we described in the last chapter, it's the difference between going to work to pay the rent as opposed to helping people get out of financial stress. Purpose gives work personal meaning – and meaning is what employees crave more than money.

In 2017, BetterUp Labs conducted a survey of 2,285 professionals across 26 industries in the US, covering a wide range of work environments, company sizes, occupations and demographics (Reece *et al*, 2017). Based on the results of a survey of workers, four findings emerged:

1 Most employees want their work to be more meaningful.

2 Employees who believe work should be meaningful are more likely to emerge as leaders and senior contributors.

3 Turnover rates are lower for employees who feel work is meaningful.

4 Employees who find meaningful work are happier, more productive and harder working.

For many, meaningful work is more valuable than a company's prestige, growth potential, or even the quality of its product, and data from 2018 shows that 86 per cent of millennial employees would take a pay cut in exchange for a job that aligns with their values (Mejia, 2018). Although people are hungry for meaningful work, many aren't finding it: in the US half of employees report that their jobs lack purpose, and an equal number feel disconnected from their company's mission (Schwartz and Porath, 2014). In the UK, a quarter of workers in 2020 felt their work was meaningless (Nolsoe, 2020). Loss of productivity due to disengagement is estimated to cost US employers upwards of half a trillion dollars per year (Sorenson and Garman, 2013). That's staggering – and clearly worth addressing.

Millennials are driving the trend

Reams of research point to Millennials as being a driving force in this shift towards valuing purpose over pay. And with good reason. Millennials' parents, the Boomers, had a clear social contract with their employers. In exchange for their hours, weeks and years of devotion to their employer, the company would compensate and be loyal to them. But the terms of the labour contract have changed for Millennials. They saw that employers were not in fact loyal and laid people off with impunity. As a result, they've come to expect companies to make the workplace a source of personal growth and shared purpose.

In its report 'Putting Purpose to Work: A study of purpose in the workplace', PricewaterhouseCoopers reiterates the importance of purpose to younger workers, finding that Millennials are looking to businesses to deliver solutions to important societal and environmental problems. And this sentiment is expected to get higher with the entrance of Generation Z into the workforce (PwC, 2016a). That same report stated that Millennials are also 5.3 times more likely to stay at a company when they have a strong connection to their employer's purpose. That compares with non-Millennials, who are only 2.3 times more likely to be concerned with their employer's purpose.

HOW MUCH DO MILLENNIALS CARE ABOUT PURPOSE? A LOT

'84 per cent of Millennials say that making a difference is more important than professional recognition.' (Raza, 2016)

'Three-quarters of Millennials would take a pay cut to work for a socially responsible company.' (Cone Communications, 2016)

'88 per cent [of Millennials] say their job is more fulfilling when employers provide opportunities to make a positive impact.' (Cone Communications, 2016)

'Three-quarters (76 per cent) of Millennials consider a company's social and environmental commitments when deciding where to work and nearly two-thirds (64 per cent) won't take a job if a potential employer doesn't have strong corporate social responsibility practices.' (Cone Communications, 2016)

'66 per cent would switch from a product they typically buy to a new product from a purpose-driven company. For Millennials, that figure goes up to 91 per cent.' (Cone/Porter Novelli, 2018)

Carol Cone, CEO of Carol Cone ON PURPOSE, says it makes sense that employees value culture over profit. She told us when speaking with us for this book:

Does anyone want to come to work to make the CEO more money? Of course not. They get excited about the end result of their work. When you have a culture that's about doing something greater than yourself, it has a huge impact.

Cone pioneered the field of social purpose in the 1980s and is widely recognized as one of the world's foremost social impact experts. In early 2020, her company, along with the Association of National Advertisers and the Harris Poll, released a study into the importance of purpose to B2B companies, as mentioned in Chapter 1. 'The B2B Purpose Paradox' shows that 73 per cent of purpose-oriented employees report job satisfaction, employees are increasingly prioritizing purpose over money and achievement in their careers, and 47 per cent of employees say purpose influences their engagement at work (Cone, 2020).

Interestingly, the report also found that B2B companies are embracing purpose for internal reasons as well as external ones. As Figure 2.2 – from the Cone study – shows, in addition to contributing to greater success, recruiting and motivating teams ranked high as reasons why companies were embracing purpose.

We think that the growing emphasis on higher purpose provides an opportunity to reinvent human resources within companies. That's because in so many cases, employees view their HR departments as more like legal and risk management entities whose role is to manage employees to the benefit of the company or leadership. Over the years, the HR function seems to have drifted away from its purpose of helping employees. In our view, HR has an important role to play in activating purpose to create motivated

FIGURE 2.2 Why B2B companies embrace purpose

Greater success than those without	82%
Supports recruiting	75%
Motivates sales teams	73%
Shows values and character in action	51%
Drives business growth	47%
Deepens customer relationships	46%
Builds future reputation/legacy	44%
Deepens relationships with employees	39%

SOURCE Cone (2020)

employees. This is something we're going to delve into in more detail later in this book.

An activated purpose can transform company culture

In 2012, Bank of America CMO Meredith Verdone faced the professional challenge of a lifetime: how to resurrect the reputation and company culture of an organization that most of the American public considered a central figure in the financial meltdown of 2008. One whose Countrywide division had pretty much popularized subprime lending. One that had an entire societal movement, Occupy Wall Street, rise up with the goal of taking down the bank and others like it. Not surprisingly, internal culture and morale were negatively impacted. Some bank employees had even become hesitant to tell strangers where they worked.

In response to this crisis of reputation, one thing became crystal clear: what was needed wasn't a new marketing slogan or internal 'rah rah' session; what was needed was a shared North Star, a convening thought that employees could rally around and that customers would find credible and reassuring.

It was with that in mind that Verdone set off on a months-long endeavour to articulate the bank's higher purpose, which ended up being stated as: *committed to better, one connection at a time*. Why *better*? Given Bank of America's reputation issues at the time, a promise of seeking to be better had the needed humility, and it was believable. As for *one connection at a time*, it referred to every touchpoint in the customer experience, as well as to the array of important life and business elements that a bank like Bank of America could link its customers to.

After introducing the new purpose in a series of town halls, the bank codified behaviour principles to guide employees' actions. The first principle had to do with *leadership accountability*. This involved, among other things, having a board that was empowered to oversee and hold management accountable for managing all types of risk. A second principle was *driving and upholding ethical conduct*. This included aspects such as driving culture and expectations for conduct throughout the employee lifecycle – including hiring, on-boarding, training, etc. It also included tools such as an employee code of conduct. The third principle was that of *creating a culture of managing risk well*. This meant encouraging the sound judgement of every employee and having each employee take ownership of risk management.

The result? A bank that financial and investing advice company Motley Fool observes is not recognizable when compared with before the financial crisis. In 2017, it noticed that Bank of America was changing its culture 'from one based on growth for the sake of growth to one based on responsible growth' (Maxfield, 2017). While Bank of America's stock price is still subdued, it has paid back the US government for its bailout and boasts a healthier balance sheet and a more motivated employee base than in previous years.

Activating purpose engages customers and consumers

As we noted earlier, the data is pretty conclusive that employees really do care about whether companies and brands they work at have a higher purpose. But what about from a consumer standpoint? Does having higher purpose help companies and brands curry any favour in the hearts and minds of consumers?

Suzanne Tosolini of the Jim Stengel Company, whom we spoke with in the last chapter, told us that in her experience, activating an authentic and meaningful brand purpose 'results in a brand that's distinctive in its category and resonates more deeply with its customers. In turn, this results in a brand with heightened awareness and loyalty, thus driving business results.'

Our own Purpose Power Index research, which we introduced in Chapter 1, confirms that position with a pretty clear answer. It reveals that consumers are much more likely to buy, recommend, want to work for and want to invest in brands they view as purpose-driven. As these responses from the PPI show, customers are more likely to buy, recommend and speak highly of those brands they consider to be purpose-driven.

We've seen this first hand in purpose activations we've created for clients – for example, SunTrust (now Truist) Bank's 'onUp' movement. By taking a stand against financial stress and increasing financial confidence, SunTrust not only rallied employees around a common mission, the movement also led to measurable increases in customer loyalty and new account additions, and decreases in attrition rates, all by operating in a way that truly helped its customers.

FIGURE 2.3 Purpose = Engagement

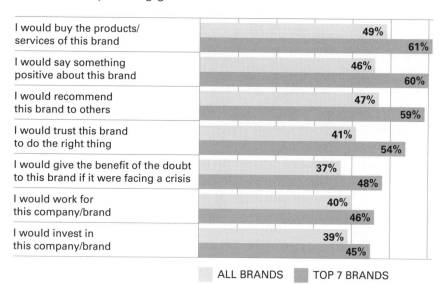

SOURCE RepTrak

Rising to the challenge

As we've discussed throughout this chapter, purpose is challenging our view of the role of corporations and brands in the world.

The long-held belief that the business of the business is to mind the business – that view from Milton Friedman on shareholder value superseding all else that's been held as the gold standard for decades – is eroding. Instead, purpose is shown to be a driving force in aligning stakeholders, company culture, employee engagement, consumer respect – and profits. Shareholder value as the sole guiding principle is giving way to the understanding that operating with morality, sustainability and integrity – and in ways that benefit all stakeholders over just a few – is what all stakeholders now expect.

And yet, there is still much progress to be made. 'The business case for purpose' from *Harvard Business Review* and Ernst & Young revealed the Purpose Gap we talked about in the last chapter. It found that 41 per cent of business leaders said there remained a disconnect between their senior executives and employees over purpose; only 38 per cent felt that their staff had a clear understanding of organizational purpose and commitment to core values or beliefs; and only 37 per cent said their business model and operations were well aligned with their purpose (*Harvard Business Review* and EY, 2015).

Part of the issue, as Dartmouth Business School professor Vijay Govindarajan points to in his *HBR* article 'We are nowhere near stakeholder capitalism', is that the compensation models have yet to match the new aspired-for reality. As long as CEOs, fund managers and boards of directors continue to be hired, compensated and held accountable to metrics such as revenues, profits, share prices and returns on investment, stakeholder capitalism will remain an ideal. 'How likely is it that a CEO would get up one day and suddenly change his or her focus from revenues, profits, and stock prices toward wider environmental, social, and governance goals?' he asks. While some might, without reframing what a company values, ESG objectives will remain secondary to shareholder value (Govindarajan and Srivastava, 2020).

But reframing metrics of success is exactly what needs to happen in the quest to be purpose-driven. We're not saying the profits don't matter – in fact, our conversation with Indian business titan Anand Mahindra later in this book will reveal that it's by prioritizing people and planet that profits will follow. We are saying that profits aren't the *only* thing that matters. The tricky part is that redefining metrics is not a blanket, one-size-fits-all exercise. We have no magic bullet for you. Instead, as Afdhel Aziz said to us ever so succinctly: you have to measure what you treasure. 'What that means is that each company needs to come up with its own bespoke measurement of how they value purpose, depending on who they are, what their business model is, what they have to achieve,' he said.

To us, all of this presents an opportunity. The will is there, as is the understanding that purpose is good for business. The problem is that so many business leaders don't know how to make their purpose a living reality. They don't know how to activate it. We believe that Movement Thinking, which we'll be addressing in detail in the next chapter, is how to meet this challenge.

Because new thinking is what's needed. This is something that Carol Cone, when speaking to us for this book, articulated so perfectly by recalling this wonderful quote from Abraham Lincoln: 'The dogmas of the quiet past are inadequate to the stormy present. The occasion is piled high with difficulty and we must rise with the occasion. As our case is new, we must think anew and act anew' (Lincoln, 1862).

We couldn't agree more.

KEY TAKEAWAYS

The question when it comes to purpose shouldn't be 'Is purpose good for the bottom line?' Instead, we contend that those interested in their company's purpose should ask, 'What are the ways in which I can use purpose to do well by doing good?' Before we launch into how to move to Movement Thinking in the next chapter, remember that activating purpose:

- drives financial performance;
- aligns stakeholders;
- transforms company culture;
- creates motivated employees;
- engages customers and consumers.

References

Artz, E and Hooper, S (2019) Collective impact and the fight for life outside, rei. com. https://www.rei.com/about-rei/presidents-message (archived at https://perma.cc/44EV-2A96)

Blacksmith, N and Harter, J (2011) Majority of American workers not engaged in their jobs, *Gallup*, 28 October. https://news.gallup.com/poll/150383/majority-american-workers-not-engaged-jobs.aspx (archived at https://perma.cc/X4WE-5S2W)

Canwell, A and Cotton, T (2018) *Purpose-driven Leadership*. https://www.ey.com/Publication/vwLUAssets/ey-purpose-driven-leadership/$File/ey-purpose-driven-leadership.pdf (archived at https://perma.cc/YWM4-CTM7)

Cone Communications (2016) *2016 Cone Communications Millennial Employee Engagement Study*. https://www.conecomm.com/research-blog/2016-millennial-employee-engagement-study (archived at https://perma.cc/2LNX-ZWQ5)

Cone, C (2020) The B2B business paradox, 11 February, Carol Cone ON PURPOSE. https://www.carolconeonpurpose.com/b2b-purpose-paradox (archived at https://perma.cc/GXN4-5ELA)

Cone/Porter Novelli (2018) *2018 Cone/Porter Novelli Purpose Study*. https://www.conecomm.com/research-blog/2018-purpose-study (archived at https://perma.cc/MB8J-549S)

Gartenberg, C, Prat, A and Serafeim, G (2016) Corporate purpose and financial performance, Harvard Business School Working Paper, No. 17-023, September 2016. https://dash.harvard.edu/handle/1/30903237 (archived at https://perma.cc/5UZE-CUJW)

Govindarajan, V and Srivastava, A (2020) We are nowhere near stakeholder capitalism, *Harvard Business Review*, 30 January. https://hbr.org/2020/01/we-are-nowhere-near-stakeholder-capitalism (archived at https://perma.cc/QMY3-ZWZL)

Harvard Business Review and EY (2015) *The Business Case for Purpose*. https://hbr.org/resources/pdfs/comm/ey/19392HBRReportEY.pdf (archived at https://perma.cc/GH3F-9VUB)

Judge, TA, Piccolo, RF, Podsakoff, NP, Shaw, JC and Rich, BL (2010) The relationship between pay and job satisfaction: A meta-analysis of the literature, *Journal of Vocational Behavior*. http://www.timothy-judge.com/Judge,%20Piccolo,%20Podsakoff,%20et%20al.%20(JVB%202010).pdf (archived at https://perma.cc/FW28-Z48Q)

Lincoln, A (1862) *December 1, 1862: Second Annual Message*, Miller Center. https://millercenter.org/the-presidency/presidential-speeches/december-1-1862-second-annual-message (archived at https://perma.cc/677N-BS8V)

Maxfield, J (2017) 10 ways Bank of America has changed in the past decade, MotleyFool.com, 1 January. https://www.fool.com/investing/2017/01/01/10-ways-bank-of-america-has-changed-in-the-past-de.aspx (archived at https://perma.cc/Q8HN-6AF9)

Mejia, Z (2018) Nearly 9 out of 10 Millennials would consider a pay cut to get this, CNBC.com, 28 June. https://www.cnbc.com/2018/06/27/nearly-9-out-of-10-millennials-would-consider-a-pay-cut-to-get-this.html (archived at https://perma.cc/Z6TZ-C83K)

Nolsoe, E (2020) Quarter of British workers find jobs lack meaning, YouGov.co.uk. https://yougov.co.uk/topics/economy/articles-reports/2020/02/20/quarter-british-workers-find-jobs-lack-meaning (archived at https://perma.cc/J4AC-6ZAV)

Orr, J (2015) Medium.com. https://medium.com/@englishsteel/this-reiemployee-is-proud-to-work-at-rei-and-in-the-middle-of-the-best-thanksgiving-week-i-ve-ever-996b7130f814 (archived at https://perma.cc/QT3J-3HNA)

PwC (2016a) *Putting Purpose to Work: A study of purpose in the workplace*. https://www.pwc.com/us/en/about-us/corporate-responsibility/assets/pwc-putting-purpose-to-work-purpose-survey-report.pdf (archived at https://perma.cc/9DC2-65Y2)

PwC (2016b) *Work-life 3.0: Understanding how we'll work next*. https://www.pwc.com/us/en/industry/entertainment-media/publications/consumer-intelligence-series/assets/pwc-consumer-intellgience-series-future-of-work-june-2016.pdf (archived at https://perma.cc/92XK-5VVL)

Raza, A (2016) Why a purpose-driven mission is key to motivating Millennials, *Entrepreneur*, 12 December. https://www.entrepreneur.com/article/284857 (archived at https://perma.cc/FF2D-6SLT)

Reece, A, Kellerman, G and Robichaux, A (2017) *Meaning and Purpose at Work*. https://get.betterup.co/rs/600-WTC-654/images/betterup-meaning-purpose-at-work.pdf (archived at https://perma.cc/T5GK-QN9A)

REI (2015) REI closing its doors on Black Friday – invites nation to OptOutside, REI.com, 27 October. https://newsroom.rei.com/news/corporate/rei-closing-its-doors-on-black-friday-invites-nation-to-optoutside.htm (archived at https://perma.cc/42KV-YCUZ)

REI (2019) REI Co-op publishes 2019 full-year financial results, REI.com, 27 April. https://www.rei.com/newsroom/article/rei-co-op-publishes-2019-full-year-financial-results (archived at https://perma.cc/B39R-5V6S)

Ritson, M (2019) A true brand purpose doesn't boost profit, it sacrifices it, *Marketing Week*, 21 March. https://www.marketingweek.com/mark-ritson-true-brand-purpose-doesnt-boost-profit-sacrifices/ (archived at https://perma.cc/9PC4-5DWV)

Schwartz, T and Porath, C (2014) The power of meeting your employees' needs, *Harvard Business Review*, 30 June. https://hbr.org/2014/06/the-power-of-meeting-your-employees-needs (archived at https://perma.cc/5GPA-Z92K)

Serafeim, G and Gartenberg, C (2016) The type of purpose that makes companies more profitable, *Harvard Business Review*, 21 October. https://hbr.org/2016/10/the-type-of-purpose-that-makes-companies-more-profitable (archived at https://perma.cc/GC6G-D52C)

Sorenson, S and Garman, K (2013) How to tackle U.S. employees' stagnating engagement, *Gallup*, 11 June. https://news.gallup.com/businessjournal/162953/tackle-employees-stagnating-engagement.aspx (archived at https://perma.cc/YTB3-AZVS)

03

Moving to Movement Thinking

This is a remarkable moment in time. An age of movements. Movements in politics and society, and sparked by brands. Movements can galvanize people, many of whom may feel a sense of helplessness and powerlessness or simply feel overwhelmed with information. Movements *move* people.

Movements are based on ideas. Ideas that inspire bigger ambitions. Ideas that can be an explosion or a contagion of truth-telling. Ideas that people rally around to drive change, to become an active part of the movement. The simple act of sharing one's story is a powerful way to help start a sweeping conversation with the goal of trying to change the world instead of conforming to it – one person tells their story, someone says that's also happening to me, and everything changes. Movement creates an incredible, amazing feeling. If you've ever been caught up in one, you recognize this feeling and the realization that 'I no longer stand alone'. When you join a movement, you can feel that your thoughts are important, you feel heard – you feel empowered.

The simple idea of this book is that leaders seeking to transform their companies, change employee habits or grow their business should activate purpose with Movement Thinking. This chapter will explain why that is, and how to go about it.

Why is Movement Thinking so powerful?

Throughout history, civilization has been shaped by movements. Movements have helped create the modern-day US democratic society from its earliest beginnings with a fight for independence. This kind of fight has played itself out in one way or another in Germany, France, the UK, Eastern Europe, the Middle East, North Africa, India, Indonesia and South Africa.

Today, movements, fuelled by social media, are turbo-charged, mobilizing millions of people of all ages, inspiring and empowering groups of people large and small to take a stand, to right a wrong, to drive meaningful change.

For example, unless you've been on another planet, you will be familiar with the anti-mask movement during the COVID-19 pandemic. This movement has played out in various places around the world and has elicited support from prominent political figures in the UK and America: Peter Hitchens of the *Daily Mail* called masks 'muzzles'; Michael Savage, a prominent American talk radio host, called masks a 'mark of submission'. The conception of 'freedom as non-interference' that underpins the anti-mask movement has the virtue of simplicity. It allows us to apply an easy metric to test our freedom: if our choices are interfered with, we are less free (Blunt, 2020). It's amazing to consider that a movement has the power to motivate millions of people to do something that can endanger their lives.

Movements key off the power of peer pressure and the magical power of belonging. Now imagine applying this same kind of power to problem-solving inside your organization. To many, it may sound far-fetched to apply the logic of social movements to the business world, but as you'll see throughout this chapter, we think they're wrong.

It has been swelling all around us in life, politics, business since the 2010s, when social media spread activism across the internet like wildfire, and when movements like the Susan G Komen walk for breast cancer, Occupy Wall Street and the Arab Spring set the early 21st century on its current course. You just have to look to more recent movements like Black Lives Matter and #MeToo, where people gathered by the millions around the world sparking global movements for racial injustice and women's rights, to see how movements continue to impact culture. With hashtags like #NeverAgain and #JeSuisCharlie, people rallied against gun violence and called for gun reform. With #FridaysForOurFuture and #ClimateStrike, students around the globe raised their voices for action around climate change. With the #UmbrellaRevolution, pro-democracy protesters in Hong Kong organized to fight against government oppression.

As these movements make headlines around the world, they break through the walls of indifference, human apathy or human distraction caused by technology enthralment, shaping our lives in many ways. The Black Lives Matter movement has resulted in widespread reflection on issues of systemic racism and unconscious bias. Workplace culture has been transformed by #MeToo, which prompted the outing of bad behaviour across all industries and sectors of business. And just look at how the students at Marjory Stoneman Douglas High School, the site of a mass school shooting, reshaped gun politics in America by saying #NeverAgain and organizing the March for Our Lives in Washington DC in 2018, a movement to stop gun violence. Aside from attracting between 1.2 million and 2 million protesters in 1,000 associated marches around the United States (Dreier, 2020), the movement led to the ban of bump stocks, stricter gun laws in Florida, and prompted companies including Best Western, Hertz and Wyndham to end their affiliation with the National Rifle Association (Rushe, 2018). It has had a lasting impact on the business of guns in America.

In contemplating the impact that the election of US President Donald Trump has had on activist behaviour, activist LA Kaufmann noted in *The Guardian* that over the course of the first 15 months of the 45th presidency, more people joined demonstrations than at any other time in American history, with numbers estimated between 10 million and 15 million (Kaufmann, 2018). Those numbers, which have surely swelled since, represent more people in absolute terms than have ever protested before in the US. Kaufmann wrote:

> Even when you adjust for population growth, it's probably a higher percentage than took to the streets during the height of the Vietnam anti-war movement in 1969 and 1970, the previous high-water mark for dissent in America, though the data for that era is much less comprehensive.

This rise in activism is much more than anecdotal; there's hard evidence to support that the numbers of protesters now outpace those of previous generations. A survey from polling firm Gallup found in 2018 that one in three Americans, or 36 per cent, reported having felt the urge to protest (Reinhart, 2018). To put that number in context, the last time Gallup asked Americans about their interest in protesting was in October 1965, during the civil rights movement, and as anti-Vietnam war demonstrations were escalating. At that time, Gallup found that only 10 per cent of Americans felt compelled to protest.

Throughout history, nothing compares with the power of movements to get things done. As famed activist Gloria Steinem once said when discussing her role in crystallizing the women's movement in the late-1960s and 1970s: 'When you tap into shared experience the world cracks open' (Apple, 2020).

Why are movements on the rise?

So why are movements on the rise now? Why are we seeing increasing unrest in Asia, Europe, North Africa and South America, as well as in the United States? Clearly, there must be something afoot that is not unique to the countries experiencing protest. There are a number of factors that are present globally that are fuelling the rise of activism.

Power shift from elites

No longer do those in power have a monopoly on the message – the editor of *Vogue* arguably has less influence than the thousands of fashion Instagrammers. Despite scandals and sometimes problematic views, the top YouTubers routinely boast tens of millions more subscribers than *The New York Times*.

Those who define culture and hold the power of the message have changed. The pyramid has flipped from a small group of people at the top to the people in the middle and at the bottom, who assert greater control of the story, the message and policy. Inside companies, that means the C-suite demanding compliance no longer works as well as a movement in which all employees feel like they belong because it's relevant and important to each of them. Technology and the internet are the reasons this is happening.

Social media

Of that technology, social media has had perhaps the greatest impact. A 2019 report from Pew Research Center, a US non-partisan public opinion research organization, found that when it comes to public attitudes towards political engagement on social platforms, Americans view social media as an important platform. Of those surveyed, 69 per cent said they felt social media was important for change and 67 per cent said the platforms create sustained movements for social change. When it came to opinions on whether social media is key to getting officials to pay attention to issues, 69 per cent said it was. Pew also found that 53 per cent of Americans had engaged in some form of political or social-minded activity on social media in the past year (Anderson *et al*, 2018).

The report also looked at #BlackLivesMatter in detail to examine how the hashtag's use evolved over the five years since its inception and to assess whether it had a significant impact on the movement. Spoiler alert: it did.

Pew's analysis of public tweets found the hashtag had been used nearly 30 million times on Twitter – an average of 17,002 times per day – as of 1 May 2018. The high water mark during that time came over a particularly deadly period from 7–17 July 2016 after police fatally shot Alton Sterling in Baton Rouge, Louisiana on 5 July 2016 and Philando Castile the next day in Saint Paul, Minnesota. The killing of eight officers in two separate attacks in Dallas, Texas and Baton Rouge, Louisiana followed in the days after. This influx of violence by and against police resulted in the hashtag being used in roughly 500,000 tweets daily (Figure 3.1).

FIGURE 3.1 Use of the #BlackLivesMatter hashtag hits record levels amid global protests over George Floyd's death while in police custody

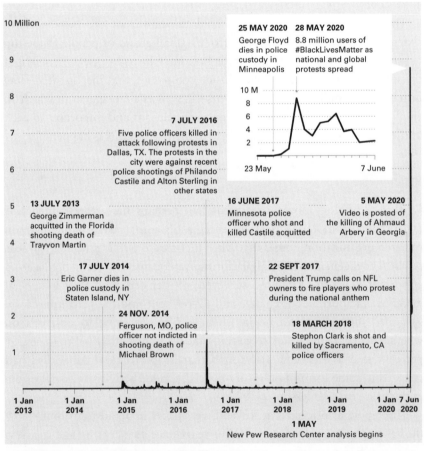

Number of public Twitter posts mentioning the #BlackLivesMatter hashtag from 1 January 2013 to 7 June 2020

25 MAY 2020   **28 MAY 2020**
George Floyd dies in police custody in Minneapolis   8.8 million users of #BlackLivesMatter as national and global protests spread

7 JULY 2016
Five police officers killed in attack following protests in Dallas, TX. The protests in the city were against recent police shootings of Philando Castile and Alton Sterling in other states

13 JULY 2013
George Zimmerman acquitted in the Florida shooting death of Trayvon Martin

16 JUNE 2017
Minnesota police officer who shot and killed Castile acquitted

5 MAY 2020
Video is posted of the killing of Ahmaud Arbery in Georgia

17 JULY 2014
Eric Garner dies in police custody in Staten Island, NY

22 SEPT 2017
President Trump calls on NFL owners to fire players who protest during the national anthem

24 NOV. 2014
Ferguson, MO, police officer not indicted in shooting death of Michael Brown

18 MARCH 2018
Stephon Clark is shot and killed by Sacramento, CA police officers

1 MAY
New Pew Research Center analysis begins

SOURCE PEW, found at Anderson *et al* (2020)

If those numbers seem high, they were nothing compared with the unbelievable surge of tweets containing the hashtag following the death of George Floyd. From 26 May to 7 June 2020, #BlackLivesMatter was used roughly 47.8 million times on Twitter, which equates to a daily average of just under 3.7 million. There were 8.8 million tweets on 28 May alone (Anderson *et al*, 2020), demonstrating how vital social media is in amplifying and unifying a movement's message.

Political conditions

In so many of the world's uprisings – from North Africa during the Arab Spring in 2011 to the 2019 pro-democracy protests in Hong Kong that lasted for 20 consecutive weekends – people are demonstrating against the same thing: oppressive and anti-democratic regimes.

While people have long voiced their displeasure over politics and political leaders through protest, new research suggests there's something different with this decade's movements. A 2019 V-Dem study by Anna Lührmann and Staffan Lindberg of the University of Gothenburg found that for the first time since the Second World War, the number of countries moving towards authoritarianism is exceeding the number moving towards democracy. While they say the evidence shows that more than half of all countries qualify as democratic, they do say 'a third wave of autocratization is indeed unfolding' (Maerz *et al*, 2020).

Increasing inequality

The gap between the rich and poor has been widening across the world. It's what sent protestors to Zuccotti Park during Occupy Wall Street a decade ago; it's why in 2019 Chile endured the worst unrest in decades; and it's why people poured into the streets in support of Black lives while lockdown orders were in effect across America due to the COVID-19 pandemic (Kaplan *et al*, 2020).

It is even why people protested those same lockdown orders – working-class people who were unable to weather the financial storm as well as the more well-heeled, who escaped to isolate themselves in their country homes – though the message with that protest might have been a bit off, since demanding a haircut, as many signs and placards read (Gregorian, 2020), might not have been quite as compelling as arguing the need to support one's family.

Angry youth

These political and social imbalances are intensifying existing pressures. And the people most up in arms about them are young. In fact, as Simon Tisdall writes in *The Guardian*, there are more young people than ever before: 41 per cent of the global population is under 24 years old. That's a lot of young people – young people who have come of age in a world shaped by the 2008 financial crisis. 'As a result, many current protests are rooted in shared grievances about economic inequality and jobs' (Tisdall, 2019).

Protest culture is probably some combination of all of these factors, but the net result is that business leaders are now dealing with a populace that is more socially engaged, more aware of what's going on in the world, and hungrier to get involved and be heard on various issues.

Why does this rise matter to company leaders? The answer is simple: because leaders can use the principles of societal movement to engage and mobilize the masses to drive change. Your customers, stakeholders and employees are all impacted by the rising movement culture we discussed above. They are the same people that might be moved to march – or likely already have. In an age when activism is becoming normalized, being unaware of, dismissive of or, worse, tone-deaf towards the issues that matter will lead you to be ignored. In this new world, your customers and employees can easily become activists – either for or against you.

What we can learn from societal movements' decay and success

One problem with protests is that they often fail to transition into a bona fide movement. In *Uprising*, Scott Goodson's first book on movements in 2011, Occupy Wall Street was in full swing. But it ultimately fizzled, proving that just having people in the streets does not necessarily equal success for a cause.

'Occupy was, at its core, a movement constrained by its own contradictions: filled with leaders who declared themselves leaderless, governed by a consensus-based structure that failed to reach consensus, and seeking to transform politics while refusing to become political,' wrote Michael Levitin (2015) in *The Atlantic*. Occupy's undoing was that it was unfocused; people who were in support of the movement didn't really know what to do to support it. A movement strategy would have kept the Occupy movement focused on driving positive change, and kept it front and centre and helped it grow instead of petering out.

Ironic as it may seem, the impact of the movement that many view as having decayed and disappeared may in fact have become stronger and clearer with time. The world's 1 per cent now possess almost as much combined wealth as the bottom 90 per cent. And while no one in Washington may have the full answer about how to fix income inequality, more elected leaders, it seems, are now openly talking about the issue and framing solutions. As Levitin says: Occupy got the diagnosis correct but real change doesn't come in slogans; it comes when the people demand it.

In contrast, Black Lives Matter has managed to have a sustained movement, though we're sure the organizers would prefer to have police brutality dealt with once and for all, rather than continually having to mobilize people. Speaking with *USA Today* in the weeks following the protests over Floyd's death, Black Lives Matter co-founder Patrisse Cullors said the movement works because the organization is usually spontaneous and decentralized, relying almost solely on local, rather than national, leadership. 'We don't get (people) onto the streets, they get themselves onto the street,' she told the paper (Miller, 2016).

This, says Greg Satell, author of *Cascades: How to create a movement that drives transformational change*, is one of the things successful movements have in common: they gain strength through small groups, not large, front-page-worthy crowds. Writing in *Harvard Business Review,* he references Solomon Asch, a prominent psychologist in the 1950s who studied conformity. He found that people conform to a majority opinion in small groups, even if they're not people they know well. 'It is when small groups connect – which has become exponentially easier in the digital age – that they gain power' (Satell, 2016).

While social media was instrumental in rallying people around Black Lives Matter in moments of crisis, the grassroots mobilization kept it going. The movement has been a sustained voice against violence against Black lives since its inception, and that consistent presence has meant that people know how to communicate, mobilize and make an impact – fast.

So what can businesses learn from the success of BLM and the failure of Occupy? In reality, Occupy was a sit-in protest in search of a movement strategy. It lacked leadership, it lacked a message other than 'greed is bad', and it had no clear practical demands about what it wanted to see change. Conversely, Black Lives Matter was crystal clear about what it wanted to see change regarding racially motivated violence against Black people. And it rallied small groups of like-minded individuals across America around a clear shared purpose.

When movements affect the world of commerce

Thus far in this chapter, we've been looking mainly at how movements work in society and culture.

But protests have been aimed at companies and brands for decades, often in the form of boycotts. Since the purpose of this book is to articulate how the power of movements can be leveraged by company and brand leaders, it's useful to spend a moment looking at how activism has shaped the world of commerce.

Whether decrying child labour at Nike factories or lobbying clothing giant Zara to discontinue its use of fur, whether making consumers aware of the devastating effects of palm oil use in KitKat or raising awareness over conflict diamonds, consumer and activist-led pressure has caused corporations to change their practices.

Indeed, Nike vastly improved working conditions at its factories after public outcry in 1998 (Wilsey and Lichtig, 2018). Following pressure from the Coalition to Abolish the Fur Trade, Inditex Group, which owns Zara, withdrew fur from all of its 2,064 stores in 52 countries (Carlile, 2019) in 2004. In 2010, after eight weeks of campaigning by Greenpeace against the use of palm oil, Nestlé promised a zero-deforestation policy in its palm oil supply chain (Carlile, 2019). And in 2018, Cartier pledged to stop buying gems from Myanmar, where the trade of precious stones funds the country's military, after human rights activists called for jewellers to boycott gemstones from the region (Carlile, 2019).

In recent years, prominent boycotts have been more politically motivated, and surveys show that large swathes of the American public are prepared to steer clear of brands and companies that don't jibe with their political outlook. In 2017, Ipsos released a report called 'Brand risk in the new age of populism' in which it found that one in four Americans had boycotted a product for political reasons (Ipsos, 2017). That same year, leading advertising trade publication *Adweek* reported that 57 per cent of consumers were prepared to boycott a brand that didn't share their social beliefs (Monllos, 2017).

That willingness to take action is how the Grab Your Wallet Alliance influenced Nordstrom to drop Ivanka Trump's clothing line (Abrams, 2017). Founded by activist Shannon Coulter following the election of Donald Trump, and named in response to and as a rejection of his infamous 'grab her by the pussy' comments uttered before his election, the movement called for economic boycotts against companies with connections to the president.

More recently, Starbucks drew public backlash for stating that employees who wore shirts or pins with BLM messaging violated its dress code policy during the surge of Black Lives Matter activity in 2020. It reversed its stance two days later after intense public pressure (Lucas, 2020).

In a world dominated by social media and the swift judgement of cancel culture – that phenomenon where public support instantly evaporates when a company or public figure makes a misstep that's objectionable – it's essential for businesses to be aware of how the rising tide of movements and activism could cause potential harm. That said, activism, as it relates to brands, needn't be negative. As we'll see below, aligning with an idea in culture can actually be key to fostering a fruitful brand movement.

Consider North Face, which in 2020 ignited a movement among companies to stop advertising on Facebook. A response to the 'Stop Hate for Profit' campaign, launched by advocacy groups including the Anti-Defamation League and the NAACP, the retailer pulled its ad dollars from the social media giant, demanding it stop allowing and amplifying messages of hate and misinformation on its platform. It was quickly joined by REI, Unilever, Verizon and hundreds of other companies (Paul, 2020). Consider Barbie, which has long faced criticism over its narrow vision of beauty. Operating in a resurgent age of women's rights, racial equality and more diverse representation, it has reinvented itself with a line of dolls that includes more skin tones, body shapes and varying physical abilities (Cramer, 2020).

Movements take hold in marketing

While not always defined in such terms, movements have been a part of marketing for decades, though they have tended to be the exception instead of the rule. When VW launched its 'Think Small' campaign in the 1960s, it was aligning with the counterculture of the time. People were drawn to VW because it stood against overconsumption and was all for eco-conscious alternatives. When Apple set out to challenge computing goliath IBM, it aimed to make computers fun. The entire culture at Apple rallied behind the idea of the 'Crazy Ones' and it infiltrated everything they did and how they advertised.

These companies tapped into a rising idea and designed their own corporate culture around it first and then launched strategic campaigns that helped give voice to a swelling cultural idea. Apple wanted to be a light-hearted counterpoint to IBM's stodgy business machines; striking and whimsical ads featuring Einstein sticking his tongue out fuelled the idea.

As we mentioned earlier, one of our earliest campaigns at StrawberryFrog was a movement for a car brand. Our first client, which launched StrawberryFrog back in 1999, came back and asked us to fix their brand in the United States 15 years later. This was a time of big cars. Minivans and SUVs were the go-to vehicles for so many Americans, but it was also the early days of conscious consumerism and not everyone was comfortable with the bigger is better mantra.

That presented an opportunity. Rather than just lean into rational and functional arguments like fuel efficiency and affordability and a low carbon footprint, the Smart Car would be an alternative to overconsumption, it would be against big, it would be 'Against Dumb', as our brand campaign was called. It would be smart. And people were compelled to act: a community of vocal advocates rallied around the brand and in a short time its audience more than quadrupled and sales grew 172 per cent. Nearly 20 years later, in a climate of renewed consumer activism, Smart Car is still seen as a conscious choice that is *against dumb*.

This was our first foray into Movement Thinking and it showed us that in marketing a movement is a brand's best friend. It allows you to use creativity for good. And when you do, the results can be extraordinary. Let's look at a few more examples.

Always 'Like a Girl'

Always' most famous and effective ad didn't even mention the product. Instead, it revealed a damaging reality affecting its youngest consumers: that doing things 'like a girl' was considered a negative.

Filmed as a social experiment, #LikeAGirl recruited real women, men, boys and pre-pubescent girls and asked them to show what it physically meant to run like a girl, throw like a girl and do other similar actions, without giving any additional context. The young girls in the film were confident and uninhibited; everyone else just flailed around like fools. The point was to illustrate how at a certain point in life, specifically puberty, young women begin to internalize the negative connotations that come from doing things 'like a girl' and lose their confidence.

It was a powerful ad for pads, but it grew into so much more. The film aired on the Super Bowl and for International Women's Day and Always encouraged girls to share photos and videos online to show the awesome ways they were being #LikeAGirl. Always took a stand against a deeply ingrained insult and sought to rewrite what it means to play 'like a girl'.

According to P&G, 76 per cent of women aged 16 to 24 said that they no longer saw 'like a girl' as a pejorative after watching the video, up from 19 per cent beforehand. And two-thirds of men said that it made them question using the phrase as an insult (Contagious, 2015).

American Express 'Stand for Small'

In the spring of 2020, American Express took the next step in its 12-year movement to help small business owners with the launch of 'Stand for Small', a coalition of more than 40 companies across media, technology, consumer goods, professional services and many other industries that have come together to provide meaningful support to small businesses as they navigate the impacts of COVID-19. Stephen Squeri, chairman and CEO of American Express, said in a statement about the initiative:

> We've always believed in the power of partnership and could not be prouder to stand tall for small with more than 40 partners to offer meaningful support to small businesses during this challenging time. The companies joining Stand for Small all have legacies of supporting the more than 30 million small businesses in the US, and collectively, our goal is to provide them with valuable resources so that we can come out stronger together once this crisis ends. (*Business Wire*, 2020)

This is the latest iteration of a movement Amex began during the financial crisis of 2008. Back then, many small businesses were struggling. American Express knew that communities need small businesses to thrive, so in 2010 it launched Small Business Saturday, a shopping holiday on the first Saturday after Thanksgiving to encourage people to shop local.

In the midst of a recession, a credit card company took a stand against big box and online shopping and stood for bricks-and-mortar entrepreneurs and community-based businesses. It gave people a day, Small Business Saturday, to mobilize. The 'Shop Small' movement instantly gained traction and by 2011 the Senate unanimously passed a resolution in support of the day, which is observed in all 50 US states (American Express, 2019).

Going into its 10th year, American Express conducted a study with Wakefield Research looking into how successful it was at moving people to shop local. It found that 77 per cent of 1,000 people surveyed were interested in spending money with small businesses on Small Business Saturday that year, an increase from 44 per cent in 2010. Amex also reported that consumers spent more than $100 billion at small businesses over the programme's nine years and that 67 cents of every dollar spent at local businesses remained in their communities – about $67 billion (Liffreing, 2019).

Bombas Socks

Over the years, we've seen that movements at companies can be more than marketing; they can be the foundation of their entire business model, like TOMS Shoes or Warby Parker with its sell-one, give-one model. They're born of a movement.

That was the case with Bombas Socks, which is often called 'the TOMS of socks'. Founders David Heath and Randy Goldberg were dissatisfied with the fact that socks were the single most requested clothing item at homeless shelters, and built a company that was for the belief that everyone deserves clean, dry feet. The Bombas product was designed with features that homeless people need, like no toe seam and extra protection against water, and with every one sold, one is donated to shelters (Berger, 2019).

In starting a movement for dry, comfortable feet, Heath and Goldberg hoped to donate a million socks within 10 years. They reached that goal in two and a half years and reached 5 million donations just a year later. It was a clearly articulated purpose and a movement people wanted to join – though we suspect a high-profile deal from Daymond John on *Shark Tank* helped fuel the groundswell!

Movements and company purpose

If the link between movements and marketing has been established, there's a new evolution in Movement Thinking: in recent years it's extended all the way through the C-suite, impacting not just ad campaigns or PR, but an entire company ethos. When David Heath and Randy Goldberg founded Bombas with a mission to give away a million socks, they established a purposeful company culture.

When we first started talking about movements at StrawberryFrog, we focused mostly on marketing. But over time we've seen the power that movements can have when applied internally to corporate culture and organizational design. Movements can impact more than marketing or PR; they can inform an entire company ethos.

Who Gives a Crap, a subscription-based sustainable toilet paper brand, offers a good example of how a company's purpose can spur a movement. Founded in Australia in 2012 with an Indiegogo campaign, the company set out to disrupt the most unlikely of industries: toilet paper. Available in

Australia, Canada, the United Kingdom and the United States, and wrapped in trendy paper packaging, Who Gives a Crap is a high-design alternative in a category full of generally banal branding.

The germ of the company didn't come from anyone saying, 'Hey, let's disrupt TP.' Instead, it was started when the founders discovered that 2.3 billion people don't have access to a toilet. To right that wrong, Who Gives a Crap donates 50 per cent of its profits to initiatives that help improve sanitation around the world. At the time of writing, the company had donated over $5.7 million to sanitation projects around the world.

This model spurred others to follow suit. The sector now includes eco-friendly, design-forward brands such as Tushy, No. 2 and Cheeky Monkey, which the company views as actually welcomed competition – sort of. On its site, it actively encourages other entrepreneurs to join their movement to create profitable businesses that give back (Who Gives a Crap, 2020).

But purpose doesn't always have to be the motivator from the start. That was the case with luxury linen company Boll & Branch. Company founder Scott Tannen told us that when he and his wife Missy set out to start the company, the goal was simply to 'make it easier for people to buy a great set of sheets'. His company's purpose soon found him, however. Formerly a digital media executive, Tannen was largely unfamiliar with the textiles industry, other than knowing it didn't have the greatest reputation.

He told us that when starting out he had the benefit of fresh eyes. As he learned about the industry, however, he didn't like what he saw. 'We kept reaching points where we'd scratch our heads and think, this can't really be how it works. It can't be possible that you don't know where the cotton comes from.' From that point, he resolved to build a business with a supply chain that was 'the way we felt it should be built'. That led him to create Boll & Branch in 2013 as the first certified Fair Trade organic and sustainable linen company in the US (Yakowicz, 2015).

In the early days of the company, Tannen told us he noodled with the idea of setting up a giving model like TOMS or other such social enterprises, but with textiles, he saw an opportunity to challenge the industry's status quo by ensuring the cotton used in its products was sourced in a way that treated everyone in the supply chain well. 'Everyone in our supply chain, from a cotton farmer right through to the C-suite, plays a part, and we believe that everyone should have the same basic value. That's the impact we're trying to make,' he said in our conversation.

Boll & Branch's attention to detail in its supply chain translates to the product it sells. As Tannen said to us, if you're not thinking about how your cotton is sourced, are you overlooking details that make your product better?

> Being thoughtful about everything is something that does manifest itself in the product. So, while a customer might not buy us because we're part of a seed cultivation project in India that makes cotton seeds more affordable to farmers, they can appreciate the level of detail that goes into how the corner threads of our sheets are tacked down.

As we frequently see with purpose-driven companies, like T-Mobile and Nextdoor from Chapter 1, Boll & Branch's purpose was activated in real time during the COVID-19 pandemic. Just as the demand for hospital beds was skyrocketing and New York City was setting up make-shift hospitals in convention centres, demand for mattresses was plummeting and previously placed orders were being cancelled. One of Boll & Branch's mattress suppliers had to furlough hundreds of employees in its Orlando factory. Based on a suggestion from one of his colleagues, Tannen told us that Boll & Branch ended up helping the factory pivot to make hospital mattresses for New York healthcare facilities while it was in the height of the first wave of the pandemic, resulting in much-needed hospital bedding while keeping factory workers employed (Chhabra, 2020). In addition, it donated 10 per cent of sales to COVID-19 relief efforts. 'As a company that exists to support everybody in our supply chain and our community, this was an opportunity for us to live our values,' Tannen said. The most important part of living those values, he said, is maintaining a healthy business, and sometimes that means helping keep partners and suppliers going in times of crisis.

CEO ACTIVISM

There was a time when the chief concern of a CEO was the bottom line, making money for shareholders, besting category competitors. All those things still matter to business leaders the world over, but there's a new, rising concern: doing what's right, not just for the business but for society.

Enter CEO activism, which is when business leaders engage in political or social issues that do not relate directly to their companies (Chatterji and Toffel, 2018) – like Anand Mahindra, the chairman of the Mahindra Group, and his quest to educate young girls in order to help reduce forced child marriage, overpopulation, environmental impact, disease, and other indirectly related issues such as the spread of terrorism and sexual exploitation. Or like former GoDaddy CEO Blake Irving, who took a stance against misogyny and transformed the company. Or Patagonia's Yvon Chouinard, who is singular in his focus to save our planet. CEOs are taking action on the issues that matter to them.

In 2016, PayPal CEO Dan Schulman cancelled plans to invest $3.6 million in North Carolina after the state passed a controversial law targeting lesbian, gay, bisexual and transgender (LGBT) citizens, and instead invested in a different state. Salesforce CEO Marc Benioff threatened to stop sending employees to Indiana and Georgia in reaction to those states' anti-gay laws. Meanwhile, and showing that CEO activism is not the domain of one political leaning, Chick-fil-A's CEO Dan Cathy was very outspoken in his denunciation of gay marriage.

As Bank of America CEO Brian Moynihan told *The Wall Street Journal* in 2018, 'Our jobs as CEOs now include driving what we think is right. It's not exactly political activism, but it is action on issues beyond business' (Chatterji and Toffel, 2018).

Indeed, as the world grappled with the COVID-19 pandemic, the CEOs of 155 companies from around the world, which together employ over 5 million people and have a combined market capitalization of over US$2.4 trillion, signed a statement urging governments to align their recovery plans with climate science. The companies – including Carlsberg Group, Electrolux, Enel, Iberdrola, Saint-Gobain, Schneider Electric – used their collective power to influence an economic recovery and a remodelling of business that prioritizes holding global temperature rise to within 1.5°C above pre-industrial levels and reaching net-zero emissions well before 2050 (Science Based Targets, 2020).

That's the kind of action people expect of corporate leaders these days. A 2018 report titled 'The purposeful CEO' from KRC Research and Weber Shandwick found 77 per cent of Americans agree CEOs need to speak out in defence of their company's values.

The positive reception to CEO activism is also increasing: 38 per cent of Americans have a favourable opinion on CEO activism, a rate which is significantly higher than in 2017 (31 per cent). And approximately half of Americans (48 per cent) think CEO activism has an influence on the government, considerably larger than a year earlier (38 per cent) (Weber Shandwick, 2018).

Necessary conditions for successful movements

While later in this chapter we're going to offer a framework for creating enterprise movements, whether internally or in external marketing, we first wanted to isolate the factors that make a movement successful. To do that we spoke with leading social movement expert Sarah Soule, professor of organizational behaviour at the Stanford Graduate School of Business. She told us successful enterprise movements tend to have three things in common:

1 They have an elite ally: they have someone in leadership to spearhead the cause.

2 They successfully frame the issue: they are clear in what they're asking of people (see 'A framework for Movement Thinking' below).

3 They embrace the osmotic effect: they are informed by and leverage what is happening in the broader culture.

The elite ally: Blake Irving

In discussing elite allies, Soule points to Blake Irving, introduced earlier as a CEO activist. When Irving took the reins of GoDaddy as CEO in 2013, the company was something of a pariah in the business world. The brand made its name on blatantly sexist television commercials featuring girls in dripping wet bikinis and other misogynistic tropes. Some were so provocative they were banned; their offensiveness affected employee morale. But Irving had a plan to turn the ship around. As he told *The New York Times* in a 2017 article, 'We needed to become the most inclusive company in tech' (Duhigg, 2017).

He did that first by pulling the chauvinistic advertising. That was the easy part. The real work came in seeking to uncover all the subtle biases that affected everything from how the company recruited to how performance metrics like communication response time disadvantaged women, who tend to be primary caregivers. It countered those biases by assessing the company's hiring, salaries, employee evaluations and promotions.

Irving departed GoDaddy in 2017, but his influence, leadership and role as an elite ally have left it transformed. According to the company's 2019 diversity and salary data, it has made gains in the number of women in technical and leadership roles, and more importantly, the 2019 data showed that GoDaddy paid men and women at parity for five consecutive years (GoDaddy, 2019).

Framing the issue: marriage equality

Implicit in our attempt to solve any problem or bring about a change is a way of thinking about it – it's what academics refer to as framing. We often don't realize that we are framing things in a particular way and that how we do so can have a huge impact on whether we successfully solve the problem. That's because the frame surrounding the issue can change perception without having to alter the actual facts as the same information is used as a base.

How a movement is framed is essential to its success because framing is essentially what you're asking people to support.

Soule says that over the years, the thinking on framing movements has evolved. She told us that in the 1990s it was thought that 'blended frames' were preferred. As an example, she points to the fight for gay rights and domestic partnership benefits, such as health and dental coverage. At the time, a significant study showed that it was important for advocates to make a connection to how affording domestic partnership benefits was good for the bottom line of a company, as well as arguing that it was simply the right thing to do.

However, she says more recent literature found that framing an issue with a clear, single objective is more effective. 'You actually have to have a pretty specific frame because otherwise, leadership doesn't know how to respond to it,' she told us.

This truth bore out during the movement for marriage equality in the US. In its effort to win the right to marry, the Civil Marriage Collaborative, a consortium of foundations dedicated to marriage equality, framed the issue as being about gaining rights in other areas, such as healthcare and the right to adoption.

The problem was that equal rights and benefits were not why most straight people got married. It was for love. Realizing this, the movement reframed the issue to one about marrying the person you love and commitment, and on 26 June 2015, the US Supreme Court made marriage equality law.

Matt Foreman, who was a member of Civil Marriage Equality at the time, wrote in *Nonprofit Quarterly* a year after the landmark victory that in hindsight the flaw in their framing seemed painfully obvious. Research showed that when asked, straight people said they got married for love and commitment. Those same straight people believed gay people, on the other hand, got married for rights and benefits. 'In other words,' Foreman wrote, 'our "rights and benefits" frame only reinforced the belief that gay people were operating from an entirely different values frame – love vs better dental' (Foreman, 2016).

This example shows that just because a frame might make the most sense, it doesn't mean it will have the greatest emotional impact. Recalling our example of the Smart Car, there might have been compelling evidence that it was more fuel-efficient, but it was capturing imaginations and aligning with the zeitgeist that was rejecting overconsumption that resulted in a lasting movement.

The osmotic effect: #MeToo

A recent example of the osmotic effect, which is how external factors affect an organization, is the #MeToo movement. #MeToo came to mainstream prominence in 2017 following accusations of serial sexual assault against Hollywood mogul Harvey Weinstein. He was the culprit that his victims were speaking out against. But its impact extended well beyond those individuals.

The movement swelled into a tidal wave of similar accusations in every industry and sector of business, which saw the dismantling of powerful men and resulted in substantial change, including US states banning non-disclosure agreements that cover sexual harassment, increased workplace protections for staffers reporting sexual assault (North, 2019) and declining reports of sexual harassment in the workplace (Keplinger *et al*, 2019).

While sexual harassment has been an incessant problem for years, it wasn't until a tidal wave of news and social media coverage of the Weinstein case erupted that the issue reached a tipping point and spurred real change in a broad sense. This long overdue cultural reckoning spread beyond the grassroots of the movement and permeated the world of business. When a concept is reaching a groundswell (or just catching on), we at StrawberryFrog refer to it as an 'Idea on the Rise' in culture – and aligning with ideas that are trending culturally is what fuels participation.

Movement Thinking > conventional thinking

If, as we just discussed, framing is a way to change someone's perception about something, then Movement Thinking is a way to frame a situation. It's a way to change people's conventional thinking; it breaks people out of their default position. Just consider these examples of how leaders from different disciplines might traditionally approach their roles:

- CEOs: Company leaders may be accustomed to giving an order and expecting change to happen. This has long been considered effective leadership, but it fails to engage the people who will ultimately be responsible for implementing change on a day-to-day basis. They're coming from a place of 'mandate-think'.

- CHROs: Heads of human resource departments traditionally come from a place of 'policy-think', where they create frameworks for employee behaviour and the administration of benefits, without taking into account the people affected by the policies.

- CMOs: Marketing chiefs have the task of selling products or attracting consumers to their business. This is often done through the lens of 'positioning-think' or 'ad think', which is focused on owning real estate in the minds of its target audience without necessarily considering whether that target audience actually cares.

The problem with these approaches is that they fail to connect with people emotionally and galvanize them to action, which is how meaningful change happens. One of the beauties of Movement Thinking is it is a way for CEOs, CHROs and CMOs to have a common framing of a challenge.

Movement Thinking, as we mentioned in Chapter 1, helps you achieve the desired change by rallying people around a common enemy and cause that stirs them emotionally and leads to action. It's a way of framing a particular change we would like to see in the world in a grievance that needs to be addressed, a wrong that needs to be made right, and a stand we're motivated to take in order to make things right.

For example, BLM addresses the issue of systematic police violence, not in terms of a rational argument for police reform, but rather it expresses the grievance of eradicating white supremacy and building local power to intervene in violence inflicted on Black communities by state actors and vigilantes. The marriage equality movement succeeded by framing its issue not as a narrow, rational argument about equal rights for gay people but rather as aimed at the broadly shared enemy of the inability to marry the person you love.

This is what movement strategy can do; it links your purpose to an idea on the rise in culture. Over the years we've launched movements for clients that tried to bring about change in school education, in taking a stand against video games and for greater imagination and free play among children, and for more responsible consumption. We developed a movement for a pet food company that launched an animal welfare initiative, and for a shoemaker that began a worldwide movement to put shoes on poor kids' feet. In each case, a company rallied people around an idea that was beginning to increasingly matter in culture, enabling customers to become activists.

A framework for Movement Thinking

Whether you're looking to move to Movement Thinking for organizational change or to achieve an external marketing objective, the principles are the same. It starts with reframing your challenge in movement terms. Here, again, are the five key building blocks of Movement Thinking in more detail.

Building block 1 – the dissatisfaction

Scholars who've studied important social movements like civil rights, gay rights or Occupy Wall Street all point to one key driver that sparks *all* movements. It's a grievance, a dissatisfaction, a wrong in the world that needs to be made right. The same is true with movements that are sparked by companies and brands. For Black Lives Matter, the dissatisfaction is police racial profiling and brutality. For REI, the dissatisfaction is around the fact that modern life is getting in the way of people's love of the outdoors. For Dove, the dissatisfaction is that too few women today feel they are beautiful.

It's important to keep in mind here that we're talking about a precise dissatisfaction in the world, in culture, society, or the customer's life. We're not talking about the dissatisfaction that your arch competitor is beating you.

Building block 2 – the change you want to see in the world

Movements are ultimately about transformation – in people, in communities and in society. Based on your grievance, what specifically do you want to change? How do you want the world to be different? For REI, it's for people to spend more time outdoors; for Dove it's a world in which the beauty of real, everyday women is celebrated.

Building block 3 – the enemy

Once you've identified a wrong that your company or brand wants to make right and the resulting change you want to see, it leads you directly to the nemesis your brand will rail *against*. Having a common, named enemy is the single biggest unifier of your movement's participants. A shared foe creates a sense of community and tribe. For SunTrust, the enemy is rampant financial stress. For Dove, it's unrealistic standards of beauty, something that bothers almost every woman. For REI, it's all the things that get in the way of spending time outdoors (eg rampant consumerism).

One of the great things about identifying your company's or brand's dissatisfaction and enemy in the world is that it immediately distinguishes you from your nearest category competitors. It gives your brand a role in society, culture and people's lives – not just within your industry or category.

Building block 4 – the stand

Once you know what your brand's against, the next logical step is to articulate what it is *for*. This is the higher-order stand you will take in the world, and is usually a direct or indirect translation of your brand's purpose. SunTrust is against financial stress and for financial confidence. Dove is against unrealistic standards of beauty and for celebrating real beauty. REI is against things getting in the way of love of the outdoors and for awakening a lifelong love of the outdoors.

We'll go into more detail a little later in this chapter about how to land on your stand and know if it's right. But a simple standard we go by is this: take the t-shirt test. Your stand should be a sentiment your movement's passionate followers would proudly wear on a t-shirt for all the world to see.

Building block 5 – the action

Movements are ultimately about getting people to *do* something to accomplish change in the world. For a movement to be successful, a company or brand has to take action that gets people to care and participate. And doing so today is easier than ever given the ubiquity of digital and social media.

REI's '#OptOutside' is the perfect example of this, as it involves both an important action and a call to action. The action was closing on one of the most popular shopping days of the year – Black Friday. The call to action was to invite America to join the company in reconnecting outdoors over the holidays, spread by the #OptOutside hashtag. More than 1.4 million people and 170 organizations chose to '#OptOutside' in its first year.

American Express's 'Small Business Saturday' is another great example of activating a movement via an action. The company identified the dissatisfaction that though all consumers have a heart for small businesses, they tended to mostly shop in big box stores. The stand of *shop small* was activated by giving consumers a specific time – Small Business Saturday – to be reminded to shop at brick and mortar businesses that are small and local.

These building blocks are important to understand because they illustrate how Movement Thinking goes beyond the traditional ways of thinking about your company or brand.

What makes Movement Thinking so effective is that people are drawn to it more than mere corporate messages; they rally around it and it stirs them emotionally. It's the difference between Dove, which unites consumers around the notion that beauty is not as narrow as typically cast in media and marketing, and Suave shampoo, which is marketed as being low-price. Dove is against unrealistic standards and for real beauty. Suave is for... value? Or the difference between American Express business cards and Stand for Small, which is for supporting local, small business, versus Capital One business cards, which are for... lower fees?

In each contrasting example, the companies have value propositions that their customers might want. After all, who doesn't like lower fees and better value? But it hardly stirs the soul. Without an emotional response, a relationship becomes functional, transactional. With an emotional relationship, your consumers become your brand advocates.

Building momentum by building a coalition

Another benefit of a movement is that you can partner with other brands, companies and individuals in a coalition to drive change. You can spark the

FIGURE 3.2   Movement framework

Dissatisfaction	What's bugging you?
Desired Change	How do you want the world to be different?
Enemy	What are you against?
Stand	What are we for?
Action	How will we rally people around our stand?

SOURCE StrawberryFrog

movement and bring others on board to leverage their networks, contacts, employees and customers. Examples of this are the Smart Car movement reinventing the urban environment, which enabled the Micro Car Company to build commons with parking authorities, rental car companies and local governments to work together to drive positive change versus simply selling and marketing another B-segment vehicle. The other example is the Boomer Coalition movement sponsored by Pfizer as a call to arms for Baby Boomers to fight cardiovascular disease and where Pfizer linked arms with the American Council of Cardiologists and the American Heart Association as a coalition.

Net-net, this gives the movement greater momentum and credibility.

How to know if your movement platform is right

One of the challenges of activating brand purpose is that purpose statements are often very lofty and hard to act upon. That means the movement you develop to activate it can also be lofty and hard to act upon if you're not careful. That's why it's imperative that your movement platform be articulated in just the right way. For us at StrawberryFrog, a movement platform typically comprises a movement name, slogan or motto, along with a brief few sentences as to the nature of the movement (typically summing up its building blocks as outlined above), often referred to as the movement's manifesto. For example, the movement platform for True North (which we introduced in Chapter 1) was 'Your True North is Calling'; a synopsis of the platform can be seen in Figure 3.3. Additionally, Smart Car's movement platform of 'Against Dumb' telegraphed the brand's stand against overconsumption in a way that was crystal clear (see Figure 3.4).

Once you've developed your movement platform, we suggest you pressure test it by getting feedback from both internal and external stakeholders. Here are some questions to explore in these conversations, and some suggestions for how to go about it and with whom.

Is it clear, meaningful and motivating?

We've found there's one pretty strong indicator that you've got a clear and motivating movement on your hands, which we alluded to earlier: the t-shirt test. Could your stand live on a t-shirt (see Figure 3.5)? Would your followers proudly wear it? Why? What would it say about them?

FIGURE 3.3   TrueNorth manifesto

Some movements start with a rally.
Others, a concert.
Ours started with a nut.

We asked:
Why can't a simple nut be more interesting?
More rewarding?
Why does a nut even have to be shaped like a nut?

Why hasn't somebody, anybody, done something more?
And then it dawned on us: Why can't we?
Everyone has a passion, a true north.
Ours is turning a simple nut into an extraordinary snack.

Your True North is Calling.

TrueNorth

SOURCE StrawberryFrog

The marriage equality movement is a great example of this. Research that the Civil Marriage Collaborative did showed that for gay people being treated the same as straight couples was very important. In day-to-day life, equal rights were, in fact, the most important thing for them. That led to a movement that framed the fight for marriage equality as one that afforded gay couples the same rights as straight couples.

But framing the movement this way failed to gain traction with the general public. Why? Because when you ask straight people why they got

FIGURE 3.4   Smart Car USA manifesto

Why do so many smart people do dumb things?

We buy stuff we don't need left and right. That's dumb.

We buy things without the least concern for the planet.

That's even dumber.

We buy stuff from the Sky Store catalogue.

Dumbest. Move. Ever.

Dumb is Venti when Tall is plenty.

Dumb requires multiple remotes.

Dumb is 2-for-1 when all you are is one.

Dumb is eating anything bigger than your head.

Dumb thinks 12 mpg is A-OK.

When it comes to consuming things, America's got a fever of a hundred-and-dumb. And there's only one prescription:

To get smart about our stuff.

By having just the right stuff, not all of it.

By buying what we need, and borrowing what we can.

So long battery-operated paper towel dispenser,

we don't need you anymore.

Come to think of it, we never did.

Let's put an end to overconsumption.

Let's take the junk out of our collective trunk.

That's the whole idea behind smart.

We're against dumb.
Come Join Us.

smart USA

SOURCE StrawberryFrog

FIGURE 3.5   Movement t-shirts

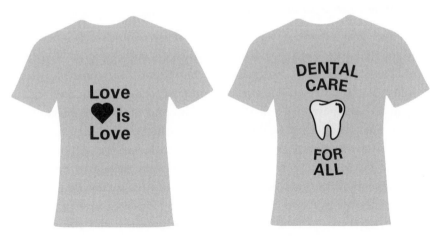

SOURCE StrawberryFrog

married, they say for love and commitment. The t-shirt test could have told the Civil Marriage Collaborative that their framing was off. The rational argument just doesn't inspire.

That's the difference between persuasion thinking and Movement Thinking. A rational, persuasive argument either convinces you or it doesn't. And when the rational argument is coming from a source that you really don't identify with, it's not likely to succeed.

By reframing the issue as the right to marry the person you love versus marrying for rights, the marriage equality movement found its allies. By framing it in terms of something that almost everyone experiences, which is to fall in love, all of a sudden you have a common enemy that everyone can identify with; the common enemy became the laws standing in the way of love.

Does it work over time?

One of the biggest challenges to sparking a successful movement inside a company is a phenomenon we call 'movement decay'. Here's what happens in many companies:

- They become genuinely convinced that purpose is important – they define the purpose, frame it into a movement and communicate it enthusiastically.
- As the message moves through the hierarchy, from layer to layer, to rank and file, much of its 'oomph' gets lost in translation.

- Over time interest in purpose wanes, clarity, enthusiasm and energy fade away, and the movement fizzles out.

StrawberryFrog's Purpose Gap tool, which we introduced in Chapter 1, can help you understand whether or not you're experiencing purpose decay over time. The Purpose Gap tool measures the distance over time and down through the organization between a purpose being announced and its continued understanding and use at the bottom of the organization 18 months later. The test of a movement is not whether it is met rapturously when it is unveiled by the leadership team, but whether it is still being used by front-line staff in 18 months. The gap between those two events and levels of people is the Purpose Gap. In essence, the tool surveys employees at regular intervals over the first 18 months and takes measures of four key movement success factors: clarity, enthusiasm, energy and commitment. Mahindra and SunTrust are two cases that demonstrate how a movement can overcome the Purpose Gap for leadership down through the organization and over many years.

Is it easy to begin activating?

Get out a sheet of paper – or if you're doing this in a group, get a whiteboard or giant Post-It – and list 10 things the brand could realistically *do* to get people to care and participate in this movement. If you're a client, your agency partners may be invaluable here. Is there an event, an action, a partnership, an employee programme, or even an ad, that springs to mind? If you're sitting there stumped, you probably need to go back and revisit your movement platform.

Some final advice – the 80 per cent rule

It's unlikely *any* string of words will leave everyone on your team feeling like your movement platform is 100 per cent nailed. That's just the nature of language. But if based on asking yourselves the questions above, you collectively feel that it's at least 80 per cent there, we recommend moving forward to start working with your movement platform. You'll have plenty of opportunities to tweak it in the weeks and months ahead based on real-world experience.

The impact of Movement Thinking

One of our former clients, VP Brand and Marketing at Etihad Airlines Tim Burnell, told us when recounting his experience with movement making while in CMO roles at Emirates Airlines and FAB: 'Despite the differences between private enterprise and society, leaders can learn much from how social movements engage and inspire people, applying the principles to create a powerful business operations and marketing process.'

Movement Thinking provides business change steps and processes that can activate purpose in a way that makes an idea stick and enables it to sustainably drive organizational culture and growth for many years. Ranjay Gulati, professor of business administration at Harvard Business School, points to global conglomerate Mahindra Group (which you'll read about in later chapters) as an example of a company that has transformed its business through a movement:

> Purpose is intended to guide business strategy and yet few leaders activate purpose in an effective way. This is cause for concern if you are a business leader, especially these days. One example of success is the Mahindra Group, a multi-billion-dollar federation of companies led by Anand Mahindra which adopted the 'Rise' purpose back in 2010 and has successfully sustained it ever since.

Becky Schmitt, EVP and chief people officer at Cognizant, said to us that when it comes to engaging people inside your organization, you need a product mindset, keeping in mind that people need to absorb your important messages in an integrated way:

> Few know how to do that. Everyone wants to change things. On top of that, you need to get the traditional HR approach out of your head and meet employees where they are. This is about a new kind of people leadership that drives change, behaviour adaptation. Movement inside an organization is a business operational model.

As we will show in this book, Movement Thinking also leads to empirically measured business results. We see evidence of that in our Purpose Power Index (Chapter 7), where top purpose brands outperform others on the statement of 'If I had the opportunity, I would work for this company', with 59 per cent of people surveyed in agreement with this statement for top purpose companies versus 29 per cent agreeing for the rest of the companies. As Kylie Wright-Ford, chief executive officer of RepTrak (formerly The Reputation Institute) and our partner on the PPI, told us, 'Now that is a competitive advantage!' She pointed out that an activated purpose can also help align leadership teams and employees behind goals to allow faster execution:

> Movement Thinking is transformative for company leaders because it helps them shift from 'initiative thinking' that is linked to annual budgets, timelines and projects to strategic thinking and creating impact over the long run. The flow-on effects for reputation and business success are clearly proven.

KEY TAKEAWAYS

As we shift our discussion to how CEOs can use Movement Thinking as a tool to transform company culture in the next chapter, it's worth reflecting on why movements matter to businesses. Not only do they isolate the cultural, racial, environmental and socio-economic stressors that people are experiencing and speaking up about, which can present significant risk or create great opportunities for your company, but movements illustrate why and how people are moved to action.

- Movements are on the rise. In an age when activism is becoming normalized, being unaware of, dismissive of or, worse, tone-deaf towards the issues that matter will lead you to be ignored. On the other hand, leaders can use the principles of societal movement to engage and mobilize their people to drive change.

- Movement Thinking helps those in the C-suite move past conventional thinking and transform companies, change habits or grow brands fast.

- In order to be successful, enterprise movements require an elite ally, the issue must be framed in a way that grabs people emotionally, and it must take into account the osmotic factors happening in culture.

- With a movement, you can partner with other brands, companies and individuals in a coalition to drive change inside or outside your organization.

- Your movement platform must be clear, meaningful and motivating, and be easy to activate.

References

Abrams, R (2017) Nordstrom drops Ivanka Trump brand from its stores, *The New York Times*, 2 February. https://www.nytimes.com/2017/02/02/business/nordstrom-ivanka-trump.html (archived at https://perma.cc/S4E2-D245)

American Express (2019) *The Story of the Shop Small® Movement*. https://www.americanexpress.com/us/small-business/shop-small/about/ (archived at https://perma.cc/2J9N-NJBU)

Anderson, M, Toor, S, Rainie, L and Smith, A (2018) Activism in the social media age, Pew Research Center, 11 July. https://www.pewresearch.org/internet/2018/07/11/activism-in-the-social-media-age/ (archived at https://perma.cc/6F3G-4P6Q)

Anderson, M, Barthel, M, Perrin, A and Vogels, E (2020) #BlackLivesMatter surges on Twitter after George Floyd's death, Pew Research Center, 10 June. https://www.pewresearch.org/fact-tank/2020/06/10/blacklivesmatter-surges-on-twitter-after-george-floyds-death/ (archived at https://perma.cc/K8XU-ZY49)

Apple (2020) Dear… – Season 2, Episode 6 [Streaming video], 5 June. https://www.apple.com/tv-pr/originals/dear/episodes/ (archived at https://perma.cc/5ST8-MCN5)

Berger, S (2019) Daymond John-backed start-up Bombas is reinventing the sock – and it's bringing in $100 million a year, CNBC, 16 April. https://www.cnbc.com/2019/04/16/daymond-john-backed-sock-start-up-bombas-is-bringing-in-millions.html (archived at https://perma.cc/3GSM-79VB)

Blunt, G (2020) Face mask rules: Do they really violate personal liberty?, *The Conversation*, 31 July. https://theconversation.com/face-mask-rules-do-they-really-violate-personal-liberty-143634 (archived at https://perma.cc/89ZN-QB44)

Business Wire (2020) American Express launches 'Stand for Small' coalition to support U.S. small businesses, *Business Wire*. https://www.businesswire.com/news/home/20200421005753/en/American-Express-Launches-%E2%80%98Stand-for-Small%E2%80%99-Coalition-to-Support-U.S.-Small-Businesses (archived at https://perma.cc/CFC9-6CN9)

Carlile, C (2019) History of successful boycotts, *Ethical Consumer*, 5 May. https://www.ethicalconsumer.org/ethicalcampaigns/boycotts/history-successful-boycotts (archived at https://perma.cc/CS8L-GPVK)

Chatterji, A and Toffel, M (2018) The new CEO activists, *Harvard Business Review*, January–February. https://hbr.org/2018/01/the-new-ceo-activists (archived at https://perma.cc/NA96-CBTC)

Chhabra, E (2020) New Jersey brand gives 1,000 mattresses to local hospitals and communities, *Forbes*, 21 April. https://www.forbes.com/sites/eshachhabra/2020/04/21/new-york-brand-gives-more-than-1000-mattresses-to-local-hospitals-and-communities/#4dda09db74a1 (archived at https://perma.cc/BQA2-GMWB)

Contagious (2015) Insight & Strategy: #LikeAGirl, Contagious.com, 21 May. https://www.contagious.com/news-and-views/insight-strategy-likeagirl (archived at https://perma.cc/PN98-LH82)

Cramer, M (2020) After all these years, Barbie is still reinventing herself, *The New York Times*, 29 January. https://www.nytimes.com/2020/01/29/business/mattel-barbie-dolls-vitiligo.html (archived at https://perma.cc/6SPG-FMR3)

Dreier, P (2020) The decade in 11 movements, *The American Prospect*, 8 January. https://prospect.org/civil-rights/the-decade-in-11-movements/ (archived at https://perma.cc/D26S-HZAP)

Duhigg, C (2017) If GoDaddy can turn the corner on sexism, who can't?, *The New York Times*, 23 July. https://www.nytimes.com/2017/07/23/business/godaddy-tv-ads-sexism.html?login=email&auth=login-email&login=smartlock&auth=login-smartlock (archived at https://perma.cc/447P-RCA6)

Foreman, M (2016) Hearts and minds: How the marriage equality movement won over the American public, *Nonprofit Quarterly*, 27 June. https://nonprofitquarterly.org/hearts-minds-marriage-equality-movement-won-american-public/ (archived at https://perma.cc/V6HG-8KL4)

GoDaddy (2019) GoDaddy releases 2019 diversity and salary data, *PR Newswires*, 12 December. https://www.prnewswire.com/news-releases/godaddy-releases-2019-diversity-and-salary-data-300973645.html (archived at https://perma.cc/86L8-TJUK)

Gregorian, D (2020) Anti-lockdown demonstrators trade guns for scissors at Michigan 'haircut' protest, NBC News, 20 May. https://www.nbcnews.com/politics/politics-news/anti-lockdown-demonstrators-trade-guns-scissors-michigan-haircut-protest-n1211366 (archived at https://perma.cc/EW9Z-GWTR)

Ipsos (2017) One in four Americans has boycotted a product for political reasons, Ipsos.com, 8 June. https://www.ipsos.com/en-us/news-polls/one-four-americans-has-boycotted-product-political-reasons (archived at https://perma.cc/F7X2-QBBV)

Kaplan, J, Akhtar, A and Casado, L (2020) A world on fire: Here are all the major protests happening around the globe right now, *Business Insider*, 4 June. https://www.businessinsider.com/all-the-protests-around-the-world-right-now (archived at https://perma.cc/7MHJ-CQ7V)

Kaufmann, L (2018) We are living through a golden age of protest, *The Guardian*, 6 May. https://www.theguardian.com/commentisfree/2018/may/06/protest-trump-direct-action-activism (archived at https://perma.cc/JQH8-DEC2)

Keplinger, K, Johnson, S, Kirk, J and Barnes, L (2019) Women at work: Changes in sexual harassment between September 2016 and September 2018, *Plos One*, 17 July. https://journals.plos.org/plosone/article?id=10.1371/journal.pone.0218313 (archived at https://perma.cc/E4QM-9BNR)

Levitin, M (2015) The triumph of Occupy Wall Street, *The Atlantic*, 10 June. https://www.theatlantic.com/politics/archive/2015/06/the-triumph-of-occupy-wall-street/395408/ (archived at https://perma.cc/4GSG-74T8)

Liffreing, I (2019) American Express celebrates 'Small Business Saturday' with Karlie Kloss, Lin-Manuel Miranda, *Ad Age*, 22 November. https://adage.com/article/cmo-strategy/american-express-celebrates-small-business-saturday-karlie-kloss-lin-manuel-miranda/2218306 (archived at https://perma.cc/NUL8-M4LX)

Lucas, A (2020) Starbucks to allow baristas to wear Black Lives Matter attire and accessories after social media backlash, CNBC, 12 June. https://www.cnbc.com/2020/06/12/starbucks-to-allow-baristas-to-wear-black-lives-matter-attire-and-accessories-after-backlash.html (archived at https://perma.cc/FDX4-KPA8)

Maerz, SF, Lührmann, A, Hellmeier, S, Grahn, S and Lindberg, SI (2020) State of the world 2019: Autocratization surges – resistance grows, *Democratization*, 27(6), pp 909–27, https://doi.org/ 10.1080/13510347.2020.1758670 (archived at https://perma.cc/Z7HG-ADAH)

Miller, R (2016) Black Lives Matter: A primer on what it is and what it stands for, *USA Today*, 11 July. https://www.usatoday.com/story/news/nation/2016/07/11/black-lives-matter-what-what-stands/86963292/ (archived at https://perma.cc/4MDN-NNRR)

Monllos, K (2017) 57% of consumers will boycott a brand that doesn't share their social beliefs, *Adweek*, 20 June. https://www.adweek.com/brand-marketing/57-of-consumers-will-boycott-a-brand-that-doesnt-share-their-social-beliefs/ (archived at https://perma.cc/R77F-UKQ4)

North, A (2019) 7 positive changes that have come from the #MeToo movement, *Vox*, 4 October. https://www.vox.com/identities/2019/10/4/20852639/me-too-movement-sexual-harassment-law-2019 (archived at https://perma.cc/7EZM-S6Y7)

Paul, K (2020) Facebook faces advertiser revolt over failure to address hate speech, *The Guardian*, 23 June. https://www.theguardian.com/technology/2020/jun/22/facebook-hate-speech-advertisers-north-face (archived at https://perma.cc/5TT3-9Z65)

Reinhart, RJ (2018) One in three Americans have felt urge to protest, *Gallup*, 24 August. https://news.gallup.com/poll/241634/one-three-americans-felt-urge-protest.aspx (archived at https://perma.cc/X3Z4-TPX2)

Rushe, D (2018) NRA under mounting pressure as companies cut ties with gun lobby, *The Guardian*, 23 February. https://www.theguardian.com/us-news/2018/feb/23/us-companies-nra-best-western-wyndham (archived at https://perma.cc/GZ2A-PPCD)

Satell, G (2016) What successful movements have in common, *Harvard Business Review*, 30 November. https://hbr.org/2016/11/what-successful-movements-have-in-common (archived at https://perma.cc/T4Q3-DMT4)

Science Based Targets (2020) Over 150 global corporations urge world leaders for net-zero recovery from COVID-19. https://sciencebasedtargets.org/2020/05/18/uniting-business-and-governments-to-recover-better/ (archived at https://perma.cc/4ABJ-CYYJ)

Tisdall, S (2019) About 41% of the global population are under 24. And they're angry…, *The Guardian*, 26 October. https://www.theguardian.com/world/2019/oct/26/young-people-predisposed-shake-up-established-order-protest (archived at https://perma.cc/CA7J-4N5L)

Weber Shandwick (2018) *CEO Activism in 2018: The purposeful CEO*. https://www.webershandwick.com/wp-content/uploads/2019/03/CEO-Activism-2018_Purposeful-CEO_FINAL_3.7.19.pdf (archived at https://perma.cc/LAV8-T2T4)

Who Gives a Crap (2020) *Our Impact*. https://us.whogivesacrap.org/pages/our-impact (archived at https://perma.cc/H4AT-CELV)

Wilsey, M and Lichtig, S (2018) The Nike controversy, Stanford. https://web.stanford.edu/class/e297c/trade_environment/wheeling/hnike.html (archived at https://perma.cc/2YAC-DJAQ)

Yakowicz, W (2015) Between the sheets: Husband and wife cofound organic, fair trade cotton bedding startup, *Inc.*, 14 February. https://www.inc.com/will-yakowicz/boll-and-branch-organic-cotton-bedding-startup.html (archived at https://perma.cc/5B22-8TF8)

04

Change the company with a movement, not a mandate

For those in the room, it was supposed to be just a regular meeting during a regular day at Verizon headquarters in Basking Ridge, New Jersey. It was a Monday morning. No one can recall the agenda. Instead, what most people who were in attendance will long remember was that there was an additional face at the table, saying nothing. This wasn't simply an additional team member coming in to take notes, or a cross-functional information-sharing session with an individual from another department. That person sitting silently amidst mid-level employees meeting about their daily tasks was Verizon CEO Hans Vestberg.

Now, for most rank-and-file employees across the corporate world, having the head honcho slide up in a chair next to you with no warning would be a panic-inducing experience. Is something wrong? Is someone in trouble? At the very least there would be an elevated level of anxiety because a standard meeting all of a sudden feels so much more performative.

But for Hans, this gesture, one that's so surprising to a workforce and so uncharacteristic of a CEO, was about demonstrating the change he wanted to see. What Hans was showing in that moment was that change inside an organization cannot be done by a mandate from the top demanding compliance. Rather, in today's peer-to-peer world, corporations must focus their attention on the middle of the organization, which determines success more than ever.

There is a new kind of leadership happening now by a select group of leaders, like Hans, who understand how movements can galvanize employees and generate trust, creativity, passions and devotion. This new leadership is a good example of Movement Thinking, which can be a tool for leaders seeking a transformative power. We believe the CEO's vision for change can become a movement that mobilizes the people that matter inside the organization, from the middle–out and the bottom–up better than top–down mandates, demanding compliance. And we think it is a company-led, cultural movement that makes the impossible possible.

Throughout this chapter, we'll look more specifically at how CEOs can successfully use movements as a tool to transform culture and activate their purpose. But first, let's get back to Hans.

A movement for new leadership

For a leader, Hans's position was an enviable one. At the time, Verizon was one of the most successful telecom operators in the world, so there was no desperate need for a turnaround, nor was he saddled with remediating a toxic culture, as is so often the case with corporate transformation. Instead, this cultural transformation was intended to evolve the company culture from a service one to one zeroed in on innovation in order to fully capitalize on all of the opportunities afforded by 5G's game-changing technology.

History proved this shift was essential. Years ago, Verizon had been close to the introduction of cloud computing but never maximized it as well as VMware or Microsoft had (Krause, 2016). Now under Hans's leadership, the organization would make a significant shift from the seller of smartphones to an innovations company capable of embracing new ideas and maximizing new potential generated in the wake of 5G's introduction.

Changing company culture and transforming employee mindsets and habits are hard at the best of times. It's particularly delicate when dealing with a company culture that's not necessarily broken but needs to rapidly evolve. When Hans took the reins of the company in 2018, he wrote a white paper that created a framework that respected the company's successes while creating the desired room for innovation. All decisions and changes would be divided into three pieces: things that needed to be preserved, or those things that the company did well; things that needed to be strengthened, or those things that fit the new vision for the company but could stand to be improved upon; and things that needed to be transformed, or those aspects of the company that needed radical change to meet the challenge of 5G. Additionally, that change would need to serve four stakeholders: employees, customers, shareholders and society.

After one-on-one sessions with Verizon employees and working groups with larger swathes of the company, he honed in on five big transformations. One was the network. With the amount of work and the degree of opportunity that were to come with 5G, having the most robust and well-supported network was paramount to the strategy. This included an enormous five-year investment in upgrading the network.

The second transformation came through a restructuring that resulted in over 10,000 employees, or about 7 per cent of its global workforce, taking a voluntary buyout (Price, 2018).

The third was the brand. Verizon's portfolio includes everything from field troops laying the network infrastructure across America for its wireless business to titles like the *Huffington Post* and *TechCrunch* for its media business, each with their own brand values. Hans unified the company under the same set of brand values by creating, as he called it, 'a branded house, not a house of brands'.

Fourth was the company's go-to-market strategy, which transitioned it from being a technology-driven organization to a customer-driven one.

Finally, there was leadership transformation, which involved training 13,000 of the company's leadership and defining a new purpose, which is articulated as 'creating the networks that move the world forward' and focuses on digital inclusion, climate protection and human prosperity.

That brings us back to that meeting. In order to activate that purpose, Hans launched an employee movement, through which he intended to get everyone, at all layers and in all corners of the business, rallied around the idea that they were part of creating the networks – be they technical or human networks – that would move the world forward. By sitting quietly in employee meetings or by not sitting at the head of every table, he was demonstrating that things were done differently now. The power to speak does not automatically default to the CEO. That power doesn't rest solely at the top but is rather distributed among middle management. Everyone had a role to play in bringing Verizon into the future.

When discussing his vision for Verizon with us, Hans said:

> Sometimes I decide that I don't speak in a whole meeting; sometimes I speak
> a lot. I'm just trying to change stereotypes and show that how we do things is
> important. We looked at everything. How do we conduct meetings? How do we

involve everyone? How do we hire? How do we empower people in a tactical organization? All of these questions are important when you do these kinds of transformations.

He added that while Verizon had a recipe for success in its history, it wasn't necessarily the recipe for the future. 'If we had our old structure, we could never enable the innovation.'

Verizon's 'Forward Together' movement

The new purpose for Verizon that Hans created – *creating the networks that move the world forward* – is not unlike other corporate purposes. What is different in the case of Verizon is the fact that Hans recognized the need to actualize the purpose among employees and stakeholders with a movement to drive both mindset and habit change.

While preparing leaders to help shepherd this change, Hans says he took a three-pronged approach that focused on self-leadership (how one learns and grows as a leader), the leadership of people and strategic leadership. By starting with a smaller group and honing their attention first on their own leadership style, he was able to set firm footings for a movement. 'I want leaders to show up because ultimately the leaders are important,' he told us.

This new purpose and company culture were then activated throughout Verizon through a Movement Inside (a concept we've dedicated the next chapter to) called 'Forward Together'. Designed to celebrate how its employees are moving the world forward together, one good deed at a time, the movement is symbolized by a purpose coin, a physical coin that was given to the top 300 leaders to bestow on members of their teams who were leading by example and inspiring those around them to put purpose at the centre of what they do. After two weeks, recipients pass it on to someone else living the brand purpose.

The purpose coin is a powerful symbol that helps Verizon recognize those who stand out as dedicated stewards of the company's shared purpose. Through creating a physical artefact that rewards individual efforts – and requires the recipient to recognize and reward those efforts in others – Hans and Diego Scotti, CMO of Verizon, created a movement that people want to participate in, not one they're told to. Behind each purpose coin exchange is a story of someone who is building human networks, fostering community and working to make the world a better place. Those stories are amplified through Verizon's daily video series, 'Up to Speed', and on social platforms. It's how fellow V-Teamers (as they're called) found out about Robert in La Quinta, who was rewarded for his consumer-centric attitude, or Diane, who was recognized for her work in helping to increase international renewable power coverage from 40 per cent to 75 per cent. By naming and faming those who are living Verizon's brand purpose, the company gives fuel to the fire (Verizon, 2020).

While Hans told us that he was only a little over a year into a five-year transformation, he said he was already seeing huge dividends. He points to the company's engagement survey results as a proof point.

The survey asked questions about whether employees felt empowered or if they felt free to speak up – important parts of the company's transformation – but Hans says he wasn't terribly concerned with the results. He was more interested in whether people even bothered to take the survey. He said the first time the survey was dispatched, it received a 53 per cent response rate. 'That means that every second employee didn't even care enough to tell management what they thought. I didn't care about the results. I just wanted people to participate.'

The follow-up survey, which was sent after 'Forward Together' was established, was completed by nearly 90 per cent of employees. 'Are we finished? No. But I definitely see results.'

Why culture change fails

What the Verizon story shows us is that organizational change is a movement that flows through layers. It is not words passed from the top and left to trickle down; it spreads from the middle–out, the bottom–up, as well as from the top. It's a movement that gains energy and momentum as it passes through the organization, transforming both the giver and the recipient. A movement can deliver on optimism, trust, conviction or creativity that's required for employees at all levels to believe it and know how to act on that purpose.

Before exploring the tools to transform company culture, we'll first look at some of the pitfalls to avoid, because, despite how in-demand culture change is, for every success story there's a litany of failed ones – according to Gallup, a whopping 70 per cent of them fall flat (Leonard and Coltea, 2013). But why? We both reflected on our own experiences and compared notes with some fellow experts to get underneath this dilemma, and several core barriers rose to the top.

It doesn't have commitment from the top

When talking about movements as a change management tool, we often talk about it being an alternative to a mandated top–down approach. That, however, doesn't mean that senior leadership is completely hands-off. Without a clear directive from the CEO, the change initiative loses credibility and it becomes extremely challenging to get buy-in throughout the organization.

It's poorly communicated

Over and over again in our work, we see purpose relegated to a quote on the lobby wall or the 'about' section of the company website. We see purpose statements that sound good but are too lofty to act upon, or are functional and uninspired. And we see entire communications programmes about purpose with too many messages, often sending mixed signals. Clearly, poor communication is an ongoing problem in change management.

As the authors of the Gallup report on change failure wrote:

> The problem is that in too many companies, front-line employees receive dozens of high-priority messages – some complementary, some competing – from executives, managers, and change leaders each day. These conflicting messages make it difficult for workers to know what tasks or metrics they should focus on during a given day to deliver a fully engaging customer experience. (Leonard and Coltea, 2013)

If there are too many drummers, how will they know which beat they're meant to follow?

It's disconnected and unfocused

Truly effective culture change has to be fully integrated in order to be sustained. Yet too often, change efforts are so disconnected that they almost cannibalize each other. We see it frequently: operations, HR, marketing, leadership can all be working at the service of the same change strategy, and yet it doesn't fit together. Ron Carucci, co-founder and managing partner at organizational design consultancy Navalent, had an interesting way of describing this phenomenon when we spoke to him:

Any one of those individual pieces could be brilliant. The HR training could be world-class, the technology could be best-in-class, but then, at the end of the day when we try to stand these changes up, it ends up looking like that person who's had too much cosmetic surgery.

Change battle fatigue

Whether it's because a company has endured several failed attempts at change or because company leadership is gung-ho about being purposeful without properly defining or activating that purpose (like when purpose is treated merely as a box to be ticked), change, when poorly managed or merely cosmetic, inspires a sense of ennui among employees. This can breed a sense of 'this too shall pass', with employees feeling like they know how to wait it out, expecting the change efforts to die. Or worse, this fatigue can breed cynicism, criticism and apathy.

Unrealistic timelines

It goes without saying that transformational change at a company requires significantly more time and resources than incremental change. Yet most change initiatives end up grossly under-resourced because CEOs drastically underestimate what change requires, resulting in insufficient funding and unrealistic timelines. Carucci put this well when we spoke to him: 'That's like somebody who weighs 400 pounds saying "I'm going to lose weight this week" and then by Wednesday saying, "I had carrots for three days but nothing happened." You can't do a five-year journey in six months.' You can certainly demonstrate quick wins within six months, but transformational change takes time.

It demands compliance rather than inspiring action

In our experience, this is probably the single biggest barrier to transformational change within organizations. That's because when change is mandated, it typically fails to give people a clear, specific direction. Stating a company's purpose or desired change is much easier than actually following through with it.

When we talked with Stanford movement and organizational design expert Sarah Soule, whom we spoke with in the last chapter, she described the phenomenon this way:

> Culture change fails when leaders mandate something and say, 'This is our new culture, we want everybody to behave with integrity, now go do it.' But then they don't tell people what that actually means or how to put processes in place to reinforce and support it; they don't model it; they don't incentivize behaviour so that people will act that way. They'll say, we value collaboration, but then they'll stack-rank everybody. Well, what does that show you about collaborating with people?

Instead, transformational change in an organization requires new behaviours from all layers of a company, and these are often at odds with corporate cultures that are often built around operational excellence and efficiency.

Soule put our feelings on this issue well when she wrote the following in *HBR* in 2017:

> Culture change can't be achieved through a top–down mandate. It lives in the collective hearts and habits of people and their shared perception of 'how things are done around here.' Someone with authority can demand compliance, but they can't dictate optimism, trust, conviction, or creativity. (Soule and Walker, 2017)

Xerox: overcoming the barriers to culture change

John Kennedy knows these challenges well. A veteran marketer with successful stints at Procter & Gamble and IBM, he joined Xerox as CMO in 2014, six years after the company spent $6.4 billion to acquire business services provider ACS, which became Xerox Services (Dignan, 2009). Because the two entities had never really come together, Kennedy was faced with the task of at long last unifying them under a common purpose and culture.

This mission was fraught with challenges. First, Xerox Services was not simply one company whose values needed to mesh with those of Xerox's document business. It was actually the product of the acquisition of dozens of standalone companies, each with its own brand values and self-identified purposes. And many of the CEOs from those companies were still a part of the merged Xerox Services business and had points of view on vision, purpose and culture. Employees from both sides of the merger had long expressed confusion as to why two seemingly disparate companies – one a document company and one a business services outsourcing provider – ever came together in the first place.

Another obstacle, as Kennedy tells it, was overcoming scepticism that was slowing progress:

> One thing I had to do was persuade some company leaders why we needed this purpose because the company had been operating without something like that for decades. And then there were different assumptions around what it was going to be used for.

Lastly was the concern that the combined companies, in Kennedy's view, simply had too many values: 'The reason that work is important is that those values are pathways to specific employee behaviours.'

Based on his experience at IBM and its 'Smarter Planet' unifying idea, Kennedy knew that a critical step in bringing the companies together was to help all employees understand what they shared in common. After several months of working with internal stakeholders, Kennedy hit two important common denominators. First, he reframed Xerox's skilled employees as 'business engineers', a concept borrowed from his experience at IBM, where employees rallied around the vision of themselves as 'IBMers'.

But the bigger challenge was helping all employees have a shared view of why they came to work every day, what their shared contribution was to customers and society:

> When defining the value that Xerox created, we really wanted it to be more than just one plus one, which is a very simple way of describing two things together. So, we started thinking, Xerox and Xerox Services were not just about documents and services, they were about workflow and accelerating and making that workflow more efficient.

Ultimately, Xerox was about *making work work better* for everyone. With this unifying purpose, Xerox was beginning a culture transformation journey against some big odds, and Kennedy had a clear roadmap in place.

It was at this point that activist investor Carl Icahn forced the split of Xerox and the Xerox Services business in 2016 (de la Merced and Picker, 2016), so the world will never know if Kennedy's culture change strategy would ultimately have worked. But what this case does illustrate, according to Kennedy, is that transforming a culture under a shared purpose is not one to be taken lightly. Never underestimate the barriers – identify them early and take them head-on, and realize that hard work and time are key ingredients.

I think that's what a lot of leaders don't understand. Purpose is the X factor in creating brand equity and the leverage point for driving a consistent experience, but the hard work is the level of commitment required to really pull it all the way through to a set of expectations that binds its way into the way your employees make decisions every day.

Fortunately for Kennedy, he had this knowledge behind him, as he was tapped to be CMO for the Xerox Services spin-off, which was renamed Conduent, making it time to go on a culture transformation journey yet again.

Movement: a CEO's secret weapon for cultural transformation

In large organizations, it's culture that determines how people do things. Culture is invisible, yet its effect can be seen and felt in every aspect of an organization. Culture is king. And how you foster culture matters. Of course, when discussing movements, we're not saying there's a single way to change an organization. But we do believe that activating purpose through movements is a better way.

As a leader of a large organization, demanding compliance is your prerogative, but if you create a movement in which people feel like they are the artists of a shared vision, you're much more likely to galvanize the whole system you're looking to transform.

We've all moved past the idolization of a single charismatic leader like Steve Jobs's stage in business. There's Elon Musk, but his model isn't for every company or every CEO. What seems clear is that a new leadership approach is needed for the new employee peer-to-peer culture. And the opposite of *one* (leader) is *everyone*. And every level. That's why our Movement Inside approach is the opposite of Steve Jobs, and why the understanding that movements create throughout the organization gives leaders a better ability in this day and age to overcome the Purpose Gap – the distance over time and down through the organization between a purpose being announced and its continued understanding and use at the bottom of the organization.

So, how do you ensure your movement is successful? In our work at StrawberryFrog creating movements for clients over the years, we've identified a number of factors that are hallmarks of robust culture-change movements.

Leadership sets – and lives – the vision

Movements are not a set-it-and-forget-it exercise because, as movements take hold, they grow and evolve. In order to be sustained, the CEO and other C-suite leaders need to be stewards of the vision.

When discussing how executives can adopt movements, Soule said to us:

> I would advise leaders that you have to be intentional about what you want. You can't just tell people to go and do something. What you need to do is model that and when you see good examples of it in your company, you see that someone is actually living the values that you appreciate and want to be the culture, you reward it and try to figure out how to scale that using all of the organizational design principles that exist.

We've observed that leaders can't ask for a change of their employees without doing that work themselves. If you, as a leader, desire to have great impact and influence, you have to realize that you are the message. In order for real transformation to occur and be sustained, it must happen simultaneously within individual leaders, between leaders, and at critical seams of the organization that supports the desired transformation.

That's what makes Hans Vestberg's movement at Verizon so powerful. He's modelling the behaviour he wants to see and is sharing the story of those living the values widely – like when he virtually passed a purpose coin via Twitter to Jeremy Godwin, who had performed above and beyond during the COVID-19 outbreak to keep employees connected with the UpToSpeed Live videos (Vestberg, 2020).

The purpose comes from within

Many purpose statements are too theoretical and hard to understand for the average person. But movements are not simply a series of predefined steps you follow to get people to do what you want; they have to relate to some truth that exists in the company. In other words, they have to be authentic.

As Suzanne Tosolini of the Jim Stengel Company said to us, those looking to instigate cultural transformation can focus too squarely on values in isolation of the hard purpose discovery work. But purpose, she says, guides those values and subsequent behaviours, which results in values that

> not only have staying power, as they are rooted in history and reality, but will also be more inspiring internally. Arguably the bigger role of purpose is culture

transformation, not external activation. If the purpose is activated within a company, it will ultimately inevitably be activated externally.

At StrawberryFrog we've proven that a movement rooted in the company culture, the brand purpose and an idea on the rise in culture is the only way to design the optimal solution. Take multinational Indian conglomerate the Mahindra Group. When StrawberryFrog started working with the company in 2008, it had a legacy of innovation but it was looking to codify and institutionalize it across the group.

Looking to position the company as a global enterprise, Chairman Anand Mahindra didn't realize that he had a purposeful movement right in front of him. The company's history was full of stories of uplifting inventions. Like when the market for its gas-guzzling jeeps collapsed during the oil crisis of the 1970s, it adapted the engine of its tractors to be used on the vehicles, making them more fuel-efficient (Joshi and Chatterjee, 2014); or when it launched India's first urban SUV, the Scorpio, in 2002; or when it launched the Mahindra Pride School in 2007 to offer workforce training to disadvantaged youth. But the organization was a federation of hundreds of companies with their own customers and business objectives managed in a matrix structure, which gave CEOs enormous independence. No one could see the culture of innovation. Worse, in trying to define who they were, they had stumbled into the classic brand positioning minefield where they were trying to establish one idea that best exemplified a tractor company and an automotive manufacturer, a top technology firm and an aerospace company. Of course, this was an impossible feat.

But it was when we conducted ethnographic research in the US, Italy, South Africa, Chile, Turkey and the home market India that we saw something that startled us: everyone said the same thing. They all had a desire to rise and to help their families and communities rise. Regardless of what sector we went to, the responses were the same.

Based on this cultural research, we were able to see the pillars of what would become Mahindra's purpose and then the 'Rise' movement to activate the purpose inside and outside the corporation (which you'll read more about in Chapter 10). 'Rise' crystallized a sweeping cultural transformation that sought to establish an overt culture of innovation based on three pillars: *Think alternatively. Accept no limits. Drive positive change.* It instantly resonated.

'When StrawberryFrog presented the "Rise" purpose and then the "Rise" movement it was eye-opening. To rise has always been a part of our DNA,'

Anand said in the years after it launched. 'The only difference is that today, we're realizing the power of it, we're articulating it, and we're building our entire future on it' (Mahindra, 2014).

Similarly, when LifeBridge Health CEO Neil Meltzer was looking to unite its group of independent hospitals within one of the largest hospital networks in Baltimore, MD, its legacy gave life to its new purpose and a movement.

LifeBridge's flagship facility, Sinai Hospital, was created in 1866 in response to discrimination. At the time, African American and Jewish medical students had no place for medical training and residency training. Having been with the hospital network for 31 years, Meltzer was proud of the culture, particularly at Sinai Hospital, where he was president before becoming CEO of the health system.

But as LifeBridge grew – the hospital network doubled in size to include 137 sites of care in a mere seven years – that common purpose started to become diluted and, over time, its focus drifted to financial stability, given the hostile reimbursement environment in US healthcare. Meltzer told us:

> In some ways, this was natural because it is fundamental as a foundation
> to provide the core clinical services required. Although we always strive
> for balance, I began to see the scales tip too far and wanted to bring the
> organization's soul back to what made me and so many others historically
> proud of LifeBridge Health. I and other leaders recognized that we needed to
> do something bold and we needed to change the culture to be more focused
> on galvanizing our team and then sharing our message more broadly to the
> communities we serve.

By digging into the roots of Sinai and celebrating all the ways the hospital network has helped people since its inception, StrawberryFrog was able to activate LifeBridge's purpose with the 'Care Bravely' movement (which we'll delve into in the next chapter). This became a rallying cry both internally and externally that reunited employees with a core part of the company's DNA.

As Meltzer told us after the movement launched, 'It allowed us to rediscover the purpose statement that has existed for a decade and infuse it with life.'

This is why experts like Carucci say purpose can't be imposed. It has to speak to some truth that already exists within an organization. 'Rise' wouldn't have been as powerful and as immediately understood by its workforce if not for the fact that it was something everyone at the company knew

FIGURE 4.1   LifeBridge Health Care Bravely launch campaign ad

SOURCE StrawberryFrog

to be true. 'Care Bravely' could have come off as a neat tagline if not for the fact that the entire foundation of LifeBridge Health was built on a legacy of helping people when others wouldn't.

Layers of leadership are empowered

We have believed for a long time that the success of a movement inside an organization is dependent on crystallizing an idea that is rooted in the culture of the company – for example, the Mahindra story – but connected to an idea on the rise in culture. Moreover, it needs to live and breathe among the C-suite, but also the top executives of the company, which requires training and coaching. But more than this, it needs to live and breathe from the middle–out and the bottom–up (remember the example by Hans Vestberg of Verizon). This will reduce the Purpose Gap.

In this new corporate world, where culture is created peer-to-peer, not top–down, there are two schools of thought on how movements spread successfully through an organization. One is about hierarchies, and the other is about linked networks.

In a hierarchical approach, leadership sets the vision, and middle management takes up the cause and spreads it to front-line employees, who ostensibly engage with it. The problem, as pointed out by Charles Dhanaraj, professor of strategic management at the Fox School of Business, Temple University, when we spoke to him, is that breakdowns often happen along the way. As the message moves through the hierarchy, from layer to layer, to rank and file – much of its 'oomph' gets lost in translation.

In its assessment of culprits causing change management failure that we mentioned earlier, Gallup pointed the finger firmly in one direction: unsuccessful ones don't focus enough on front-line managers. That's because they're a vital connection to the employees who deliver that new experience to the customer.

Anand Mahindra says empowering middle layers of management and affording them autonomy to make decisions that best align with the company's purpose is particularly essential in a matrixed organization. In his federation of companies, as he refers to Mahindra, he actively fosters a culture of autonomy and empowerment within the ranks of management. This is not a natural stance for many leaders and one that's not universally understood.

When we spoke, Anand shared a story of how his approach has been questioned. Anupam Thareja is a venture capitalist and a partner with Mahindra in its Jawa motorcycle business (an endeavour that revived a classic motorcycle brand), and was a sceptic of Mahindra's federation structure. Anand told us:

> He always told me he thinks I empower people too much and therefore things don't move as quickly as they should. He then said he'd changed his view and had become a supporter of the federation concept because when looking at the companies in his portfolio, the ones that were surviving were those that were agile and nimble. He said to me, 'I'm thinking that, frankly, more than Mahindra's ability to raise capital, it is the autonomy you've granted your sector that will enable them to make decisions, that will make their company adaptable.'

The change starts small

'Start small to grow big' has been one of our mantras for years. We saw earlier in this chapter in the Verizon example how this approach can be successful. We've found that while ambitions may be big when embarking on a new corporate purpose journey, culture change or launching a movement, the reality is that it's essential to start with small groups, not the entire organization at once.

Cascades author Greg Satell, whom we spoke with in the last chapter, echoed this, noting that in his study of societal movements, often the worst thing you can do early on is to go big by doing something like sparking a mass protest. 'This invites your most ardent critics to come out and take you on publicly.' Starting small, with the group or groups of people who already support your cause, and then have them spread it to others who are like-minded, is much more often the key to success.

Spreading enthusiasm for purpose through networks is an alternative to doing so through hierarchies. Under this theory, change occurs when small, loosely connected groups unite behind a common purpose versus when the desired change is cascading through organizational layers. Transformation happens side-to-side.

Satell served up big data giant Experian as an example of achieving transformation through creating a networked culture. Company leadership noticed that employees who were members of 'Le Tour de Experian', a bike club that raised money for charity, were creating boundary-spanning relationships and connections across segments and layers of the business. Those bonds were resulting in unexpected collaboration across the organization. By identifying and empowering this interest group, Experian leadership was able to leverage the collaboration.

As he wrote when discussing this case:

> What's interesting and salient about how the network culture was built at Experian is how it all seems so mundane. Many firms have clubs, employee groups, and volunteer efforts. Seminars aren't particularly unusual, either. Yet it's not any one program or platform, but how those initiatives are optimized to widen and deepen informal bonds across the organization, that makes the difference. (Satell, 2019)

It's communicated through story and with emotion

Over hundreds of cases and challenges, we've learned that the power of the movement happens through emotional messaging. Disseminating a movement through an organization is an emotional rather than rational exercise; it's much more about heart than head. But even more, it needs to be designed to galvanize your people.

When we began working with LifeBridge Health, the easiest solution to unifying the disparate cultures of its multiple healthcare organizations would have been to explain to all stakeholders what they had in common and why it made sense that they were one. But in truth, that had already been done, and it had failed to engage people. It was only when we rallied people around the 'Care Bravely' movement through emotional communication and storytelling that employees saw their shared purpose and were galvanized to participate.

Temple University professor Charles Dhanaraj explained this to us by saying that 'you don't drive purpose by a statement; you drive purpose through narratives. When the stories come down and become part of folklore, people get it. That has to happen internally as well as externally.'

To illustrate the power of storytelling, he shared an interaction he had with a Mahindra driver in India who met his plane and was driving him from the airport to visit the headquarters. The company had been thrust into the spotlight because of 'Rise' and Dhanaraj, a professor with an interest in strategic partnerships, global innovation and emerging markets, thought Mahindra was a compelling case.

Dhanaraj says that, at the time, he was unconvinced by the movement (we'll forgive him his mistrust). 'My take at the time was that it seemed like more marketing lingo than genuine purpose.' Until he listened to his driver. Having no idea who Dhanaraj was or that he was en route to meet with Anand Mahindra and other key executives, the driver spontaneously started talking about the 'Rise' movement and was able to recite all the pillars of the strategy. He was putting the company's language into his own words. 'This was an extraordinary example of how a company successfully actualizes its purpose down throughout the entire organization, including a driver for the company who had no idea what my interests were or why I was heading to Mahindra.'

We design movements carefully to maximize words and language so that complex ideas can be understood emotionally and with simple human words. When you can do this, you can make a significant impact with tens of thousands of employees across disciplines and cultures. Dhanaraj said:

> Language is everything. If the language becomes so sophisticated and stays only in the boardroom, it doesn't live. In order for a brand to live its purpose it has to be embedded in a language that can be on the streets, it has to live through stories.

It has to live with cab drivers.

Stanford's Sarah Soule confirms the importance of communicating with emotion:

The leaders who don't do cultural change well miss that. They miss story, they miss emotion, they miss getting people on board on a very instinctual level. They just throw it out there and people are lost. And they may not even believe it and it's just a bunch of terms that mean nothing and don't resonate emotionally.

Movements rethink traditional equity

CEOs and CFOs wishing to think more radically in times of great change might think of movement as a way to update the old ways we think about equity – in other words, a different way to think about defining company shares and the motivations for people to invest and keep ownership of those shares. Historically, our notions of ownership in companies have been framed in terms of different kinds of shares, driven by financial superpowers of Wall Street – common shares, preferred shares, voting shares and so on. But all that was born in a very different time. Let us speculate how things could be different.

Perhaps movements could represent an alternative kind of ownership system and a more important ownership system for today – ownership of what really matters about what a company offers and the activity that comes with that. Let's think about these as M (Movement) shares.

Perhaps these would be shares that are issued only at certain times of the year, and purchasing them would symbolize solidarity with the company and its stand. For example, Verizon might issue special Forward Together shares, the proceeds of which would help fund Verizon's efforts to move the world forward through good deeds.

So, one could ask some interesting questions of leaders, in a language and through a frame they understand: how many M shares have you sold – internally and externally? Do you know? How many are you issuing every year? Are you giving them the same diligence and attention in the goals you are setting for your company as you are with the more traditional kinds of shares? Which are more important for your success and momentum today and tomorrow, do you think?

There is precedent for M shares in the growth of ethically conscious funds and investment products increasingly offered to consumers. Since these will only continue to grow in interest among conscious consumers, as the CEO or CFO, why not get ahead of the rest and be the first to design M shares, enabling people to literally buy into your movement? As Afdhel Aziz said to us, it's an enticing way to measure what you treasure.

Movements make you 'anti-fragile'

Another way that movements can be indispensable to CEOs is in helping them respond to times of crises. At the moment we're writing this, the COVID-19 pandemic is front of mind, but that's merely the current crisis. There have been others – it seems not so long ago we worried about the global economic crisis of 2008 – and there will be more – climate change is that looming issue that has been momentarily kicked down the road while the world deals with COVID-19. As we've seen in this crisis, and as we mentioned in Chapter 1 in the discussion about T-Mobile and Nextdoor, companies need to move fast.

A company's longevity and ability to ensure change are of great interest to CEOs and business leaders, so naturally it's something that Anand Mahindra thinks about often. How do you ensure your company is relevant as consumers, the financial markets and the planet all change? Given that we spoke with him in mid-2020, right when the COVID-19 pandemic was in full swing and starting to reveal its long-term impact, it's no surprise that the topic of longevity was on his mind.

In trying to articulate the characteristics of companies that would endure, he came up with this: beauty and meaning:

> At least two things will be critical and which people will always look for in a product or service. They will look for things of beauty and things of meaning. Those are the reasons why people gravitate towards a product.

It's why people buy Dyson – not simply because of its technology, but because they look beautiful in your room. It's why people buy Patagonia – to signal that they believe in the meaning of the product. And meaning, of course, is directly connected to purpose. 'Things of beauty and things of meaning make you anti-fragile. If you want to be anti-fragile, make products, or deliver services that have meaning and which are beautiful.'

While anti-fragile is another way of saying resilience through purpose, the words themselves reveal the downside of not being resilient: *fragility*. This is especially important in a post-COVID world. As Anand wrote in a piece on post-COVID capitalism in *The Telegraph*, the pandemic demonstrated that what people value is rapidly changing:

> Crises reveal what should be truly important to us. The bottom line is that interconnectedness, of people with each other and with the planet, is non-negotiable. Business leaders who do not get it are going to see their

company's brand value erode before their very eyes. Purpose-led capitalism, where enlightened self-interest aligns with community interests, is the future for business. (Mahindra, 2020)

It's likely no surprise to hear that we wholeheartedly agree. As we said at the start of this book, this realization is what helped define StrawberryFrog's own purpose to use creativity for good. Underpinning this has always been the belief that it is in the interests of business to drive positive change and help people and the planet thrive. When consumers live long, happy, financially stable lives, they buy more of your product. And to paraphrase the words of Byron Sharp, the author of *How Brands Grow*, generating new consumers is your company's biggest challenge (Sharp, 2010). If companies poison their consumers or employees or make their lives miserable, they'll lose their consumers and employees. Better to make their lives better, healthier, and then each time you and the consumer meet, you'll feel better with each other. A brand purpose can help you get there. But it's toothless unless you flip the switch and turn it on. That's where a brand movement can be transformative.

KEY TAKEAWAYS

In the next chapter, we're going to outline in detail how to launch a Movement Inside and share examples of companies that have enjoyed transformative change because of it. But before we engage in that conversation, it's essential to remember that transformational movement doesn't just happen. You don't just put it out in the world and see what happens. It's far too monumental of an undertaking to just 'see what sticks'. Instead, a movement requires:

- visionary leadership and unequivocal support from the top – only then can it move people to act from the middle–out, top–down and side-to-side;
- a purpose that comes from within, that is authentically rooted in the company's history;
- layers of leadership that are empowered so they can bring the purpose and movement to life in all areas of your company;
- a focus on the small groups that can be movement champions;
- communications that are rooted in story and emotion.

References

de la Merced, M and Picker, L (2016) Xerox, in deal with Carl Icahn, to split company in two, *The New York Times*, 29 January. https://www.nytimes. com/2016/01/30/business/dealbook/xerox-split-icahn.html (archived at https://perma.cc/GV3L-SM8U)

Dignan, L (2009) Xerox buys ACS for $6.4 billion, *CNET*, 28 September. https://www.cnet.com/news/xerox-buys-acs-for-6-4-billion (archived at https://perma.cc/U8ZU-YGHY)

Joshi, D and Chatterjee, D (2014) 40 years ago… and now: How the Mahindra Group survived crisis, Rediff.com, 15 September. https://www.rediff.com/ business/report/40-years-ago-and-now-how-the-mahindra-group-survived-crisis/20140915.htm (archived at https://perma.cc/4CUT-GB76)

Krause, R (2016) How Amazon, Microsoft, Google crushed Verizon, AT&T in the cloud, *Investor's Business Daily*, 29 August. https://www.investors.com/news/ technology/how-amazon-microsoft-crushed-verizon-att-in-the-cloud/ (archived at https://perma.cc/A5DL-Q42K)

Leonard, D and Coltea, C (2013) Most change initiatives fail – but they don't have to, *Gallup*, 24 May. https://news.gallup.com/businessjournal/162707/change-initiatives-fail-don.aspx (archived at https://perma.cc/949J-SWRV)

Mahindra, A (2014) Mahindra Rise: Insights from Anand Mahindra, Chairman, Mahindra Group, YouTube, 19 September. https://www.youtube.com/watch? v=_lwOpcyjL-4 (archived at https://perma.cc/LUE6-B8AG)

Mahindra, A (2020) Post-Covid capitalism should care for people and the planet, *The Telegraph*, 12 June. https://www.telegraph.co.uk/business/how-to-be-green/ post-covid-capitalism/ (archived at https://perma.cc/2VVP-NNSE)

Price, E (2018) 10,000 Verizon employees have accepted the company's buyout offer, *Fortune*, 10 December. https://fortune.com/2018/12/10/verizon-buyouts/ (archived at https://perma.cc/GMC9-MASJ)

Satell, G (2019) *Cascades: How to create a movement that drives transformational change*, McGraw-Hill Education, New York

Sharp, B (2010) *How Brands Grow: What marketers don't know*, Oxford University Press, Oxford

Soule, S and Walker, B (2017) Changing company culture requires a movement, not a mandate, *Harvard Business Review*, 20 June. https://hbr.org/2017/06/ changing-company-culture-requires-a-movement-not-a-mandate (archived at https://perma.cc/8HNC-VMYM)

Verizon (2020) Coining our new purpose, 15 January. https://www.verizon.com/ about/news/speed-january-15-2020 (archived at https://perma.cc/R9RW-GUXX)

Vestberg, H (2020) @hansvestberg, Twitter, 27 April. https://twitter.com/ hansvestberg/status/1254839480399335424?lang=en (archived at https://perma. cc/5QQ9-HDPZ)

05

Movement Inside

Galvanizing the people that matter inside your brand

As Jennifer made her way into the emergency room at Baltimore's Sinai Hospital, she was trembling. Compounding all this, her head was spinning, she was dizzy, and the nurses could see her sweating as she told them about the pounding in her chest. The teammates inside the hospital knew what the issue was immediately. In fact, even though the hospital workers didn't know her by name, they certainly knew her face. Like millions of Americans, she always came into the hospital emergency room desperate for help, but she was also exasperated that she was in emergency care... again. She was an emergency room super-user. While hospitals are accustomed to seeing repeat patients at urgent care facilities, super-users are those who present themselves to the hospital multiple times. A mother of three who had difficulty controlling her diabetes and frequently sought help for her swings in blood sugar, Jennifer had been to Sinai Hospital, part of LifeBridge Health, over 100 times in one year.

Unlike other service businesses, the point of hospitals is not having repeat customers; they're intended to help people in moments of crisis, make them well and, hopefully, never see them again. Something was wrong in Jennifer's life. But what?

Like many Americans, Jennifer sought ongoing care at the emergency room rather than dealing with the root cause of the disease. So, teammates from LifeBridge Health (LBH), one of the largest health services groups in Maryland, decided to pay her a visit. While diabetes is managed through supplemental insulin and other medication, it's also significantly affected by diet. The team from LBH saw that Jennifer didn't have a working stove. Too often, physical health issues stem from environmental factors, which, if addressed, can drastically improve patient outcomes. The LifeBridge team went to the local department store and a nurse promptly took out her own credit card and ordered Jennifer a stove; she knew that she'd be reimbursed, no questions asked. The LifeBridge team also filled Jennifer's fridge with healthy food and arranged for three nutrition classes so that she could learn the basics of nutrition, which she didn't know. The nurse didn't ask anyone if this was okay. She just did it because Jennifer needed the help. Jennifer hasn't been back as a patient.

From purpose to a new organizational culture

This story helped thousands of employees of LifeBridge Health feel the LBH purpose in their bones. The leaders of LifeBridge Health used this insight and others like it to design a strong and original purpose that reflected the DNA of the institution. But more, they codified it and turned it into a strategy that could unite a confederation of famous and well-known hospitals and their teams into one unified force for good. Neil Meltzer, CEO of LBH, Brian Deffaa, CMO, and the leadership team united behind a movement to galvanize the employees called 'Care Bravely'. It was a Movement Inside to shape the collective culture and understanding of 'how we do things' at LifeBridge Health.

For organizations seeking to become more customer-focused, as in the case of LBH, or more innovative, as in the case of Mahindra (which we will get to in Chapter 10), culture and employee habit change are two of the most challenging parts of the transformation. In the peer-to-peer culture inside large organizations, change no longer can be achieved through top–down mandates from the CEO demanding compliance. Leadership can inspire and empower optimism, trust, conviction or creativity with a Movement Inside, not with a mandate from the top.

With the world changing quickly and employees being knocked from all sides during the COVID-19 pandemic, most corporate executives feel the pressure to drive transformation, or deal with the cultural and societal issues that employees are facing such as financial, emotional and physical wellbeing. In the beginning, corporate leaders often reach for easy solutions or low-hanging fruit. They focus on training and improving the capabilities of product teams. There are now quite a few organizations offering training in design thinking, lean startup and agile product development. While these grassroots movements are well and good, it is also starting to dawn on most executives that lean startup training is not enough.

As we've seen thus far in this book, the principles of social movements have been applied widely to motivate businesses' external audiences, consumers and other stakeholders. But in recent years it's become increasingly clear to us, having worked on a number of transformational and cultural change programmes, that those same movement principles are a powerful tool for leaders to transform companies and change employee habits.

What is Movement Inside?

We call that a Movement Inside, and it can help the CEO or CHRO solve numerous business problems. It enables leaders to take complex and some-times rather dull topics and make the company strategy interesting, because if you think about it, when was the last time you heard a genuinely interest-ing message from the leader of a company? It's a powerful tool to change culture and rituals within your organization.

In this chapter, you will find examples of how Movement Inside can unleash the power of the company's purpose, can be used to help employees become healthier, and can be used for employees to adopt a more innovations-focused culture. It can drive pride and turn an organization rooted in the industries of the past into a powerhouse of fresh thinking that accelerates its rise on the world stage.

Simply put, Movement Inside is transformative. It is a means of uniting a company's people around a shared purpose to achieve change. Often, as in the LifeBridge Health case, that change is cultural. Stories like Jennifer's give extraordinary meaning and emotional vigour to galvanize employees. These stories live within the walls of almost all large organizations and become part of the folklore people hear about when they begin working there. While they can provide employees with a powerful sense of pride, with the focused framework of a Movement Inside, leaders can use these stories to intentionally engage and mobilize their workforce. In the process, they can institutionalize new organizational norms and behaviours. Throughout this chapter, we'll discuss how a Movement Inside provides a more strategic and overt framework to crystallize and activate a brand purpose, just like LBH did with 'Care Bravely'.

A movement of care

There is always a business objective underpinning a Movement Inside. When LifeBridge Health came to StrawberryFrog, the company was looking to unite its federation of independent hospitals and healthcare facilities within one of the largest hospital networks in Baltimore, MD. As we mentioned in Chapter 4 when we introduced LifeBridge Health, its flagship Sinai Hospital was created as a teaching hospital, and teaching was part of the fabric of the organization.

But over the course of seven years (between 2012 and 2019), the hospital network doubled in size to include 137 sites of care. Such rapid change had a dramatic effect on the culture of the organization, CEO Neil Meltzer said in conversation. With the growth, he says LBH went from being a hospital system to an interdisciplinary 'integrated delivery and financing system', which included a series of non-profit companies and an insurance product. The various parts of the system were growing bigger and moving physically further from each other. 'We're very much diversified from where our roots began.'

But its roots actually posed a problem when it came to finding a common purpose that people could align around. That's because, as Meltzer says, the purpose of a free-standing radiology centre is very different from that of a hospital or urgent care centre or hospice:

> I realized we needed to do something to create a spark and ambition, an
> attitude that brought us back together. We needed a rallying cry. We always
> had a purpose statement around care, and we would use it periodically, but it
> no longer felt like it was part of the DNA of the organization because it really
> was created at a time when we were a much smaller organization.

The 'Care Bravely' movement

To address this business objective, StrawberryFrog designed 'Care Bravely', a purpose, and then a Movement Inside activated the purpose. 'Care Bravely' means 'to act with the awareness of our power to bring hope, relief and healing for the benefit of our patients at their most vulnerable moments'. This established a focused LBH culture through actions and storytelling, coaching and ambassadors.

'Care Bravely' brought to the forefront all of the ways employees across the LifeBridge Health network are delivering exceptional care. It set expectations for how teammates treated each other and how they treated their consumers and patients. It institutionalized Jennifer's story into simple steps that everyone could take to feel a part of the 'Care Bravely' movement. We talk a lot about how movement can galvanize employees. 'Care Bravely' galvanized employees across the federation of buildings and under different legacy hospital names. And it enabled Neil Meltzer to run the organization with greater loyalty and passion among the healthcare workers, culminating with his organization being named one of the best places to work in 2020.

THE 'CARE BRAVELY' MANIFESTO

As Neil Meltzer, CEO of LBH, says, '"Care Bravely" means seeing each individual as a person, not simply a patient. To make going above and beyond our normal. It's a mindset that we bring to all that we do. Not just care for every person but to *care bravely*.'

FIGURE 5.1   LifeBridge Health manifesto

Welcome to LifeBridge Health, 12,000 give-a-damn human beings dialed into breaking out of the status quo.

Since 1866, we've been bravely serving those in need without bias and we're still here today changing how care is done.

That doesn't just mean a few shiny new machines or a fancy new wing. You need equipment; sure.

You need knowledge; yes. But you need something more than tubes, technology and a degree.

You need to care. Really, really care.

You need persistence to see past medical symptoms and treat root causes.

You need empathy to help people as they scale the scariest, the hardest, the most vulnerable moments in their lives.

You need to care like there's no tomorrow. And then do it again the next day.

That's the brave, new kind of care we're creating. Every time we scrub in.

Care that sees patients as people and puts people before profits.

Care that enlists science in the service of better lives, families and communities.

Care that means doing the right thing, even when it's the hard thing.

At LifeBridge Health, we see care not as just a service, but a promise to every patient we sit down with.

And then we stand up again to face the mountain together.

Care Bravely

LifeBridge Health

SOURCE StrawberryFrog

Bringing the movement to life

Every movement has a motto. We crystallized LBH's movement with those two words: *Care. Bravely*. The movement came to life intentionally, through orchestrated actions and training, and with a powerful communications programme that made use of LifeBridge Health's own people, inspiring them to take on the 'Care Bravely' norms and motto. It started with an internal website where thousands of employees submitted genuine stories about when they provided brave care or saw their colleagues provide 'Care Bravely' stories like Jennifer's. Or the physical therapist who learned enough Spanish to foster a patient's dog that only understood Spanish commands, until that patient was discharged from rehabilitation. Or the security guard who turned a wheelchair into a spaceship to bring joy to a paediatric behavioural health patient.

Working closely with StrawberryFrog, the LBH leadership team designed and curated a series of iconic 'Care Bravely' launch events across all LifeBridge Health facilities to introduce and spread the movement. All 12,000 LifeBridge Health employees attended, received 'Care Bravely' swag and were encouraged to join the movement at WeCareBravely.org.

'Care Bravely' ambassador programme

To speed mobilization of the movement, we sought out 100 rising-star employees to be a part of the first-ever three-month 'Igniter' leadership training to learn the values of 'Care Bravely' at LifeBridge Health. StrawberryFrog's Movement Inside coach, Eric Horwitz, facilitated training sessions to help our 'Igniters' unlock their potential with tools and ongoing support to spread and live the movement. Each was sponsored by a member of the C-suite and was in constant contact with them through the first six months of the programme. These 'Igniters' were the key to cascading interest in the movement throughout the organization.

Horwitz told us that from his experience, HR leaders play a crucial role in this process. That's because they have the breadth of knowledge and understanding of the organizational culture to determine who among their ranks has the organizational influence and is well respected enough to become an ambassador of a movement. 'Once doctors heard about the programme and others heard about it, they wanted to join,' he recounted to us.

Furthermore, to spread the movement we produced films, stories, digital prompts and nudges, and social media all targeting LifeBridge employees.

We then went outside the organization to our communities with posters, digital and TV advertising on all major stations. WeCareBravely.org further educated employees about the movement, housed 'Care Bravely' films that featured employees' acts of brave care, and allowed employees to share real stories of people they saw *caring bravely* at LifeBridge Health. Meltzer said:

> Our people are the touchpoints across the health system so we celebrate employees at all our organizations. By bringing our own people into the movement, and thus engaging them, they are helping to build this new culture. And we were able to create a new sense of ownership and excitement within our culture and see our employees put our 'Care Bravely' movement into action in their everyday work.

Results

Since the launch of 'Care Bravely' in 2019, LBH has seen a dramatic deepening of engagement, as evidenced by 80 per cent of staff completing their employee engagement survey. Meltzer also attributes the Great Place to Work designation directly to the movement. And in spite of a number of external factors working against the organization, the 2019 fiscal year ended up as the most profitable in the 21 years since the inception of LifeBridge Health. As Meltzer told us when reflecting on his 'Care Bravely' journey, culture change is often the most challenging part of any organizational transformation. It demands new leadership skills and behaviours, which can be the opposite of focusing on operational efficiency. That's what makes movements so powerful if they can be achieved from the inside–out.

Chief Marketing Officer Brian Deffaa says his goal with the movement was to create a revolutionary way of thinking and doing. He wanted an idea that would serve as an internal rallying cry for LifeBridge employees inside the organization as well as an external beacon to the consumer and the community that defines the LifeBridge culture and experience. By creating a purpose-based movement, which encompassed both objectives, he says they did just that.

> Creating a brand is one thing. Activating it and having it resonate or 'stick' is something else entirely. To really take hold and galvanize an organization, it must be based on traits of the organization but also the culture. It must overcome the very real cynicism of 'tag-line du jour' and become a genuine ground–up movement for change.

Deffaa added that it was only by igniting a movement that they 'shaped culture and moved the people that matter to LifeBridge Health'.

This is also what Meltzer says was most significant about the movement:

> What we created wasn't an advertisement, it wasn't a marketing campaign, it was really a movement that was used to coalesce a group of disparate people in three states and allowed us to engage our workforce in a way they've never been engaged before. Not only did it engage the hospital network's people who worked across three US states, it celebrated who they are and the work they do. We were intentionally trying to do something that was a little bit different than everybody else. We wanted something that could morph over time without losing the feeling of what we are trying to create. More importantly, it allows us to rediscover the purpose statement that has existed for a decade and infuse it with life.

The benefit of activating a purpose with Movement Inside

It's increasingly clear that people want more meaning in their work. They are also more sceptical than ever about the real commitment of leaders to new initiatives around purpose – and their likelihood to endure. Employees will believe it when they see it. All talk and no action undermines the CEO's position and the opportunity for purpose to drive organizational and employee behavioural change.

UK-based strategic maestro Adam Morgan, author of *Eating the Big Fish*, recently added this thought when we spoke:

> Perhaps this is just, once more, 'this year's leadership speech'. And, of course, most leaders simply don't know how to lead through purpose or feel genuinely comfortable doing so. Successfully creating a Movement Inside around the purpose shifts the framing question for middle managers from 'How serious are they (leadership) about this?' to 'How serious are we about this?', and it gives a platform for culture carriers at all levels in the company to show the potential of purpose in their different spheres of work and application.

Employees are your best brand ambassadors. When it comes to making habit change happen, HR leaders want to know how quickly they can get their people there. How do we make it happen? What is a proven mindset and habit-changing process that is sticky and drives change? In this chapter let's look at recent examples where large organizations use Movement Inside to do just this, to help create a willingness to change, and find smarter ways than what was done before.

You can challenge your orthodoxies

Getting from where you are to where you need to be starts with exercises to help companies challenge their own orthodoxies – those biases in the industry, company and among leaders that stifle creativity and change. Those same feelings of 'who we are' or 'how things are done here' can be barriers. The process to design Movement Inside starts with exercises to test those deeply held beliefs to see if they align with your purpose and the movement that will bring the strategy to life for years to come.

That's what Christy Pambianchi, EVP/CHRO at Verizon, did as she helped CEO Hans Vestberg roll out the 'Forward Together' movement. If Verizon was going to be the *network that moves the world forward*, it had to make sure it was moving forward as well. Challenging the orthodoxies held by employees allowed Verizon leadership to ensure they were asking the right questions and solving the right problems. Pambianchi says they did that by asking leaders the question: what is a core belief that you believe are orthodoxies that, if challenged, open up new opportunities?

Verizon leaders and employees then underwent a reframing exercise – identify a potential orthodoxy, ask 'What if this is no longer true?', and consider what new questions and possibilities emerge. This was followed by a question sprint where participants built new questions to help one another bust orthodoxies.

The purpose of the exercise was to break people from the tendency to fall back on past experiences. Pambianchi told us:

> We may have reached the top of Mount Everest with 4G and are basking in the glow. But now there's a whole new mountain to climb with 5G. And what got us here might not get us there. So what we've been doing with our transformations is try not to look backward and say these were not good choices, or these were not good systems, and instead ask ourselves, what would success in this new environment look like?

You can align HR to purpose

Pambianchi says this thinking has also helped her reform how her team approaches human resources. Instead of hiring for specific skills or university grades, she says she inspires her team to hire based on employee values and traits.

She reinforces this by starting each of her meetings with a statement rooted in the company's purpose: 'We deliver the talent that creates the networks that move the world forward: how are we going to attract the right people?'

'The purpose of human resources is to deliver the talent that creates the network to move the world forward, and we're going to do that by attracting people who are excited about our purposes, share our values,' she told us. This has resulted in a number of changes around how the company hires, how it builds out job taxonomies and career paths, and it's transformed Verizon's incentive and employee programmes. These moves, she says, help people understand how serious the company is about its purpose.

You can galvanize the people that matter to your brand, inside and out

Movement Inside is an important tool for leaders because we're seeing that employees are increasingly unhappy at work. In its June 2020 report on employee engagement in the United States (Harter, 2020), Gallup found that only 31 per cent of employees are engaged. That means the vast majority of American workers are psychologically unattached to their work and company. The story is worse globally. Gallup reported that in 2017 only 15 per cent of employees worldwide felt engaged in their work (Gallup, 2017).

Having unengaged employees and stakeholders is one of the biggest hurdles facing CEOs aiming to establish a more adaptive and innovative environment. So the question becomes, how do you change the culture of an organization when no one reads your CEO or CHRO email? This is often the most challenging part of the transformation.

Movement Inside is not simply an employee engagement programme or internal marketing push. It is designed to get employees rallied around a higher purpose they want to participate in because it is meaningful to them personally.

As Ruzbeh Irani, erstwhile chief brand officer and now president, group human resources and communications of Mahindra, said of the company's 'Rise' movement:

> It crystallized the culture inside our multidisciplinary, multicultural organization. It galvanized all our employees. It gave us a better understanding of ourselves, it unleashed our magical powers to think differently and to act. It is a lens we use to evaluate employee performance and to recruit top talent. Moreover, it enables us to bind a diverse group of people from many different companies – from automotive to agribusiness, from aerospace to technology – with a common purpose we all share.

Stephan Scholl, CEO of Alight, the leading global provider of benefits administration and cloud-based HR and financial solutions, takes this a step further. He suggests that when looking to connect with employees – especially those in different locations – and ignite purpose within an organization with a movement, one that is personalized can achieve this even faster:

> Never before have employees or company leaders faced the kind of change accelerated by the pandemic. While connecting people with the right information when they can't be in the same place is important, demand for virtual solutions will remain after the crisis. Which is why we are focusing on personalization, on genuinely understanding each employee so that companies can provide a more personalized physical, emotional and financial wellbeing.

Movements give employees an inspiring reason to get up and go to work every day – and in doing so revolutionize employee engagement. So, the million-dollar question is: how do you successfully move to Movement Inside?

New leadership for a new culture

In many, if not most, companies, culture change or enhancement initiatives get interpreted and acted upon differently in separate silos within the organization. Human resources is doing one thing, IT another, marketing still another. And all this coming from an edict from the office of the CEO. That's why, as discussed in Chapter 4, movements are effective tools for CEOs looking to transform company culture.

Movement Inside is intended to get all the arrows going in the same direction, under an inspiring North Star that's the company's higher purpose. We've found over the years that there are four pillars that guide the successful development of a Movement Inside.

Pillar 1: reframe your purpose via Movement Thinking

This is the most important foundation for success in activating purpose and requires you to ask yourself: does your purpose, as it's currently framed, make employees feel their work is truly meaningful? Does it make them proud to work at your firm? Many do not, and it's not just a matter of language or even a concept – but rather a matter of framing.

That's what we did with SunTrust Bank (now Truist). While *lighting the way to financial wellbeing* is a great purpose, the movement accelerated the

FIGURE 5.2   Getting to purpose resonance

Reframe your purpose in movement-think terms	Address Barriers early and head on	Leverage Networks for momentum	Pivot when necessary to maintain energy
You need a shared enemy, and a stand that helps you fight that enemy.	Attack the obstacles, whether it's sceptical people, organizational inertia, etc.	Spreading enthusiasm for purpose through networks is more effective than through hierarchies.	Continually monitor employee sentiment for loss of enthusiasm and energy to know when a change of approach is needed.

SOURCE StrawberryFrog

speed of adoption and accelerated the momentum behind helping people *move from financial stress to financial confidence*. That movement was activated inside the company with 'Momentum onUp'. Thereafter SunTrust provided programme access to over 200 large organizations across the US to help them spread financial literacy to their employees.

The principles of Movement Thinking are outlined in Chapters 1 and 3, but they bear repeating here because putting your purpose through these principles is essential to reframing it for a Movement Inside:

- Dissatisfaction – what's your grievance?
- Desired change – how do you want the world to be different?
- Enemy – what are you against?
- Stand – what are you for?
- Action – how will you rally people around your stand?

Pillar 2: address barriers early and head on

It's easy to assume that activating your higher purpose via a movement will be popular with all your stakeholders. After all, who doesn't want to try to relate what we do every day to making life and the world better? But within every organization, there is a slew of people who can stand in the way – those who say 'this too shall pass', the cynics, the sceptics and the nay-sayers. It's important to know that you'll never get 100 per cent of people on board, but you can connect with and hopefully pre-empt the most prominent and influential potential detractors.

But people aren't the only obstacles to movement success; there are others that are less visible and thus harder to overcome. Organizational inertia is perhaps the biggest of these as many larger organizations in particular are bureaucratic and lethargic with a seemingly built-in bias for stasis. This is often caused by problematic structures like rigid dividing lines between departments and functions that keep employees separated in silos, cultural norms that favour keeping to the tried and true, and rigid policies that inhibit the organization's ability to change. Before embarking on your movement journey, it's vital to map out the barriers to change and put in place a plan to address the most important ones.

Pillar 3: leverage networks

It's easy to assume that the hardest work is defining your purpose and framing it appropriately in movement terms. Assuming you do that correctly, activation should be relatively easy, right? Unfortunately, that's often not the case. Even the most compelling movement platform can fade or fizzle quickly without constant pressure on activating.

There are two approaches we've seen work in getting and keeping the movement mobilizing across your organization. The first tries to take advantage of your organization's existing hierarchy, recognizing that no matter how flat or egalitarian we claim or desire our organization to be, the truth is that nearly all of them have top management, middle management and front-line workers. In this approach to mobilizing your movement, the vision comes from the top, it's taken to heart by middle management, and it's adopted at a grassroots level of the rank and file. We call this 'top–down, bottom–up, middle–out'. As we discussed in Chapter 2, there's strong empirical evidence to support the notion that under this approach, middle management has a critical role to play, as the engine keeps the enthusiasm going.

The other approach – as we discussed in the last chapter – is through networks. These are 'teams of teams' within your organization, be they informal (eg clubs, groups of acquaintances, subject-matter enclaves, etc) or formal ones (eg the 'Care Bravely' ambassadors from the LBH example earlier). The movement begins to spread when these small, loosely connected groups unite behind a common purpose and begin talking it up to others. Eric Horwitz, who facilitated LifeBridge Health's Movement Inside, said that networks are particularly beneficial in the face of generational differences: 'Younger people don't see leaders as credible or trustworthy and grassroots activities have more credibility.'

And as Greg Satell, author of *Cascades*, said when we spoke to him in the last chapter, small groups can grow exponentially when they're unified by shared values that are focused on a shared purpose:

> When you have small groups who are interested in things, you have to ask how can you empower them and how can you convene them and allow them to connect in ways that make them feel like they can take ownership? It's a non-linear phenomenon.

Pillar 4: pivot when necessary to maintain energy

The most successful Movements Inside in our experience have placed a premium on measurement. They have identified key metrics they want to see move before they begin an activation, and take readings frequently to gauge when the loss of enthusiasm and energy is occurring or when a change of approach is warranted. For Movements Inside, employee sentiment is often the most important indicator, with things like overall morale, degree of engagement with the workplace, understanding of and enthusiasm for the company's purpose, and so on. But other yardsticks can be important as well – anything from Glassdoor ratings to placement in 'best places to work' rankings. As a movement matures, it needs to pivot to build on successes and address shortcomings.

COVID-19 AND THE CHANGING ROLE OF HR

The old HR model is no longer fit for purpose. We asked a few leading CHROs about what is happening in people management, and the emphasis is on change. Risk management has given way to a more empowered, more engaged cultural leader in the CHRO. They are the rising stars coming out of the pandemic, supporting CEOs by driving more cultural and behaviour leadership. CEOs in the past have led the organization through giant company moments. What COVID-19 has done, however, is to put the role of people leaders and HR leaders on a pedestal as they have been asked to stand out and more visibly help CEOs manage internal culture and transformation, and lead their companies forward.

We work with many HR leaders and we're seeing how their role is changing. We help them design internal movements to deal with employee wellbeing in a full-spectrum way. It's incredibly challenging: how do you positively change company culture and the behaviour of your employees, with stress and uncertainty running high in all quarters?

The CHRO's moment is now

While HR has typically been one of those core functions that exist behind the scenes, the role and response of HR leaders and departments were thrust into the spotlight during the pandemic. Based on the attention paid to HR policies during that time, the responses that reshaped work life around the world and the lasting effects of those responses, you could call the early 2020s the 'CHRO moment'.

As the pandemic was unfolding, we talked to several HR executives about their leadership during such turbulent times, including Truist's Kimberly Moore-Wright, Becky Schmitt of Cognizant, Ruzbeh Irani of Mahindra and Verizon's Christy Pambianchi.

For instance, Kimberly Moore-Wright played a significant role in helping lead the establishment of a new culture at Truist, a major financial company born from the merger of BB&T and SunTrust Bank, and launched it in the months leading up to and in the middle of the pandemic. Fortunately, the bank had a clear purpose, and moreover, as CHRO she played an active role in bringing the purpose to life:

> This has been an extraordinary time where we have used our purpose to make important decisions for our teammates, such as implementing work-at-home strategies, modified branch hours, and augmented compensation for our essential teammates. Also, our 'Together Safely' strategy is focused on ensuring the safety and wellbeing of our teammates as we begin a very careful and mindful approach to bringing teammates back to our work facilities. These efforts have helped accelerate Truist's purpose-, mission-, and values-driven culture as we work together to create and drive meaningful change for our teammates, clients, and communities. (Goodson, 2020)

At Verizon, Pambianchi told us in order for employees to believe in a transformation, the claims of that change have to be reflected in what they experience as an employee – otherwise, they just aren't going to believe in the transformation. In a broad sense, she says that if a company like Verizon stated it was going to be agile and innovative and allow risk-taking, but then didn't recognize and reward that behaviour, employees would interpret those claims as hollow.

> From an HR leader's perspective, whatever those tenets are, you have to take a clean look at all the HR systems, policies, hiring practices, reward systems, and if they don't fit with the new parameters of the stated desired culture, they should be redone. Because that's what employees are going to feel. That's one reason it's a key moment for HR leaders.

This, she says, is especially true during a crisis like COVID-19:

> Coronavirus is a human crisis. So it's causing businesses to call into question all of their policies around how they treat their employees – how are they going to run their business, how are they going to keep their employees safe? So it's a huge moment for HR leaders to step up and put their money where their mouth is. At Verizon, we pivoted 100,000 people to work from home, put in caregiver leave and all kinds of policies that didn't just say we cared about their health and safety, but showed them.

Movement Inside engages the whole person

Sometimes it's easy for leaders to forget how much the people working at their companies have on their plates. They have a day-to-day responsibility for operational excellence, operational efficiency, and it's really hard to look out into the horizon and start to think about innovation. This is to say nothing of their lives outside of work where they're raising kids, paying bills, and doing their best to stay happy and healthy.

Movement Inside is a way to treat the whole human as both an employee and a person. This matters because when it comes to where they choose to work and how they show up at work, more and more people are being led by their personal sense of purpose. They want to be with a company whose mission and values fit with their own.

As the LifeBridge story demonstrates, a Movement Inside can transform the experience employees have at work, strengthen the relationship they have with their employer and improve the service they give customers. That's because when people are engaged in a goal beyond simply making a paycheque and delivering profits to a company, they are happier.

But what happens when life outside of work isn't that happy? That was certainly the case in 2020 with its perfect storm of cultural upheaval, from protests around racial injustice and stress around financial and physical wellbeing resulting from the COVID-19 pandemic. People were forced into their homes – cramming work, family and life into whatever four walls they had (if they were fortunate enough to work from home during the health crisis). HR departments were thrust into the limelight as they quickly had to devise work-from-home policies, caregiver leave for those with ill family members, and financial and mental health support for those who were struggling.

This is to say nothing of the fact that these days, employees are harder than ever to engage. They're under greater stress both at work and at home. Their mental, physical and financial wellbeing are threatened. They tune out company messages and programmes.

When your employees face new threats to their mental, physical and financial wellbeing, the order of difficulty in driving change is no doubt magnified. How do you keep employees motivated and engaged at such a time? How do you detect and protect their wellbeing issues, be they physical, mental or financial? How do you maintain a great culture when there is no office?

The good news: HR leaders in search of new solutions can tap the principles of social movements to improve and transform employee mindsets, behaviours and actions in turbulent times like these. Creating an internal movement is the solution to these challenges, and doing so empowers HR leaders to meet the moment. HR leaders can deal with these issues by activating and actualizing purpose inside their organizations. And that's where Movement Thinking can be transformative. Here are some ways that the whole person can be engaged.

Designing a movement for financial wellbeing

SunTrust's 'onUp' movement didn't simply ignite a crusade for financial confidence among the general public; it sparked a conversation about a huge issue facing SunTrust teammates themselves: financial stress.

It started with a programme for financial literacy among all SunTrust employees. Internal mobilization included performance change programmes, actions and an 'onUp' purpose ambassador programme. It was complemented with external communications including the national launch of the 'onUp' movement at the Super Bowl, and events for both employees and the communities in which they and their families live. 'onUp' gave SunTrust employees the motivation and confidence to speak up and have hard conversations about money – with both their financial advisors and their families.

Susan Somersille Johnson, now Chief Marketing Officer at Prudential (former Chief Marketing Officer of SunTrust), said to us:

> We launched our 'onUp' movement and we've been living and breathing it ever since. We've done a lot towards integrating it deeply into the organization. The main reason our purpose has been productive is that the whole organization is behind it, it's not just a marketing initiative.

As we mentioned earlier, SunTrust also launched 'Momentum onUp', a workplace financial wellbeing programme used by more than 200 companies, including Home Depot, Waffle House and Delta, to improve the financial stability of their employees. Johnson said:

> The 'onUp' movement has empowered people to confront a taboo topic: money. Businesses are making it part of their benefits programmes, and people are sharing the resources and their stories. Our goal is to help people take control of their finances so they can enjoy the moments that matter to them most.

Designing a movement for physical wellbeing

To an employee at a large company, benefits are perhaps one of the most important priorities. Leaders in those companies spend an extraordinary amount of time designing the right benefits. As such, one of the most powerful ways of activating purpose among employees is through benefits. That's because all the enrichment and engagement programmes in the world won't do employees any good if their physical health isn't protected. The 'Better Living' Movement Inside of Walmart is an excellent example of how a movement for wellbeing can transform the way associates (what Walmart calls its workforce) experience the company.

When he joined Walmart as Senior Vice President, US Benefits, Adam Stavisky saw several areas to focus his attention: help Walmart associates better understand the benefits that the company provides, meet employees where they are, make change and innovation happen quickly, and measure it.

Walmart has more than 1.5 million associates in the US. But as with many large organizations, associates did not always pay close attention to 'open enrolment' materials and were thus not aware of, and therefore underutilizing, many of the health benefits and services available to them. The problem to solve was to change the pace quickly, and find the recipe to get the right level of engagement and information to associates.

As Stavisky said to us when recounting his initial challenge, the traditional engagement model large companies use with their employees for benefits is proving increasingly less effective. So he needed something new to engage Walmart's US employees in a conversation about better health:

> We need to drive real and lasting change quickly. The unmet need is to meet different employees where they are. Benefits are often a personal topic, so it's challenging to change habits quickly. We asked ourselves: how do we make that happen? How do we create not just a willingness to change but a desire to learn and change?

To help change people's behaviour quickly, we launched the 'Better Living' Movement Inside at Walmart, intended to ensure that the physical wellbeing of its workforce was being optimized. The movement took what had been dry, clinical information and turned it into motivating and engaging communications. We created a series of videos, targeted people with digital media buys and created opportunities for them to engage with the messaging. We mobilized associates by creating a new integrated ecosystem with a mix of owned and paid channels.

By talking to employees in an empathetic manner, delivering it with high-quality video in channels they used (eg mobile) and getting the message off the break-room wall, Walmart used a Movement Inside to bring people along what could have been a difficult journey towards better physical health. Stavisky added, 'This is about better health and creating a willingness to change and do what we didn't do before in innovative and effective ways.'

Reflecting on the journey to remake the way Walmart communicates internally, Stavisky told us that Movements Inside companies represent a different kind of leadership. It's a shift from the corporate centre imposing a view on others, to one where the movement reflects peer-to-peer culture, and finds its own inspiration because it reflects what employees as a community care about:

> A movement provides business change steps and a process, which is hard to do. When people are included in information they feel better and treat customers better. This approach creates a willingness to change and do what they didn't do before in innovative new ways.

Designing a movement for mental wellbeing

As we've noted throughout this book, rarely has there been a more precarious time for employee mental health than the one that America – and elsewhere – experienced in 2020. Fear and outrage about police brutality became widespread as more people captured and shared it on video. And all this just as people were still reeling from the fallout of the COVID-19 pandemic.

During this time clinicians, hotlines and employee assistance programmes were reporting high rates of fear, uncertainty, grief, loneliness and exhaustion. These feelings, especially when they become chronic, lead to a greater risk of clinical depression, anxiety, PTSD, suicide and substance abuse. These lead to higher rates of disability, reduced productivity and low employee morale. Unlike many disasters, the COVID-19 crisis was protracted.

Even before the ominous events of 2020, employee mental wellbeing was under siege. Depression is the leading cause of disability worldwide, according to the World Health Organization, and from 2000 to 2016, the United States experienced a 30 per cent increase in suicides, making it the 10th largest cause of death (Brueck, 2018). A report from Blue Cross Blue Shield found that rates of depression in the US went up 33 per cent from 2013 to 2016 (Blue Cross Blue Shield, 2018).

Employees who had to adjust to new vulnerabilities, uncertainties and business practices as a result of COVID-19 were re-traumatized through repeated exposure to images and threats of violence. For some, this moment was a wakeup call to make important and necessary changes, but for many, there was a cumulative deep emotional overload and exhaustion. The time caused companies to reflect on how they could help their employees cope.

Scott Tannen, CEO of Boll & Branch, whose sustainable luxury linen company we introduced in Chapter 3, says the mental health of his employees was central to how his company responded to the COVID-19 pandemic and the social unrest following the Black Lives Matter protests. He responded by giving employees paid communities days to contribute to their communities however they saw fit and imposed a Slack siesta – one hour a day where people were relieved from always-on communications. It was his way of fostering the mental health of his people.

Dr Anne Hallward – former Harvard Medical School Fellow in Psychiatry, founder of Safe Space Radio and StrawberryFrog – collaborator says it's important for leaders to understand that everyone has a sense of vulnerability to illness, loss and an uncertain future:

While some individuals are relatively insulated from direct risk, there is a sense of 'we' that can help reduce shame and foster a culture of mutual support and compassion for those struggling through this cultural moment. This is especially true if that support is coming from management in palpable ways.

An innovative employee wellness movement can give company leaders and internal teams a powerful new tool to deal with these issues. This should enable collaboration among department heads, and give employees a sense of belonging and the feeling that they matter; their concerns are heard and are being taken seriously. Employees should feel that they can trust and be part of the process and that they are being given choices and the power to support one another along the way.

What makes this challenging? The stigma of mental health problems is powerful. Many still fear they will be seen as weak, a failure or defective if they acknowledge having mental health issues, which leads to shame and a reluctance to seek help. People often hide their struggles, which puts them at risk. Sociologist Erving Goffman defines stigma as a sense of spoiled identity that you cannot wash off (Goffman, 1986). People fear that their reputation will permanently suffer if they are seen as needing help. Companies need to explicitly address stigma and provide privacy and confidentiality in order for new programmes and initiatives to be effective. Research about reducing stigma clearly demonstrates the value of leadership in sharing stories of vulnerability in order to shift the culture within an organization.

The key to reducing stigma and fostering a culture of mutual support and compassion is communication and connection. This is where designing a Movement Inside among your employees comes in. Your company's engagement and communication style can make or break relationships with employees. Many companies are messaging employees to inform them about wellbeing programmes and resources. The problem is that most employees tune these messages out. Thirty per cent of employees admit they don't read emails from their employers, according to APPrise (Albrecht, 2016). Only 13 per cent report using their company's intranet daily, and 31 per cent admit they have never used it, according to Prescient Digital Media (Prescient Media, 2020).

Nothing's more important than your employees' mental health. And this time of uncertainty and vulnerability makes it clear that changing how you engage with employees for greater mental health impact must become a priority. A Movement Inside will help you develop greater employee engagement, reduce mental health stigma, and ultimately provide tools and solutions to support your employees' everyday mental wellbeing.

Communicating your Movement Inside

We've emphasized repeatedly that a movement is not just a communication campaign. Having said that, we've observed that a major reason movements fail to take hold – particularly inside a company – is poor communication. In our work inside companies big and small, not only creating Movement Thinking but communicating it through the organization, we've developed these principles that guide our work:

- **Start with the human, not the company**
  What is relevant to them and their families? Design the movement around what is relevant to them and then tie it back to the company or your purpose.

- **Deliver what they need, not what you need to say**
  There's a tendency in employee communications to start with what is an intended message – and then tailor it to the audience. Instead, always start with the employee and what they need (and continue putting the employee first in everything you do). Then determine what to say.

- **Frame your movement**
  Be sure it's framed in such a way that people really understand what's at stake and that they have a personal as well as a social obligation to see that change through. The goal is to incite action. We want people to participate.

- **Make your communications consumer grade**
  People are used to seeing high-quality communications on TV and online. As a result, basic-looking communications coming at them from their own company fail to engage.

- **Create symbols**
  If you think about social movements, they create visual identities. They have symbols that they use that people within that movement wear or hang in their room or hang on their computer. You need to create symbols. Those symbols are like the visual manifestation of the ideas that you're trying to express and it starts to create visual references so that people in the outside world can see that there's this group of people together. Is it an internal video that arouses emotion? Is it a t-shirt that communicates your purpose and elicits pride? Is it highlighting the stories of employees living your brand values?

- **Act swiftly**

  One of the things we've learned over the years is that for a movement to succeed, it's got to have fast, iconic actions. People live in a changing world, and habit-changing and actions need to happen quickly. People need to see this strategy happen in real life. They need to see it actually coming to life in front of their eyes. It can't be a theoretical journey over 18 months. They need to see things start to happen so that they feel a momentum being built and the cadence that is necessary to prevent decay. Communicate the vision and early wins in a way people will respond to and you're more likely to elicit action.

- **Meet them where they are**

  The most relevant communication will fail to connect with employees if it is delivered at a place and time that are not relevant. Employers typically do not use the channels employees use most. You need to build a community and a place for this movement to form. It could be a place where people engage virtually. For example, WhatsApp has a really simple platform that you can use to engage a community over geography or even across different business units inside a company. What's important about that community when you form it is that you make sure you give people perpetual messages and continuously give them opportunities to engage.

KEY TAKEAWAYS

When you activate your purpose internally, it will help you change the course of your company. Challenges can be overcome through the momentum and engagement it will create, and it can improve employees' lives. To a CEO or CHRO, Movement Inside has the power to bring life to the important actions you are taking and those company stories like Jennifer's, turning them into a powerful culture that frees the organization to leap forward and drive radical growth. It is also an essential foundation for communicating and activating your purpose externally, which we'll discuss in our next chapter on Movement Outside. By activating your purpose inside, it helps leaders to be believed when the time comes to communicate your purpose to consumers.

Before moving to activating your purpose outside your organization, remember these key elements of a Movement Inside:

- A Movement Inside can change company culture and employee behaviour better than a CEO mandate by inspiring creativity, trust and motivation among employees.

- A Movement Inside allows you to challenge existing biases and orthodoxies, so that employees understand, engage with and are hired to align with the company's purpose.

- A Movement Inside can engage employees as a whole person by addressing specific pain points, such as mental, physical or financial wellbeing.

- A Movement Inside demands engagement through consumer-grade communications that meet people where they are.

References

Albrecht, H (2016) 4 marketing strategies to make HR better and employees happy, *The Employee App*, 11 August. https://www.theemployeeapp.com/ entrepreneur-4-marketing-strategies-you-need-to-make-hr-better (archived at https://perma.cc/2YVQ-RLKF)

Blue Cross Blue Shield (2018) *Major Depression: The impact on overall health.* https://www.bcbs.com/the-health-of-america/reports/major-depression-the-impact-overall-health (archived at https://perma.cc/GNB8-8YFJ)

Brueck, H (2018) The US suicide rate has increased 30% since 2000, and tripled for young girls. Here's what we can do about it, *Business Insider*, 10 September. https://www.businessinsider.com/us-suicide-rate-increased-since-2000-2018-6 (archived at https://perma.cc/34V6-3MVA)

Gallup (2017) State of the global workplace, Gallup.com. https://www.gallup.com/ workplace/238079/state-global-workplace-2017.aspx (archived at https:// perma.cc/B7B3-DFFY)

Goffman, E (1986) *Stigma: Notes on the management of spoiled identity*, Touchstone, New York

Goodson, G (2020) The CHRO's time has come, *Inc.*, 11 July. https://www.inc. com/scott-goodson/the-chros-time-has-come.html (archived at https://perma.cc/ 2D8L-VP6C)

Harter, J (2020) Historic drop in employee engagement follows record rise, *Gallup*, 2 July. https://www.gallup.com/workplace/313313/historic-drop-employee-engagement-follows-record-rise.aspx (archived at https://perma.cc/5HW5-THHZ)

Prescient Media (2020) *Social Intranet Study Report*. https://www.prescientdigital. com/downloads/social-intranet-study-2012-purchase-the-full-report (archived at https://perma.cc/Q2GL-XPHM)

06

Movement Outside

New marketing, branding and advertising
for a new customer culture

Every aircraft that falls from the sky is breaking news. Yet, in the United States during the past few years, the equivalent of 13 jumbo jets' worth of people have died each month from a single cause, one that tragically few, if any, talked about. These deaths received scant attention and few headline news stories. That's because the people who represent those 13 aircraft full of people – upwards of 70,000 a year – died from accidental opioid addiction (CDC, 2019).

This epidemic of death has touched families across the United States and is something Peter from Massachusetts knows all too well. We first met Peter (anonymized for his privacy) in 2015 at the Nantucket Project – an ideas festival held on the island off the coast of Rhode Island every August. Peter and his wife live on a leafy tree-lined suburban street, the kind you see in Hollywood movies. He told us about how on that street one family had a teenager who tragically had developed cancer. It was heartening, he told us, to see how the community rose to the occasion and helped the family in that home. People wished them well, they brought gifts and dropped off food at their doorstep. It was beautiful, Peter said.

He then told us how a couple of years later Peter's own son was in need of support and care. After suffering a sports injury in high school, his son was taken to the emergency room. Within 10 days of his surgery, he was back in the ER as a drug-seeking patient and what followed was the horror story most parents dread. Peter's son had become dependent on prescription opioids – doctor-prescribed painkillers. In the years that followed, after the insurance ran out, his son turned to street drugs. The family tried to intervene repeatedly, but to no avail. His son died of an overdose.

What stood out during those days, Peter said, was how differently he was treated on the street he lived on. When word got out that his son was addicted to drugs, the family was avoided like the plague. No one came over, no one brought gifts, no one dropped food off for the suffering family. A typical businessman in a pressed shirt and with tidy hair, Peter was quickly thrust onto the front lines of the opioid epidemic. He never thought he'd be an activist, but his son's death changed that. Peter's son was a good kid and didn't need to die. He sought help for an injury and, in return, his life was destroyed. By the time we met Peter, he had vowed to understand the root cause of this epidemic and try to get people to do more to stop it.

Before we continue our discussion about how to launch a Movement Outside, we want to pause and acknowledge something contentious: companies and brands can radically grow and thrive in the age of movements by designing a marketing movement rather than doing an old advertising campaign. That's how we helped Orexo break into the United States market while helping people like Peter lead a mass movement that ignited a national conversation about a preventable epidemic.

Righting a societal wrong with Orexo

Like all movements, the issue of doctor-prescribed painkillers was a wrong that needed to be righted. Where to begin? To us, the way Peter's son was treated was a stigma, a social issue that deserved – no, demanded – a movement mobilizing the industry, the media and Americans. The scourge of accidental opioid addiction was taking its toll across the United States and around the world and needed to be outed. As we've discussed, the desire to right a wrong is a core principle of any movement. In the rest of this chapter, we'll discuss how to create a Movement Outside that engages customers and external stakeholders, but not before we finish the story of how we helped others avoid Peter's fate.

If we look at the opioid epidemic alone, it's killed hundreds of thousands of Americans and damaged the lives of millions more. Of those prescribed painkillers, 5 per cent will become addicted (NIH Medline Plus Magazine, 2011), and once their health coverage for opioid treatment runs out, many turn to street drugs. And it's easy to understand why – a single medically assisted treatment (MAT) dose can run upwards of $60; a bag of heroin on the street is $5.

At the time few, if any, in the medical community were openly talking about this accidental opioid addiction – the pharma companies were not talking about it; the government wasn't talking about it. Serendipitously, Swedish-based pharmaceutical company Orexo called us wanting to launch a better MAT for drug addiction into the US. The company wanted us to develop and launch a creative advertising campaign to position its product Zubsolv, which had better efficacy and safety as well as the same active components as previously approved MAT buprenorphine. We told them not to do an advertising campaign; instead, we said, you need to launch a movement.

A movement to galvanize the people that matter to your brand

How does a company identify and crystallize a movement idea that is relevant to customers and prospects? An idea that galvanizes thousands or maybe millions of people? And how do you find an idea that is relevant to the brand, the company's purpose, and yet not gratuitous? For Orexo – which is the story about how a challenger brand entered the United States and aspired to grow market share – we needed to shed light on an ugly truth.

To do that, we created 'Out the Monster', a movement that set out to erase the stigma of accidental addiction. A two-minute unbranded film introduced the idea of addiction as a monster, a grotesque nightmare that ruins lives and kills thousands. Viewers were directed to outthemonster.com and the site invited people to show support for the monster's victims through social media. A 40-page hardbound book that told the monster's story was distributed to 50,000 doctors and healthcare professionals across America. All elements of the campaign focused on bringing the conversation out of the shadows and into doctors' offices.

'Out the Monster' was the movement that ignited a conversation about this deadly epidemic that lived in the shadows in America and that no one was talking about. What convinced us that we were on the right path was Robin Koval, President and CEO of Truth Initiative, who said, 'When corporate America joins the fight against the opioid crisis, their employees and their families benefit. We hope more companies join us to expand the reach of this campaign and save more lives' (Truth Initiative, 2019).

What Orexo accomplished was remarkable. In many ways, its MAT was simply a better mousetrap, a more effective version than what its competitors offered. But the way it was introduced to the market was anything but normal. The ambition of the 'Out the Monster' movement was to essentially ignite a national discussion of this deadly epidemic that no one wanted to talk about.

It was literally like bringing the issue of accidental opioid addiction out of the shadows and into dinner-table conversation. Our hypothesis, which turned out to be accurate, was that when we brought the monster out of the shadows and into proper conversations, people would want to stop this. Thousands of social posts and news articles were ignited and conversations were had across the country – all ignited by this movement from Orexo. Rather than simply doing another traditional pharmaceutical advertising campaign that ran on the 6pm news with interchangeably good-looking people and a litany of warnings, this movement made the brand and the company executives thought leaders. And the result: Orexo saw a 27 per cent growth in sales, had 185,000 engaged advocates and movement joiners, and organically reached nearly 11 million people through the movement – Orexo's 'Out the Monster' movement played a role in finding a solution to a big, ugly societal issue.

Good for society, good for business

As we mentioned, with Movement Marketing, you can identify the right idea on the rise in culture that can help your company and brand grow its share of the market, or, if you're the market leader, grow the market. As you've just seen, Orexo is a good example of this in action.

We were hired by Orexo to launch and grow its share of MAT medication. Instead of a traditional pharma advertising campaign to grow share against the leading brand, we designed and launched a movement that served to both help Orexo achieve business goals and drive positive change in society. This case demonstrates that when you link what's good for society with business goals, it can be good for sales growth and measurable business results.

Movement Marketing, or Movement Outside as we call it, is the opposite of traditional advertising. Movement Marketing organizes people and communities against the problem or enemy; it takes a stand; it crystallizes these ideas on the rise in culture, stoking emotions and passions in order to drive change.

How you design the movement strategy matters, as does how marketers connect the movement back to the brand purpose or brand benefit in some tangible and credible way. Without this, you run the risk of people calling BS or seeing your investments and efforts decay and fall short of your business goals. When you consider the weight consumers put on deciding for brands that drive some form of good, you understand the potential and transformative nature of a marketing movement.

FIGURE 6.1   Movements versus advertising

Movements	Advertising
Sustainable	Finite cycle
Rooted in passion	Rooted in product
Multi-platform	Traditional media
Create conversation	Talks about the self
Mobilize people	Influences thinking
Inclusive	Exclusive

SOURCE StrawberryFrog

Over the past 20 years, we have developed effective and successful Movement Marketing strategies across all geographies and sectors, from corporate brand movements (Emirates Airlines and Google) to big-ticket product movements (Smart Car, Mitsubishi Colt) to fast-moving consumer goods movements (Quaker, Stacy's Pita Chips, Sabra Hummus, TrueNorth Snacks, Pritt, Jim Beam, Lipitor). In that time, we've learned a thing or two of value when taking this approach, as well as the pitfalls and where to avoid the landmines. Designing a movement to activate a purpose or to be the purpose is a science. All brands can spark a movement, but not all brands deserve a movement.

Why start your own movement?

So how does a smart brand respond in a time of heightened passions and greater activism? Rather than becoming more cautious or putting one's head in the sand in the hope of avoiding any kind of backlash, we believe brands must connect with that passion and activism somehow. If you fail to respond to this shift in the culture, you run the risk of being out of step with your customers. Your company could end up looking like a 'status quo' brand in a revolutionary world.

Rather than simply developing a traditional advertising campaign, if you want radical growth, better to align your brand purpose with a movement on the rise in culture that is already shared by millions of people. If movements are happening all around, your business needs to somehow become involved in movements – or better yet, start one of your own.

One important point to reiterate: Movement Outside needn't be political. When we helped launch Mahindra Group's 'Rise' movement (described as one of the best purpose examples in the September–October 2019 issue of the *Harvard Business Review* [Dhanaraj *et al*, 2019]), the goal was to inspire more innovation throughout the world. For other clients, we've launched movements that tried to bring about change in schools and more responsible consumption. And as we worked on our book about activating purpose, we encountered everything from a major bank launching a movement against financial stress and for financial confidence, a toilet paper brand with an idea to stand with the hard-working families in America, and a major health network that ignited a movement for partnership in health. In each case, a company rallied people around an idea that mattered to people inside and outside the organization, an idea on the rise in culture, enabling customers to become activists. In the process, each company demonstrated that it was engaged in people's lives and cared about something more than just profits.

This isn't just a new spin on old corporate social responsibility programmes. It's not about giving to a laundry list of charities. To spark a Movement Outside, you must do more than make donations. The company must become an activist itself on behalf of something it believes in – something that also matters deeply to its customers. As we said in the last chapter, the most successful movements start on the inside before being introduced to the public.

It's also much more than traditional advertising, which is increasingly ineffective, especially among the under-25 crowd, even with the best creativity in the world. Increasingly we live in a peer-to-peer world dominated by social media, and with it comes a desire to connect with brands that share our values and crystallize how we feel about genuine human issues. As Matt McGowan, director and general manager of Snapchat, said to us in a conversation about that social media platform's largely Millennial and Gen Z users, 82 per cent of Snapchatters in the US and almost half of Canadian Snapchatters believe they have a personal responsibility to create the change they want to see in the world, and they want to support brands that align to their personal beliefs. Furthermore, 47 per cent of Canadian Snapchat users agree that they're more likely to buy from brands that support their local community.

The desire for positive change is there – you just need to harness it. This can be achieved through shared values that people move together. Whereas advertising is exclusive, dependent on traditional media and large media plans, movement is open, a sustainable marketing model, and multi-platform. A movement can live in the hands of consumers.

How to ignite and build a Movement Outside

A movement is when a big idea inspires mass engagement by the culture. For years now, we have studied and developed movement strategies for brands. There are two types of movements: mass participation (where your big idea is embraced by pop culture) and social movements (where your big idea actually changes society or culture). Both are ways of amplifying your big idea. The business value of mass engagement by the culture includes earned media (on top of paid media) and greater penetration, conversion and loyalty through word of mouth. Net, they help build share. Big traditional advertising agency corporations with a business model to deliver traditional advertising are the old world. Movements are the new world.

Most movements consist of four stages: formulate, agitate, explode and fuel.

Formulate: define the behaviour change

1 Define the change you want to make. This will include the behaviour you want your consumers to have in relation to your brand, and/or the social or cultural change you want to drive. This change should be relevant to your business challenge *and* brand purpose.

2 Understand your target 'people'. Why do they behave as they currently do? What is important to them – in the category and, importantly, in life? Look for fundamental human insights and how these link back to the brand's purpose.

3 Be purpose-inspired and benefit-driven. People long to be part of something bigger than them. As such, big ideas that are true to your brand purpose have a strong potential to become a movement. Equally, any brand movement needs to ultimately serve a benefit equity and drive share harder. (Note: the closer you get to a social movement, the more explicit your purpose is likely to be in the work.)

Agitate: start small to grow big

4 Insightfully provoke a discussion. Your goal is to overcome a state of complacency. This requires you to turn a deep human (versus product) insight into a sharp instigation that stirs your audience's souls.

5 Create 'must-share' content with sticky language: consumers must want to share your content and message. Your movement must also come with memorable language that the culture can adopt.

6 Influence the influencers. Get great content to your most passionate fan base first and to those people who most influence your mass consumers. PR and social media play a big role here.

Explode: ignite mass participation

7 Have a simple call to action. Be clear on what you are calling on your consumers to do. What must they do to be part of the movement?

8 Ignite in key flashpoints. These are platforms where people will be disproportionately receptive to your movement messages and where your influencers can help explode your message. These flashpoints will be supported by 'always on' communication. Note, this stage is most relevant for social movements.

Fuel: keep the fire burning

9 Let social and cultural media be the oxygen. Movements need a place to form, so it's critical that social media channels are open and readily available for engagement.

10 Nurture in real time: going from agitation to explosion doesn't just happen. It requires watching where the sparks start and engaging in the conversation there. You need to actively stoke the fire, adding bursts of fuel to make the flames jump ever higher.

How a bank ignited a movement with 6 million participants

Unlike advertising campaigns, which have both start and end dates with very precise messaging associated with them, Movement Outside can evolve and be sustained over a matter of years. Just look at SunTrust Bank (now Truist).

In 2020, SunTrust Bank passed 6 million participants in the 'onUp' movement, which we introduced in Chapter 5, in addition to gaining the bank a host of other internal employee loyalty and external growth results. How did it get there?

Let's go back to 2015 when our research found that 80 per cent of Americans couldn't put $2,000 together in a crisis, trust in banks was low and financial services was one of the least purpose-oriented industries, with undifferentiated products and services.

At the same time, SunTrust had defined its purpose as *lighting the way to financial wellbeing*. While that indicated its hopes and aspirations for how the bank could help its customers, it didn't clearly articulate *how* it could do that or what was in it for clients. That's when Susan Somersille Johnson – then CMO of SunTrust, now CMO of Prudential – came to us to design and launch a movement to activate the bank's purpose, rather than doing a traditional brand advertising campaign. Johnson recounted to us:

> From our research, we knew that everybody, regardless of income level, can have financial confidence. With that insight we said, 'Okay, SunTrust, you're purpose-driven and we just found out that everybody can achieve this. What are we going to do about it?' StrawberryFrog helped take our purpose and turn that into the 'onUp' movement, allowing us to take a stand for financial confidence and help get everybody there.

The 'onUp' movement started inside the corporation. The goal was ensuring that SunTrust teammates felt confident in their financial footing. As we mentioned in the last chapter, SunTrust's Movement Inside focused on helping its employees with its own financial literacy and featured an ambassador programme to bring the movement to life person by person throughout the organization.

As Johnson said, 'We started with ourselves and then once we had a workplace solution, we were ready to launch our movement out to the world.'

The best way to bring big ideas to life is by writing a manifesto. SunTrust knew that when they read our 'onUp' movement manifesto. The best way to get the big idea to stick in someone's mind is to wrap it up in a good yarn. The power of making a point through storytelling is why phrases like 'killing me softly' or 'walking on thin ice' are alive and well in our culture, despite being over a thousand years old.

The manifesto illuminates the fundamentals of the idea, the experience, the message and the advertising, and shows how the creativity will feel.

If people have too narrow a focus or definition when it comes to creativity, the manifesto can broaden the mind. The manifesto gets you out of thinking about the style and calling it creativity, and rather focusing on the big idea that guides it all.

A client who knows nothing about creativity might believe you if they feel the manifesto emotionally – especially if you are taking a cultural stand for or against something like we did for the 'onUp' manifesto.

With the manifesto, clients begin to know what the big idea is and begin to spot it, and begin to demand it in all the work. Everybody has to begin to exercise their creative muscle by looking at the movement manifesto.

Staying with that idea of needing to look outside the industry for inspiration, the manifestos written at StrawberryFrog look to culture and society outside of creativity, and also intentionally use a reaction:

SUNTRUST'S 'ONUP' MANIFESTO

If you worry about money, you're not alone. In fact, for 75 per cent of
    Americans, money is a cause for concern and a source of uncertainty.

And these feelings have left millions feeling stuck in place.

Unclear on where to turn. Unsure of how to move forward.

That is why, the time is right, to spark a movement.

To help people transform their concern into confidence.

To provide positive motivation and forward momentum.

To guide them towards their goals and their dreams.

One smart step at a time.

This is a movement about moving forward.

And we're lighting the way.

Onwards and Upwards.

OnUp.

To introduce the 'onUp' Movement Outside, SunTrust held mass movement rallies in three of its largest markets, resulting in an iconic experience. Onstage with Johnson was CEO Bill Rogers, CFO of the company Aleem Gillani and several other leaders from the C-suite, along with musical acts and sporting celebrities. 'onUp' was launched to all Americans during the 2016 Super Bowl with the bold target of getting 5 million people involved in the movement in five years. In 2020, within four years, SunTrust had 6 million participants. How did SunTrust get from where it was to where it wanted to be?

Turning passive purpose into active results

After that launch in 2016, SunTrust launched the 'onUp' movement outside the bank with a complete movement programme, including the onUp.com website. The site was invented to be more of a content platform like a TV channel than a traditional bank website, where participants joined, their progress was tracked, and where relevant information and education promoting the easy learning about budgeting and financial literacy lived. Advertising in TV, out of home, print, radio, digital and social media told the world about the 'onUp' movement and drove people to the site. Added to that was the building of the onUp Experience at SunTrust Park (now Truist Park), home of the Atlanta Braves, in order to bring the movement to the people in culture – not in the bank, but where people love to be – at the ball game. onUp On Tour brought the movement to small towns across the country, where 'onUp' activities from SunTrust brought many locals out to participate in the 'onUp' experience first hand.

The 'onUp' movement was designed to sit above product and service marketing and advertising. And as the movement gained traction and momentum, these product messages started to become integrated into the movement work, at first subtly and then, over time, more overtly.

Description: TV spot, Braves Stadium

This commercial features a stadium attendant who has the confidence to sing a rousing song in the middle of the stadium, amazing his fellow attendants as they look on. It establishes confidence as the fundamental benefit of a relationship with SunTrust.

Description: TV spot, Winter Olympics

This commercial depicts a young girl having a star turn as a figure skater in a large stadium in front of a huge audience. The copy reads, 'It takes confidence to dream big' and ends with the SunTrust motto of 'Confidence starts here'.

Five years into the movement, 'onUp' continues to thrive. It avoided decay by being led from the top by Bill Rogers, SunTrust's CEO, and through an engaging and creative programme that refreshed the movement annually, avoiding movement decay, which is a threat to any successful change management or engagement programme.

This leadership was essential, Johnson said to us:

> What I've learned and what I love to say is that movements are CEO-led and CMO-designed. I mean, it has to be 100 per cent CEO-led because every leader has to be on board and they won't be on board in the beginning, so you can't do that unless the CEO leads the vision.

SunTrust's keys to success

According to Johnson, there were a few key factors that contributed to the success of 'onUp', even following the merger of SunTrust with BB&T to create a new brand entity, Truist (which we discuss in Chapter 8).

SET A TARGET

The first was that a bold target was set. Without one, she says, a movement can meander or veer as it naturally evolves. It needs a clear destination. 'There's nothing like a target to motivate people to move together. So, when we set the 5 million people in five years target, that was the rallying cry.' Not only that, the 5 million target was divided into four areas – individuals, communities, corporations and teammates – so that all of SunTrust's employees and business units understood how they would contribute to that goal. 'Everybody had a piece and we had something tangible. It was important to have structure because movements go in whatever direction they want, but at least we had a goal.'

MAKE IT RELEVANT TO EVERYONE

The challenge with a corporate purpose statement is to make it relevant to all stakeholders, inside and out. You need people to be able to see themselves in it in order for them to participate. That was easier to do with the external movement than internally. But one depended on the other. Johnson told us she spent a lot of time with executive leaders connecting the purpose to their business, acknowledging that there were varying degrees of interest across the organization:

> The challenge was to get everybody on board because you need the whole company. The connection with each business line, that was a difficult part. And in the end, every leader held part of the target and we did put the 5 million on the enterprise scorecard.

She points to SunTrust's wealth group as an area where connecting to 'onUp' wasn't immediately clear because, as she says, many people think that wealthy people are 'already up'. After discussions with that group and those business leaders, she realized that, in fact, 'onUp' connected because people still want to make sure their kids are financially confident, that they know how to manage their money, and that they can be self-sufficient, which isn't a given. 'It took time and discussions but we realized they connect a lot because they want to make sure their kids go on up.'

Over in the bank's mortgage group, changing the name of one of its units helped it connect the mission to both employees and clients. Rather than being Collections, which evokes a sense of fear and dread, it was renamed the Home Preservation department. The name change helped people understand why they got out of bed to go to work every day. The bank's purpose is to keep people in their homes. In turn, it changed the relationship consumers had with the bank as they were more likely to see it as an ally rather than something to be wary of.

'You've got to find a way so that every banker can understand the role they play at the moment,' Johnson told us. 'It's not just volunteerism and philanthropy. That's their everyday job. I think that's the key – connecting the purpose as an everyday job.'

KEEP IT FRESH

That connection is what led people like Ryan, a SunTrust Purpose Ambassador, to coach a customer from being unemployed to becoming an employer. It's also how 'onUp' remains fresh, says Johnson. In order to become a Purpose Ambassador, SunTrust teammates have to apply, and each year, a new crop of eager employees bring their new ideas to the movement and then translate those ideas to SunTrust customers.

If changing faces keep things fresh, so does the changing world outside of SunTrust. Since movements are always based on what's happening in culture, an idea on the rise, they're able to respond to real-world events. Johnson said:

> I think one thing that StrawberryFrog really helps us with in addition to the movement strategy is staying close to culture and keeping us grounded in the zeitgeist of the country at any time. So, our message changes with whatever is going on.

This is how Johnson pivoted the 'onUp' messaging from financial confidence to one of financial resiliency during the COVID-19 pandemic. The entire platform was updated with resiliency messaging, including specific resources, content, and toolkits around financial and mental wellbeing.

TRACK RESULTS

As is common among chief marketers, Johnson is highly driven by data and results. That's how she can say with certainty that the 'onUp' Movement Outside has been successful for the bank. Aside from surpassing the 5 million goal – 6 million had taken part in 'onUp' at the time of writing – the movement has had a demonstrable impact both inside the business and outside. Our research with the Purpose Power Index (which we'll get into in detail in the next chapter) shows that SunTrust is perceived by consumers as being the most purposeful bank.

SunTrust's own data shows that retention rates are two times higher among teammates who participated in the movement than among those who didn't, and they're more likely to say they work at SunTrust. Customers are 50 per cent more likely to add new accounts since the movement started and participants are 7 per cent more loyal to the bank. Ninety-nine per cent would recommend the programme to others. Finally, 'onUp' has been successful in its goal of helping people become more financially confident and stable. Participants living by a budget have increased from 43 per cent to 87 per cent, their emergency savings improved from 68 per cent to 90 per cent, and their retirement contributions up from 68 per cent to 98 per cent.

In terms of how the bank is marketed to consumers, Johnson says that when movement messaging is included, results are unequivocally better:

> I can tell you with confidence that weaving 'onUp' messages with product messages is more effective than only product messages. And this is, you know, an age-old debate among marketers because everybody just wants to push the product, push the product. We find that when we send people messages about the movement interspersed with messages about our products, they're more likely to buy.

Why be a patient when you can be a partner: the 'Together We Well' movement

Northwell Health is another organization that understands the power of Movement Thinking. When we started working with Northwell, New York State's largest healthcare provider, the leadership asked us to help them take the brand to the next level. Our instinct was to identify an issue in the culture of health that Northwell Health could lean into and change. In healthcare, patients seek help when they become ill. We wanted to ignite a movement for partnership in health, throughout a person's life.

Why be a patient when you can be a partner?

Instead of another brand advertising and clinical campaign, we came up with 'Together We Well', a movement to drive partnership in health. This enabled Northwell to be the brand that empowers people to take an active role in their wellbeing by leading a movement for equal partnership between the doctor and the person. This is about a new kind of collaboration, not blind following. 'Together We Well' is the movement motto, a rallying cry or a call to action that we use. It concisely captures our movement. Sometimes it becomes a tagline for the movement, but not always. It became a sustainable platform for ongoing conversation.

'Together We Well' was brought to life through a manifesto. The manifesto lays the emotional groundwork for the movement. It's a call to arms. It's a creative document, but not a TV script. It inspires the movement actions that the brand eventually makes:

NORTHWELL HEALTH'S MANIFESTO

Why be a patient?

Patients are treated.

Patients are compliant.

Patients... have to be patient.

Instead, why not be a partner? For life.

Because think about it.

Nobody knows you better than you.

You know when you're feeling good.

And when something feels off.

So, ask questions.

Share your history. Your hunches. Your theories.

And choose the right health partner.

Who doesn't just treat illness, but promotes wellness.

One that knows when to listen, and when to lead.

Because if you're told, you'll forget.

If you're shown, you might remember.

But if you're involved, you'll understand.

Why be a patient... when you can be a partner?

Together We Well.

In recounting the early conversation around Northwell's journey to a movement, Ramon Soto, senior vice president and chief marketing and communications officer, told us about the moment he realized the need to activate the hospital's purpose. He was at a CMO conference with several of his C-suite peers and the conversation turned to how to become more customer-centric. As the leaders of confectionery, telecoms and technology businesses were talking about how their brand purpose was helping them engage with consumers, Soto realized there was more work to be done to make Northwell Health more purposeful.

As one CMO was talking about how to use brand purpose to become more consumer-centric from a confectionery perspective, Soto told us he was dumbfounded:

> Here I was representing health, which is one of the most core, fundamental things in life, and yet it's a low-interest category until it becomes a high-interest one when you're sick. So, what category has a greater need to create a relationship with consumers and more power to unleash a movement than healthcare?

The hospital network had already begun to address employee engagement during the process of integrating a diffuse confederation of hospitals that had been acquired by Northwell under one banner. Soto said that in two years, employee engagement rose from 46 per cent to 86 per cent, so he knew at Northwell there was latent power that could be unlocked to transform the organization:

> We're a fatter society, a sicker society and we pay more for healthcare than any other Western industrialized nation. You know, people need to rise up and scream at the top of their lungs and evangelize that people need to frankly take more control of their health. It all starts with a base of employees who believe.

That's why, he told us, a movement struck him as the perfect next chapter. By framing healthcare in its broadest definition – which includes not just the physical but also the emotional and social sense – we were able to help Northwell Health present itself to the world as a partner in healthcare.

One of the goals of 'Together We Well' was to galvanize both the employees of the large organization, over 77,000 strong, and consumers. The words and imagery used to bring this to life conveyed the idea of the movement in an emotional way. 'I love both the play on words and the flexibility of "Together We Well",' said Soto. 'It was a nice articulation of the relationship we want to have with consumers and is motivational enough for them to engage with this partnership in their healthcare. And, frankly, it's aspirational.'

Little did he know just how flexible the platform was. Before Northwell was even able to launch 'Together We Well' to the public, the COVID-19 pandemic hit New York like a tsunami and Northwell was thrust onto the front lines. Suddenly, healthcare was the most high-interest category going. This afforded Northwell the opportunity to use its 'Together We Well' platform to help address New Yorkers' concerns. How it showed up during COVID-19 demonstrates how a movement can help transform a category. Rather than using bland, inward-facing messages like *we're here for you*, as its competition did during the crisis, Northwell's movement invited people in to be partners in their health.

It did that in three phases, addressing in real time how people were feeling. For instance, the initial shock of COVID-19 brought with it incredible amounts of fear. In New York, people were dying at an alarming rate and case counts were almost uncontrollable. Some of the most indelible images from those early days of the crisis were those of the refrigerated trucks needed to handle the overflow from the morgues. It was utterly terrifying stuff. Northwell knew it needed to build confidence in consumers to assure them they had a partner to get them through the crisis. Within a matter of days, we created 'Information is Healthy, Fear is Not', the first salvo in the 'Together We Well' movement, to rally people around information over anxiety. We created printed materials to help people navigate a completely new and frightening reality with a measure of calm and knowledge, and launched a rousing ad with consummate New Yorker Ray Romano.

Once the initial fear levelled off, we shifted Northwell's messaging to one of gratitude. As Soto told us, no other institution in the United States treated more COVID-19 patients than Northwell Health. He estimates over 50,000 patients came through the hospital network, 14,000 of those requiring inpatient care in the early days of the pandemic. 'We treated more COVID cases than states that are hotspots now have in totality,' he said at the time that southern US states were experiencing spikes in cases. Because of that, Northwell knew all too well how fatigued and drained its workers were. To help celebrate them, and to fortify them in their efforts, Northwell launched 'Thank You Heroes', a campaign that tapped into the social norm of cheering for front-line workers that was developing in the city. Through TV and print, the campaign demonstrated the strength and resolve of the hospital network's workers.

As the healthcare system's response to the crisis became more established and people's fears settled, it was time to mobilize the full movement. The third phase of Northwell's response to COVID-19 became the official launch of the 'Together We Well' platform and was anchored by 'Fearless Leader', a powerful animated film that featured a young girl bringing people together.

As Soto said to us months after the onset of the crisis:

> COVID changed everything. With its ruthless and its stealth-like nature and the fear that it instils, it was the cultural disruptor. It disrupted everything. But it also presented this window of opportunity to create different relationships with consumers. Health and wellbeing is incredibly top of mind now. I'm hopeful all these things change how we all interact and this will change the dynamic of healthcare.

As summer turned to autumn in 2020, the leadership at Northwell, including Don Simon, Jen Nelson and Joe Leston, worked with StrawberryFrog to remind New Yorkers that whatever comes next, Northwell is ready. This was beautifully brought to life in a new creative campaign featuring the voice of Steve Buscemi, the New York actor, director, writer, producer and former firefighter, illustrated with murals on walls around New York City and the suburbs.

What it takes to launch a Movement Outside

Movements are powerful and, as we've seen in this chapter, they're capable of addressing difficult societal issues like doctor-prescribed opioid use. They can unify sprawling organizations under one shared vision. They can empower individuals to take control of their finances and, in turn, create better lives for their families and be prepared for unforeseen challenges. All of this can make a movement seem like an enticing proposition, but both Susan Somersille Johnson and Ramon Soto offer some advice for marketers contemplating a movement.

A movement takes courage

When Johnson was first considering a movement, she had some reasonable trepidation. SunTrust was, to her knowledge, the first bank to start a movement. She didn't know if it would work. A conversation with Andrew Young, an American politician and an early leader in the civil rights movement, changed that:

I remember talking to Ambassador Andrew Young and he gave me great comfort. He said they weren't sure about all the tactics of the Civil Rights Movement but they just kept trying. He said to me, 'We didn't know if it would work but we just kept going.' And so, keep going, keep doing what you're doing.

That advice, she said, gave her the courage to bring 'onUp' to life:

We didn't know if it would work, so from a business perspective, we had to start on faith in our values and good business judgement. Ultimately, you have to build proof that it works, which we did, but while you're building those results, you have to go on faith in your values and confidence that you've done everything you can.

A movement requires clarity

When we spoke, Johnson also articulated something we tell clients all the time: purpose is not philanthropy. When embarking on a movement, it's essential to be clear on that point:

The biggest mistake is to equate purpose with philanthropy or corporate social responsibility. Purpose has to be integrated into everything that you do and you have to work hard to make sure everybody sees themselves and their team in the purpose – it can't be a separate initiative.

A movement takes commitment

Ramon Soto told us that his experience with Northwell's 'Together We Well' revealed the level of commitment required to launch a movement:

If you're going to do it, you have to be all in. That requires a really thoughtful reflection on your brand purpose and you have to be a committed student of your consumers. The power of a movement is unlocked when you completely take the outside perspectives, but then firmly root it in who you are as a company. If you don't, you run the risk of creating something that feels like another campaign.

The FrogLogic approach

Movements like 'onUp' and 'Together We Well' came to life using FrogLogic, the approach and toolset we employ to land on a movement platform that enables you to activate your brand purpose. It involves three phases: ready, set and leap.

At its simplest, the 'ready' phase involves doing your due diligence regarding the 'three Cs' – consumer, company and category – and using these to populate a strategic template via a facilitated work session. This kind of approach is pretty typical of any consultancy or agency you might work with. What sets FrogLogic apart is its emphasis on movement versus traditional advertising, which we've talked about extensively throughout these pages. But there are two other big differences: how we gather insights to drive our thinking – specifically, we conduct all our learning through an ethnographic and cultural lens; and our focus on understanding where consumers and culture are going versus where they are or have been. Let's take a closer look at those.

The ethnographic lens

We tend to opt for ethnographic research over traditional methods (eg focus groups) because it's a more empathic and prescient approach to understanding both consumers and brands. Ethnography is a branch of anthropology that explores culture from the point of view of the subject of the study. It takes place in a research subject's 'natural habitat' (home, office, etc) and casts the researcher or moderator as a participant observer. As such, it allows us to hear and understand things people might have a hard time telling us, things they might not even be consciously aware of – and even things we might not have known to ask about. We conduct ethnographies live or virtually over computer or mobile.

Soto told us that for him, the insight that came from Northwell's ethnographic research was enlightening. 'It was actually quite powerful, as it gave us a deep look into how somebody consumes healthcare. We don't see that half of the equation in the way we typically go to market.' Instead, he said, the hospital is used to seeing the sliver of the interaction with an institution, not how people live their lives with their health challenges:

> We think we know a lot but there is so much more to understand – the fear, the anxiety, their needs, their challenges, what makes people happy, what makes them frustrated. It was eye-opening to see how healthcare still needs to go quite a far way to be seamless and be helpful. It was a really nice exploration of that and taking the broadest aperture of what a consumer goes through. It really reinforced the need for partnership.

The cultural lens

One of the most crucial things our FrogLogic approach does is to help get our clients' companies and brands out of category competition and into competing in culture. Why? Too often, the harder we compete within a product or service category's existing parameters, the more we end up seeming like our competitors rather than different. The best we can hope for is to be seen as a somewhat different version of them.

We use a wide range of types of analysis to help us break a brand out of its category and into culture. These include 'the usual suspects' of cultural trends analysis and secondary research. But we also employ tools like semiotics, which is the study of signs and symbols in culture, and which can be useful in understanding how a brand fits in society and where it might go in the future. 'Brand archetypes' analysis, which are universal brand 'types' that everyone connects with intuitively, is another tool we use to place a brand within the broader culture. 'Brand archetypes' include 'The Hero' (eg Nike, BMW), 'The Caregiver' (eg Johnson & Johnson) and 'The Outlaw' (eg Harley-Davidson), to name a few. If, for example, we know that Jim Beam is an 'Everyman' brand, we also know it competes alongside other 'Everyman' brands like Wrangler and Budweiser, not just other whiskeys like Jack Daniels. We land on a brand's archetype by doing a deep dive into the history of the brand's communications, actions and marketing to look for archetypal markers.

Bear in mind we're NOT saying category competition isn't important. Of course, we need to be on top of what competitors are doing. And ultimately, being different from your direct competitors is a great outcome. But doing only that can make your brand a captive to category competition, rather than help you break free from it altogether.

Understanding where consumers are going

Traditional research like surveys and focus groups is important, but it usually gives us a snapshot of what people are thinking and feeling right now. Consumers simply aren't very good at telling us what they'll be like in the future, which is a shame because that's usually what we need to know to move a brand forward.

One way we frequently counter this problem is by doing what we call a 'Visionary Salon', which is a gathering of experts and other cultural mavens whose background promises to shed light on where people and culture are headed. For example, to understand where healthcare consumers are headed for Northwell, we gathered perspectives as diverse as a healthcare venture capitalist who is constantly hearing pitches from startups, and thus knows also about what's next, to a holistic wellness guru to a healthcare futurist, all of whose points of view helped us map out a trajectory for the brand.

FrogLogic session

Once we've gathered inputs on consumer mindset, hit on an idea on the rise as well as product and brand truths, we're ready to populate our movement framework (see Figure 3.2 in Chapter 3). This is the template that allows us to refine our thinking and land on a movement platform. StrawberryFrog typically does this on its own and comes up with 'strawman' movement ideas, but where the rubber meets the road is in our facilitated FrogLogic work session. There we gather all relevant stakeholders, review our insights and strawman ideas, and then discuss and debate them. During the session, participants have the opportunity to adopt one or more of the ideas, adapt them or create new ideas as a team. Our objective coming out of the session is to land on one or two movement platforms to proceed with into our 'set' phase.

To illustrate how this works, let's use a real-world example from a few years ago: TrueNorth, a new snack food brand we helped Frito-Lay develop and introduced at the start of this book.

Frito-Lay, food company and maker of Lays potato chips, wanted to target a health-conscious Baby Boomer audience and had developed a protein-dense nut snack product that delivered well on functional health and emotional taste/craveability benefits. But since there were several competitive products already available, what would make this one stand out and resonate culturally? Could a nut snack spark an actual movement?

Our ethnographic research with Boomers told us that connecting with them wasn't just about generational insight, but rather about life stage. Specifically that people in their 50s onwards, regardless of their walk of life, are looking to ensure they are finally living their life's purpose. We found that it is during these decades in life that many actually do find their higher calling – something we dubbed a *true north* (thus the product's name).

The movement was called 'Your True North is Calling' and was launched with a user-generated content campaign challenging Boomers to send us their 'True North' stories of finding their purpose later in life. Thousands entered and the effort generated significant PR buzz. The winners were featured in a TV campaign that debuted at the Oscars. You can see our True North movement framework in Figures 6.2 and 6.3.

FIGURE 6.2 Movement building blocks

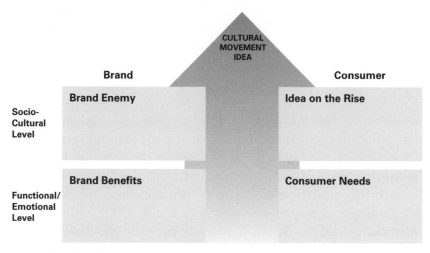

SOURCE StrawberryFrog

FIGURE 6.3 Movement building blocks: True North

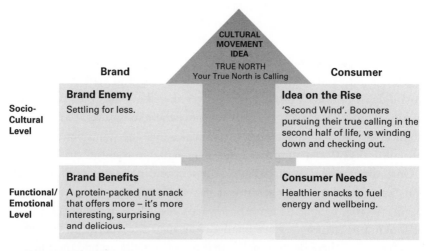

SOURCE StrawberryFrog

KEY TAKEAWAYS

As we've seen throughout this chapter, a Movement Outside can inspire people to take control of their finances, as with SunTrust's 'onUp'; it can create opportunities to become partners in their healthcare, as we saw with Northwell Health; and it can address and help change societal issues, as with Orexo. More than marketing, these movements are an example of purpose in action. The next chapter will show that this behaviour on behalf of brands matters to consumers. When brands are active in their purpose, customers notice and reward them accordingly.

When considering launching a Movement Outside, remember:

- A Movement Outside is one that aligns brand purpose with an idea on the rise in culture. This is why understanding the rise in activism, as we discussed in Chapter 3, is so important. If you're on top of what matters to your customers, you'll find the clues required to engage them in a movement.

- A Movement Outside requires courage, clarity and conviction. In short, you've got to be all in.

- The FrogLogic approach to movement-making breaks you out of category convention and helps you compete in culture.

References

CDC (2019) *NCHS Releases New Monthly Provisional Estimates on Drug Overdose Deaths*, Centers for Disease Control and Prevention, 11 September. https://www.cdc.gov/nchs/pressroom/podcasts/20190911/20190911.htm (archived at https://perma.cc/Y6V7-GJCX)

Dhanaraj, C, Malnight, T and Buche, I (2019) Put purpose at the core of your strategy, *Harvard Business Review*. https://hbr.org/2019/09/put-purpose-at-the-core-of-your-strategy (archived at https://perma.cc/6ZKJ-4SH7)

NIH Medline Plus Magazine (2011) Opioids and chronic pain, 6 (1), p 7. https://magazine.medlineplus.gov/pdf/MLP_Spring_2011.pdf (archived at https://perma.cc/9D4D-V9MQ)

Truth Initiative (2019) How an email from a grieving father inspired a Fortune 500 company to fight opioids, 7 January. https://truthinitiative.org/research-resources/substance-use/how-email-grieving-father-inspired-fortune-500-company-fight (archived at https://perma.cc/22MZ-KPEL)

07

Purpose Power Index

New winners and laggards

In early 2016, two standout NFL players on the San Francisco 49ers – Eric Reid and Colin Kaepernick – took a knee during the singing of the US national anthem. They had been following social posts about the incredible number of unarmed black people being killed by the police. After hours of careful consideration, including a meeting with Nate Boyer, a retired Green Beret and former NFL player, they came to the decision to kneel in peaceful protest to give a voice to the voiceless (Reid, 2017). Kaepernick told NFL Media at the time, 'I am not going to stand up to show pride in a flag for a country that oppresses black people and people of color' (NFL, 2016).

Two years later, in 2018, a new advertising campaign from Nike proclaimed: 'Believe in something even if it means sacrificing everything.' These words were placed over a black-and-white close-up of Colin Kaepernick's face. It declared that in the fight for racial justice, Nike stood with those willing to forego personal gain for the greater good. With this 2018 campaign, which included a rousing commercial imploring people to dream crazy, it was making its stance known.

Kaepernick quickly became a high-profile symbol for the Black Lives Matter movement and his actions drew both support and ire. Other athletes across a variety of sports staged their own protests (Mather, 2016), though none was vilified quite as much as Kaepernick, who became a target in one of President Trump's famed tweetstorms (Belson, 2017).

The demonstration came at a huge cost for Kaepernick. After filing several grievances against the NFL, in which he claims he was black-balled, he was eventually iced out of the league (Mather, 2019). Despite his struggles in the league, Nike stuck with its man, with whom it had a relationship since 2011. That said, Nike's affiliation with the former quarterback also came at a cost to the company. People were so incensed by the company's support of the athlete that boycotts were staged; some even burned their shoes. But the brand was so resolute in its belief that it was willing to forego those sales in favour of doing the right thing. Nike itself was standing for what it believed in, even if it meant sacrificing profit.

By these actions, you'd think that Nike was considered a purposeful brand by the public. It was taking a stand against racial inequality and aligning itself with an idea on the rise. And it was doing so even though its revenues might suffer. Noble, right?

As it turns out, you'd be wrong. When it comes to the brands that consumers perceive to be purpose-driven, Nike ranks below where you'd find it on other brand indexes, such as the Interbrand Best Global Brands list, where it ranks 16 out of 100 (Interbrand, 2019). We know this because the Purpose Power Index provides empirical evidence showing there's often a disconnect between a brand or company's actions and how those actions are perceived by the public.

In 2019, StrawberryFrog set out to better understand purpose and designed the Purpose Power Index in partnership with Kylie Wright-Ford, CEO of consumer research firm The RepTrak Company. We believed that business leaders were sailing without a compass, that what purpose needed was empirical data to prove the lifting purpose brings to companies and brands. What we saw was a lot of anecdotal evidence supporting the need for purpose but little data. So, having the results of the first-ever empirical measure of brand purpose has enabled us to evaluate the purpose brands and to identify the criteria for winners and laggards. That's how we discovered that despite the fact that Nike's Kaepernick campaign eventually paid off – Kaepernick was named *GQ* Man of the Year and Nike saw a 31 per cent spike in sales (Raggs, 2018) – the brand was still not considered by the public as purposeful in the PPI results. In fact, it didn't even rank among the top 100 purposeful brands.

Why? As the PPI data shows, having just a social activist platform is not enough. Consumers are savvy, so if they don't see your products as very purposeful or they take issue with how you treat your employees, they take notice and reward or rebuke brands and companies accordingly. This can certainly explain the disconnect between Nike's ambitions to take a stand on social issues and consumers' perceptions of how purposeful it is. For example, despite its daring 'Dream Crazy' campaign with Kaepernick, only 4.8 per cent of Nike's directors were Black or African American in 2019 (Nike, 2019).

That's why, as we've been arguing throughout this book, leaders need to put purpose at the core of their strategy. It isn't simply a marketing platform; being purposeful starts at home. You have to start inside by addressing the systems and policies that run counter to your purpose, align all stakeholders and get employees on board, and then communicate your purpose externally, because if you don't have your own house in order, you're building on an unsteady foundation.

As Temple University professor Charles Dhanaraj, whom we introduced earlier, recently wrote in the *Harvard Business Review*, companies have long been encouraged to build purpose into what they do, but they usually approach it as an add-on, like community philanthropy or as a way to improve employee morale. But these are superficial activities and they don't reach all the way through an organization. Dhanaraj wrote that in his study on purpose he noticed that high-growth companies had moved purpose from the periphery of their strategy to its core, 'where, with committed leadership and financial investment, they had used it to generate sustained profitable growth, stay relevant in a rapidly changing world, and deepen ties with their stakeholders' (Dhanaraj *et al*, 2019).

That's something that Nike CEO John Donahoe acknowledged in a June 2020 letter to employees. 'While we strive to help shape a better society, our most important priority is to get our own house in order,' he wrote while announcing Nike's $40 million commitment over four years to support the Black community in the US (Thomas, 2020). What's noteworthy is at roughly the same time an Instagram account called 'Black at Nike' launched with messages from anonymous current and former Nike employees sharing experiences with racism at the athletic-wear giant, according to the account creators (Ciment, 2020).

In previous chapters we've discussed why purpose is important to your business; we've talked about the transformational power of Movement Thinking to activate purpose; how Movement Inside creates a sticky culture and changes behaviour better than top-down mandates; and we've talked about Movement Outside as a new way to engage consumers and grow your business. Now it's time to find out what consumers, those people on the receiving end of your purpose strategy, really think about brand purpose. Do they notice what brands are doing vis-à-vis higher purpose? Do they care? This chapter will look at what our findings from the Purpose Power Index indicate are necessary to get consumer credit for higher purpose – and some brands that are firing on all cylinders.

The Purpose Power Index

Increasingly, consumers are looking for the businesses and products they engage with or buy to share similar values. That means it's no longer enough to make the best product; how you make it can matter just as much to your customers. Evidence of this can be found in Carol Cone's 'B2B Purpose Paradox' study, which reported that 76 per cent of Americans would refuse to purchase a product if they found out a company supported an issue contrary to their beliefs (Cone, 2019). Similarly, Stanford University's Closer Look series, 'The double-edged sword of CEO activism', found that 56 per cent of consumers don't respect CEOs who remain silent on important issues (see Figure 7.1), with 64 per cent believing CEOs should lead the way on change (Larcker *et al*, 2018). And the 2020 'Strength of Purpose' study of 8,000 global consumers and 75 companies and brands (commissioned by New York-based global communications agency Zeno Group) found that when consumers think a brand has a strong purpose, they are four times more likely to purchase from the company, four and a half times more likely to champion the company and recommend it to friends and family, and six times more likely to protect the company in the event of a misstep or public criticism (Zeno Group, 2020).

Traditionally, it has been impossible to measure brand purpose, leaving brands to rely on metrics such as sales and engagement and loyalty to measure its worth, all of which can come without purpose. That's why we came

FIGURE 7.1 Global consumers on CEOs and change

64% of global consumers believe CEOs should take the lead on change rather than waiting for government to impose it.	**56%** say they have 'no respect for CEOs who remain silent on important issues'.

SOURCE Larcker *et al* (2018)

up with the PPI, an empirical way to measure the consumer perspective. Does higher purpose really matter to the general public? Does it provide a clear business advantage? Who is getting it right and why? Because when assessing whether higher purpose results in business benefits, it's important for a company to understand how its higher purpose registers with its consumers.

How the PPI works

So how did we determine exactly how consumers perceive purpose? Given that we know many companies have a purpose statement and ambitions to be purpose-driven, and knowing that so few companies are good at activating their purpose, we needed to find criteria that would look at purpose as a belief system; purpose had to be defined as seen in the eye of the beholder as opposed to words on a boardroom wall.

To understand who's leading the pack when it comes to purpose, we worked with analysts at RepTrak and created an algorithm to score companies and brands, not on how purposeful they think they are, but on the degree to which consumers *see* them as driven by higher purpose. Our breakthrough was to identify and validate four factors that determine how purpose-driven a brand is.

The PPI algorithm requires strong agreement on at least three of the following four elements in order for a brand to be considered purpose-driven:

- **Beyond profits:** The brand has a higher purpose that's bigger than just making money.
- **Improving lives:** The brand, through its business practices and actions, improves the lives of people and their communities.
- **Better society:** The brand does things to benefit not just shareholders, employees, or customers, but society as a whole.
- **Better world:** The brand is committed to changing the world for the better.

Our model is a proven way to assess the degree to which a consumer believes a company or brand to be purposeful and provides a score out of 100, which allows for normative comparisons of brands.

We then chose 204 US and multinational companies, both big and small with high and low familiarity, and surveyed over 7,500 US consumers, which resulted in more than 17,500 individual ratings.

What we found

One of the major findings in the PPI is that purpose does indeed matter to the public, clearly driving behavioural intent (see Figure 7.2). The research also revealed that the top purpose-driven brands are not the 'usual suspects' of brands that topped lists of most valuable brands in 2020 – we're talking Apple, Google, Microsoft, Amazon and Facebook (Swant, 2020). These brands either fail to crack the top 20 or are nowhere to be seen in the top 100 in the PPI research.

But a darker finding also emerged. Not only do consumers find few brands to be strongly purposeful – they find most brands to be UN-purposeful. In fact, only 3 per cent of the 204 brands in the study were seen as strongly purpose-driven. On the flip side, nearly two-thirds (64 per cent) of brands were viewed as weak or poor on being purposeful. These low scorers include some brands that are typically considered successful global brands, even highly purpose-driven, but none makes the PPI Top 100.

That top 3 per cent of purpose-driven brands are limited to an elite group of seven. They are Seventh Generation, Method, TOMS, REI, Stonyfield Organic, Wegmans and USAA.

As it turns out, consumers have high expectations when it comes to purpose and brands are not meeting them. They're also much more likely to buy, recommend, invest in and want to work for brands they consider highly purpose-driven.

What's interesting about the highest scoring brands is that several are what archaeologist-turned-strategist currently working at IDEO Nina Montgomery calls 'born with purpose'. In her research while writing *Perspectives on Purpose*, she found that purpose-driven brands tend to fall into three categories:

- **Born with purpose:** those companies that are purpose-driven from the start. These are brands like Method, REI, TOMS Shoes, or Who Gives A Crap (the sustainable toilet paper that builds sanitation infrastructure with a portion of its profits), which build their business model from the ground up around a sense of greater good.

FIGURE 7.2 Purpose Power® 100: Few brands are strong on purpose

Seventh Generation	TOMS	Method	REI	Wegmans	Stonyfield Organic	USAA	Allbirds	Chick-fil-A	Ben & Jerry's
North Face	Kellogg's	UPS	Etsy	Burt's Bees	Microsoft	Hobby Lobby	Warby Parker	Canon	Kimberly-Clark
Intel	Tesla	Samsung	Google	Whole Foods	Patagonia	Campbell's	Lego	Dell	Honeywell
Nationwide	McCormick	Bosch	General Mills	Whirlpool	Caterpillar	General Pacific	Clorox	Unilever	LinkedIn
IBM	Deloitte	Hershey	Kraft Heinz	FedEx	Ikea	Cisco	Roche	Oracle	AbbVie
Disney	3M	Walgreens Boots	Netflix	GM	Sony	Eileen Fisher	Danone	Aetna	British Airways
Zappos	Container Store	Lime	Body Shop	United Healthcare	Michelin	PepsiCo	Ericsson	MAC	Honda
Toyota	PayPal	Nissan	Nintendo	Amazon	Liberty Mutual	Inter Continental	Xerox	Dick's Sporting	Airbus
Nestlé	SAP	Fuji Film	CVS	SC Johnson	GE	Toshiba	Bridgestone	Timberland	Accenture
Coca-Cola Company	Good Year	Prudential	P&G	Visa	Siemens	Total	Bayer	Target	Adidas

STRONG   AVERAGE   WEAK

SOURCE RepTrak and StrawberryFrog

- **Reborn through purpose:** those companies that, often through an enlightened leader, recalibrate to make purpose core to their strategy. These are companies like Verizon, Mahindra and GoDaddy, which, through visionary guidance from CEOs, have made significant changes.
- **Purpose through an existential crisis:** those companies that seek purpose as a way to ward off existential threats to their business.

While being born with a purpose, or those purpose natives, certainly makes it easier for consumers to fully understand and internalize a company's belief system, being purposeful is not simply the domain of B Corps and those with charitable business models. It just means they're often a little further ahead in their purpose journey.

What the top brands have in common

So, what makes the top seven PPI brands stand out? What do they share in common? It's not simply a business model or sector that gives companies an edge, as the top brands range from sustainable brands to those with giving models, from a bank to an outdoor-gear retailer to a grocery chain. We've found that most purpose-driven brands share three things in common.

1. The top purpose brands tend to be associated with a movement

Of those seven brands out of the 204 included in the research that scored highly on purpose, the most notable thing is that they tend to be associated with some sort of movement or idea on the rise that exists in culture:

- **Seventh Generation:** The household products company is known for being associated with the sustainability movement.
- **Method:** With its fetching cleaning products and a rousing rallying cry of *people against dirty*, Method is also deeply tied with the sustainability movement.
- **TOMS Shoes:** The pioneer of the one-to-one giving model, TOMS gives shoes to those living in poverty.
- **REI:** Through its business practices and its outward communication, the outdoor gear company is a loud voice in the environmentalism movement.
- **Stonyfield Organic:** Driven by the belief that healthy food means healthier people and a healthier planet, this yoghurt brand has been an organic maverick since 1983.

- **USAA:** Created to serve members of the military, this financial institution is synonymous with proud service.

2. The top purpose brands act boldly and communicate authentically

As we've said repeatedly, many brands forget to actually do something with their 'why'. Too often it sits dormant in the 'about' section of their website, or on company coffee mugs or posters. Or brands expect it to self-activate through simply creating a poignant anthem video about their purpose. The problem, of course, is that it seldom does.

According to the PPI data, there are two defining characteristics of top purpose leaders that separate them from the rest of the pack: acting boldly on their purpose and communicating it authentically (see Figure 7.3). Top purpose brands like Seventh Generation and REI build credibility by starting with an action and then communicating through a movement versus traditional advertising and communications.

3. The top purpose brands are purposeful inside and out

The PPI research reveals that consumers' purpose is not simply a 'why' statement. It is a complete narrative in their minds about your entire company or brand, how it operates in the world, how it treats people, and what issues it champions. And this narrative is not built by a single action or communication. Digging deeper into the PPI data, we discovered that there are four

FIGURE 7.3 Purpose leaders act bravely and communicate authentically

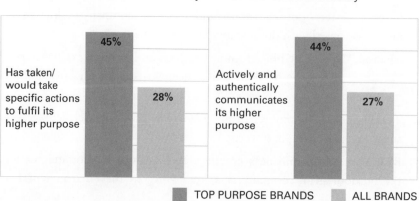

SOURCE RepTrak and StrawberryFrog

domains of purpose activation (see Figure 7.4), and consumers see the top purpose leaders as excelling in not one or two, but in all domains.

FOUR DOMAINS OF PURPOSE ACTIVATION

- **Purposeful products, services and operations:** This means a company sells products and services that make the world better and are operating in an environmentally responsible way.
- **Community and philanthropy:** The company promotes charitable giving, supporting the welfare of communities.
- **Employee advocacy:** The company is seen as caring for the health and wellbeing of employees.
- **Social activism:** The company takes a stand on major societal issues.

What you'll see here is that two of these domains – purposeful products, services and operations, and employee advocacy – are things that can be addressed with a Movement Inside. The other two – community and philanthropy, and social activism – can be activated with Movement Outside. This insight helps bring the results of the PPI beyond a place-in-time study into something that is actionable and can be addressed with a movement.

FIGURE 7.4 Purpose activation domains

Social Activism From promoting fairness and equality – including gay rights, gender equality and rights of racial minorities – to campaigning for data privacy

Employee Advocacy Cares for the health and wellbeing of its employees

Community and Philanthropy Promotes philanthropy and charitable giving, and supporting welfare of communities where it operates

Purposeful Products, Services and Operations Selling products and services that make life better and contribute to society

Being environmentally responsible in how it operates

Actively innovating solutions to advance mankind

SOURCE RepTrak and StrawberryFrog

PURPOSE POWER INDEX SNAPSHOTS

The Purpose Power Index revealed that the public is very astute when it comes to understanding and rewarding purpose. Here is a snapshot of three of the top seven purpose leaders.

Seventh Generation

Seventh Generation, a certified B Corp, was founded in 1988 and is guided by its purpose of *transforming the world into a healthy, sustainable and equitable place for the next seven generations*. It has consistently delivered on that promise.

Aside from the fact that its products are all plant-based, the company is a leader in sustainable packaging – it is committed to making all of its packaging 100 per cent post-consumer, recycled plastic by 2020 (a goal that by mid-2020 it admitted it had not fully achieved) and is moving to introduce 50 per cent of its packaging to be made of biodegradable, non-plastic containers by 2025 (Seventh Generation, 2019).

It is a corporate leader in the fight for ingredient disclosure regarding cleaning products, which was amplified with the #ComeClean movement. Those efforts have influenced various bills for ingredient transparency in several US states (Seventh Generation, 2017). The company also built a movement known as #GenerationGood that is centred around a shared spirit of leaving the world a little better than it was found. The movement encourages people to make moves for collective good (often through small acts like carpooling or sharing healthy food tips). The company is also an active voice for voter rights, sustainable energy and clean water initiatives.

Seventh Generation retained its sustainability focus even following being acquired by Unilever in 2017. In a letter to employees, CEO Joey Bergstein said Unilever was 'not only committed to boosting our shared social and environmental mission, they're giving us new power to achieve it' (Bergstein, 2018). To ensure that the company under Unilever would stay true to its mission, it assembled a Social Mission Board that meets bi-annually to check the company on its own mission and focuses on sustainable and diversity proceedings (Seventh Generation, 2018).

Seventh Generation's efforts to prove that business can be a force for good in the world resonated with PPI respondents. The study found that people perceive the company as one that lives out its mission daily. That the company acknowledges its impact on future generations and thus makes decisions with longevity in mind was endearing to respondents and helps keep its mission within the spotlight. It is unfettered in its pursuit of commerce that is transparent, socially conscious and environmentally ethical, and corrects itself and its efforts every step of the way. The mission is truly the guiding light for the company and everything it does is a reinforcement of that mission.

Stonyfield Organic

The story of American dairy company Stonyfield Organic dates back to a New Hampshire farm in 1983. At the time co-founders Samuel Kaymen and Gary Hirshberg were running a non-profit organic farming school. Their mission was to support family farms, keep food and food production healthy, and do so in ways that protect and respect the environment. To fund the school, they started making yoghurt from the milk of its seven dairy cows. Nearly 40 years later, Stonyfield is a clear leader in the organic movement and continues to produce its products free of pesticides and chemical fertilizers. It has pioneered planet-friendly business practices, including making yoghurt cups from plant-based materials instead of petroleum, offsetting emissions and producing renewable energy. Its ethos is summed up in its declaration that Stonyfield is *good on purpose*.

The company also positions itself as a steward of a healthy planet and those values are consistently demonstrated and applied through its activism on issues like climate change, the use of pesticides and environmental toxins, humane animal practices and organic farming. It is also pushing for pesticide-free green spaces across communities via Stonyfield's #PlayFree initiative.

All of this contributes to the perception of Stonyfield as an organic maverick. Despite existing in a rather mundane product category, the company is rewarded by consumers for the way it activates its purpose beyond the bottom line.

Wegmans

Wegmans is proof that a supermarket can be more than the place you simply buy your groceries. The American chain is dedicated to helping people live healthier, better lives through food. That commitment is expressed in the statement: *Every day you get our best*. That manifests in everything from the products on shelves to in-store customer service.

President and CEO Colleen Wegman, who took the reins of the company from her father Danny Wegman in 2017, has continued to advance the company's social impact through charitable donations to organizations and programmes supporting its five key giving priorities: reducing hunger, helping young people succeed, promoting healthy eating and activity, strengthening neighbourhoods, and supporting United Way initiatives. Each year, Wegmans donates 18.6 million pounds of food to local food banks and programmes that feed the hungry through its Perishable Pick-Up Program (Wegmans, 2020). The company is also committed to reducing food and plastic garbage in stores with their zero waste initiative.

As a result, PPI data shows that Wegmans is perceived as a generous supermarket that delivers on freshness and customer service in its stores. That perception was reinforced by the 2019 Harris Poll Reputation Quotient®, a study of the '100 most-visible companies', in which Wegmans ranked number one (Tobin and Greenwood, 2019). It also placed third on *Fortune* magazine's 2019 list of the 100 Best Companies to Work For (Wegmans has been on the list every year since it began; in 1998 and in 2005 it ranked first) (*Fortune*, 2020). Wegmans is an excellent example of how customers reward companies for excelling in the four domains of purpose activation: purposeful products, services and operations; community and philanthropy; employee advocacy; and social activism.

Why purpose requires it all

A master marketer, Nike knows how to tell a compelling story in a rousing, anthemic way. It certainly did this with its 'Dream Crazy' campaign, which joins an illustrious canon of knockout Nike advertising. And still, it fell short of being considered purpose-driven. These four pillars offer an explanation. While Nike took a huge risk by splashing Kaepernick's face on its ads, as the PPI reveals, great advertising alone does not immediately translate to purpose. Or as Jeff Beer wrote for *Fast Company* in a retrospective on the campaign: 'That may be the Kaep ad's most damning legacy: that it was all just an ad' (Beer, 2019).

Even though we believe that Nike's intentions to use its megawatt voice to speak out against racial injustice were genuine, without actions internally to back it up, it wasn't enough to click for consumers. Aside from its lack of diversity, which it acknowledged and is working to remedy, the company has also struggled with poor workplace conduct. This resulted in the immediate resignation of its president in 2018 (Aiello, 2018). The company came under fire in 2019 when six-time Olympian Allyson Felix was forced to leave the brand over its maternity policy (Felix, 2019), as well as for an inequitable corporate culture for women (Thomas, 2018). Not to mention a 2019 *New York Times* headline story about Mary Cain, a young runner from Bronxville, New York, who was pressured by male coaches to get thinner and thinner until, as she wrote, her body started breaking down (Cain, 2019). Following this report, Nike announced it would start an investigation into Cain's allegations. On 9 December 2019, hundreds of Nike employees protested the company's support of running coach Alberto Salazar and the treatment described by Cain and other Nike-sponsored female athletes (Draper and Creswell, 2019); by January 2020, Salazar was placed on the United States Center for SafeSport's temporarily banned list, a disciplinary action that could result in a lifetime ban (Minsberg, 2020).

This all registers with consumers.

REI: the complete package

On the other hand, outdoor sports retailer REI is a good example of a company telling a complete purpose story. If you recall from the opening of Chapter 2, REI has made a huge impact with its social activist platform '#OptOutside', wherein it closed all its stores on Black Friday and gave its employees a day off to hit the great outdoors. It's true that this platform is front and centre in the public realm, as it supports the company's mission of supporting a life well-lived outdoors while making a statement against overconsumption. But the company does a lot more than give its people a day off.

In 2019, it deepened its social activism around sustainability with '#OptToAct', which encouraged people to engage in 52 weekly challenges to reduce their environmental impact, get active and leave the world better than they found it with events like community clean-ups.

Its purposeful products, services and operations are evidenced in its strenuous Product Sustainability Standards, which outline its actions on fair and safe supply chains, chemicals management, land stewardship, animal welfare and environmental management (REI, 2019).

REI also performs well in the employee advocacy domain. It has for 23 consecutive years been on *Fortune*'s '100 Best Companies to Work for List', with employees quoted as saying, 'There are few places that come close to the level of passion that I've experienced at REI; a passion for the outdoors, excellence, doing the right thing, and for purpose over profit' (*Fortune*, 2020).

And REI regularly gives back nearly 70 per cent of its profits (REI, 2017; Chen, 2019) to the outdoor community, investing in over 400 non-profits annually.

It really is a company firing on all cylinders when it comes to higher purpose.

Purpose and partisanship

One of the fascinating revelations that came from the PPI is that political affiliation can be an important driver. When it comes to purpose, politics matters.

This runs contrary to the speculation that brand purpose is limited to those drawn to progressive, left-leaning brands. Our research shows that purpose crosses the political divide and people on both the left and right sides of the political spectrum give brands credit for having a higher purpose. They just credit different brands.

For example, Chick-fil-A and Hobby Lobby, two brands associated with religious freedom (which actually translated into actions that diminished gay rights and gender equality), score highly in the PPI research among Republicans (see Figure 7.5). Meanwhile, eco-friendly REI and TOMS score highly among Democrats. As an aside, demographics (eg gender, generation, income) didn't seem to impact which brands consumers consider purpose-driven.

FIGURE 7.5 Top Republican and Democrat purpose brands

Republican	Democrat
Chick-fil-A CAT	Seventh Generation
Hobby Lobby	TOMS REI

SOURCE StrawberryFrog

This all begs the question: what do you do as a consumer when a brand's values collide with your own? Or worse, what if their basic views and principles target you?

Take Chick-fil-A. Despite the fact that its philosophy statement declared that it was more about selling chicken and that the company should be a part of customers' lives and the communities it serves, the fast-food chicken chain found itself in the crosshairs of a partisan battle in 2019 when LGBTQ activists targeted the company for its support of Christian charities that were openly anti-same-sex marriage (Lucas, 2019).

Following years of pressure from protests (and the nearly immediate closure of its first UK expansion), it shifted focus exclusively to education, homelessness and hunger and ceased donating to organizations with anti-LGBTQ viewpoints – positioning the change as coming from a need to clarify its position and message.

At the same time, the company has an extremely charitable arm. The Chick-fil-A Shared Table programme donates surplus food to shelters and soup kitchens and feeds first responders to disasters. In addition, it has the Restaurant Team Member scholarships for local fundraising. The Chick-fil-A Foundation focuses on youth outreach and education. And the Chick-fil-A Peach Bowl, which is college football's most charitable bowl organization, holds the college bowl record for charitable/scholarship contributions with $21 million donated since 2002.

The fact that Chick-fil-A scores relatively highly on the PPI, certainly higher than the other fast-food brands, indicates that the company has handled controversy well. Through its words and actions, it has managed to distance itself from polarizing views. And it's done so in a way that seems to have made inroads with those on the left politically while remaining strong among those on the right.

When bold action doesn't connect

For Dick's Sporting Goods CEO Ed Stack, the school shooting at Marjory Stoneman Douglas High School, which we mentioned in Chapter 3, was the straw that broke the camel's back. The fact that the shooter, who killed 17 students and staff, bought the gun at a Dick's store was the tipping point. Stack needed to make a change. He declared that the stores would halt the sales of assault weapons and no longer sell to people under 21 (Siegel, 2019).

It was a bold action that aligned with the protests and calls for gun control that erupted after the 14 February 2018 shooting. And yet, the company scored surprisingly low in the PPI. The data shows that several brands that are taking controversial actions to improve society have yet to be recognized for it.

Why? Part of the problem can be that people didn't necessarily believe the CEO's claim; the store pulled assault weapons off its shelves in 2012 following the shooting at Sandy Hook elementary school in Newtown, Connecticut, which killed 26 people, but eventually resumed sales. Another reason could be that people didn't quite connect a company that was known for a lifetime of pro-gun beliefs with anti-gun activism.

But the bigger issue according to our PPI data is that many people didn't even know Dick's had halted the sale of assault weapons. In our survey, we asked consumers the degree to which they associated Dick's with the issue of gun safety and very few indicated they did.

Since then, Stack has continued to speak out for gun control, telling Vox, 'If we do [remove guns from stores] and it saves one life, don't you think it's worth it?' (Nguyen, 2019). The company has also destroyed $5 million worth of weapons and in 2020 stated it was removing guns at an additional 440 stores (Zhang, 2020).

It seems that corporate America isn't always getting credit for its activism, but cases like Dick's also illustrate that communicating purpose to people in a way they innately understand takes time.

Being purposeful is good for business

As we enter what we are calling the purpose economy, the purpose will continue to be a top priority for company and brand leadership. You can see why in the PPI results: the winners found in most studies of top brands, like Apple, Google and Amazon, don't register with consumers as being purpose-driven. And yet, that same research shows that consumers are not naive when it comes to purpose; they have high expectations that brands are largely failing to meet. This is making room for those with a higher mission at their core, as identified in the PPI. These leaders are large and small, they're disruptor brands and established incumbents, and, it's worth noting, many of them are associated with important and sometimes controversial social issues and movements. The implications of this study amount to a challenge for those in the C-suite: will you boldly activate your purpose by sparking a movement, or will the new breed of brand leaders lead the charge?

KEY TAKEAWAYS

Consumers are the unknown factor when it comes to brand purpose and company movements. It's true that you can never know exactly what's in the hearts and minds of the public, but the Purpose Power Index was a breakthrough that got us pretty close.

- As the Purpose Power Index shows, consumers are savvy when it comes to rewarding brands as being purpose-driven, though they only considered 3 per cent of brands in the survey as having a higher purpose.

- The PPI data revealed that there are four domains of purpose activation: purposeful products, services and operations; community and philanthropy; employee advocacy; and social activism. In order to be considered purpose-driven, however, brands have to excel in them all, not just one.

- Bold action and authentic communication are key to being considered purpose-driven. As we'll see in the next chapter, that is even more critical when a company finds itself in a merger situation.

- Bold action, when not communicated properly, can fail to connect. That's partly why a brand like Dick's Sporting Goods, which banned the sale of guns in its stores after another school shooting, was not rewarded for its leadership on gun control.

References

Aiello, C (2018) Nike executive resigns amid complaints about workplace conduct, CNBC, 15 March. https://www.cnbc.com/2018/03/15/nike-executive-resigns-amid-complaints-about-workplace-conduct.html (archived at https://perma.cc/HS9U-K8YA)

Beer, J (2019) One year later, what did we learn from Nike's blockbuster Colin Kaepernick ad?, FastCompany.com, 5 September. https://www.fastcompany.com/90399316/one-year-later-what-did-we-learn-from-nikes-blockbuster-colin-kaepernick-ad (archived at https://perma.cc/E22C-45QB)

Belson, K (2017) Fueled by Trump's tweets, anthem protests grow to a nationwide rebuke, *The New York Times*, 24 September. https://www.nytimes.com/2017/09/24/sports/trump-national-anthem-nfl.html (archived at https://perma.cc/KPY6-HR6U)

Bergstein, J (2018) A message from our CEO, SeventhGeneration.com, 31 July. https://www.seventhgeneration.com/blog/ceo-message (archived at https://perma.cc/8DC3-GL4H)

Cain, M (2019) I was the fastest girl in America, until I joined Nike, *The New York Times,* 7 November. https://www.nytimes.com/2019/11/07/opinion/nike-running-mary-cain.html (archived at https://perma.cc/AX84-MP42)

Chen, C (2019) How REI has managed to lead with its values and still turn a profit, *Business Insider*, 26 December. https://www.businessinsider.com/rei-company-values (archived at https://perma.cc/H3VA-HAYQ)

Ciment, S (2020) Former and current Nike employees are sharing their experiences with racism at the company via an anonymous Instagram page – and it's part of a growing trend on social media, *Business Insider*, 14 July. https://www.businessinsider.com/black-nike-employees-allege-racism-at-company-in-instagram-account-2020-7 (archived at https://perma.cc/S38J-ZWW5)

Cone, C (2019) *B2B Purpose Paradox*, Carol Cone on Purpose. https://www.carolconeonpurpose.com/b2b-purpose-paradox (archived at https://perma.cc/7EXZ-WDPS)

Dhanaraj, C, Malnight, T and Buche, I (2019) Put purpose at the core of your strategy, *Harvard Business Review*. https://hbr.org/2019/09/put-purpose-at-the-core-of-your-strategy (archived at https://perma.cc/5GQJ-QW83)

Draper, K and Creswell, J (2019) At Nike, employees march to protest support for Alberto Salazar, *The New York Times*, 9 December. https://www.nytimes.com/2019/12/09/sports/olympics/nike-protest-alberto-salazar.html (archived at https://perma.cc/E7T7-3YYL)

Felix, A (2019) Allyson Felix: My own Nike pregnancy story, *The New York Times*, 22 May. https://www.nytimes.com/2019/05/22/opinion/allyson-felix-pregnancy-nike.html (archived at https://perma.cc/HV8N-JDA9)

Forbes (2020) Great place to work, *Forbes*. https://www.greatplacetowork.com/certified-company/1000409 (archived at https://perma.cc/T23R-K4D9)

Fortune (2020) 100 best companies to work for, *Fortune*. https://fortune.com/best-companies/2020/wegmans-food-markets/ (archived at https://perma.cc/AP7J-RVL9)

Interbrand (2019) Best global brands. https://www.interbrand.com/best-global-brands/ (archived at https://perma.cc/25MA-TCYE)

Larcker, C, Miles, S, Tayan, B and Wright-Violich, K (2018) The double-edged sword of CEO activism, Stanford, 8 November. https://www.gsb.stanford.edu/sites/gsb/files/publication-pdf/cgri-closer-look-74-double-edged-sword-ceo-activism.pdf (archived at https://perma.cc/7Q33-9QZM)

Lucas, A (2019) Chick-fil-A no longer donates to controversial Christian charities after LGBTQ protests, CNBC, 18 November. https://www.cnbc.com/2019/11/18/chick-fil-a-drops-donations-to-christian-charities-after-lgbt-protests.html (archived at https://perma.cc/9L5X-QC5B)

Mather, V (2016) Megan Rapinoe, wearing a US uniform, kneels for the anthem, *The New York Times*, 16 September. https://www.nytimes.com/2016/09/17/sports/soccer/megan-rapinoe-in-an-american-uniform-kneels-for-the-anthem.html (archived at https://perma.cc/3YE2-ZT5E)

Mather, V (2019) A timeline of Colin Kaepernick vs the NFL, *The New York Times*, 15 February. https://www.nytimes.com/2019/02/15/sports/nfl-colin-kaepernick-protests-timeline.html (archived at https://perma.cc/P6V4-E5VR)

Minsberg, T (2020) Alberto Salazar is suspended by SafeSport after accusations of verbal abuse, *The New York Times*, 31 January. https://www.nytimes.com/2020/01/31/sports/olympics/alberto-salazar-ban.html (archived at https://perma.cc/VQD6-NAM9)

NFL (2016) Colin Kaepernick explains why he sat during national anthem, NFL.com, 27 August. https://www.nfl.com/news/colin-kaepernick-explains-why-he-sat-during-national-anthem-0ap3000000691077 (archived at https://perma.cc/PWE7-URQ6)

Nguyen, T (2019) Dick's Sporting Goods destroyed $5 million worth of guns it pulled from its stores, Vox.com, 8 October. https://www.vox.com/the-goods/2019/10/8/20904713/dicks-destroyed-guns-5-million-dollars (archived at https://perma.cc/89H2-NU74)

Nike (2019) *2019 Representation in Leadership*, Nike. https://purpose.nike.com/fy19-representation-and-pay (archived at https://perma.cc/94Q3-A77N)

Raggs, T (2018) Nike enjoys 31 percent bump in online sales after debut of Colin Kaepernick campaign, *Washington Post*, 8 September. https://www.washingtonpost.com/news/early-lead/wp/2018/09/08/nike-enjoys-31-percent-bump-in-online-sales-after-debut-of-colin-kaepernick-campaign/ (archived at https://perma.cc/WBC7-WVT6)

REI (2017) REI Co-op gives back nearly 70 percent of profits to the outdoor community after year of record revenues in 2016, REI, 15 March. https://www.rei.com/newsroom/article/rei-co-op-gives-back-nearly-70-percent-profits-to-outdoor-community-after-year-record-revenues-in-2016 (archived at https://perma.cc/6WPJ-5CQT)

REI (2019) REI product sustainability standards, REI.com, 1 October. https://www.rei.com/assets/stewardship/sustainability/rei-product-sustainability-standards/live.pdf (archived at https://perma.cc/EF9Y-M28P)

Reid, E (2017) Eric Reid: Why Colin Kaepernick and I decided to take a knee, *The New York Times*, 25 September. https://www.nytimes.com/2017/09/25/opinion/colin-kaepernick-football-protests.html (archived at https://perma.cc/FN7W-DBMD)

Seventh Generation (2017) Driving momentum in the #ComeClean fight for ingredient disclosure [Blog]. https://www.seventhgeneration.com/blog/driving-momentum-comeclean-fight-ingredient-disclosure (archived at https://perma.cc/P5VW-67J2)

Seventh Generation (2018) Meet the Seventh Generation Social Mission Board [Blog]. https://www.seventhgeneration.com/blog/meet-seventh-generation-social-mission-board (archived at https://perma.cc/MUW6-T8F4)

Seventh Generation (2019) 2019 corporate consciousness report. https://www. seventhgeneration.com/insideSVG/reporting (archived at https://perma.cc/ LQB8-HLSP)

Siegel, S (2019) Dick's Sporting Goods overhauled its gun policies after Parkland. The CEO didn't stop there, *Washington Post*, 31 May. https://www. washingtonpost.com/business/economy/dicks-sporting-goods-overhauled-its-gun-policies-after-parkland-the-ceo-didnt-stop-there/2019/05/31/9faa6a08-7d8f-11e9-a5b3-34f3edf1351e_story.html (archived at https://perma.cc/P7CV-2KXG)

Swant, M (2020) The world's most valuable brands 2020, *Forbes*. https://www. forbes.com/the-worlds-most-valuable-brands/#2dae9d35119c (archived at https://perma.cc/7ZKR-PQFM)

Thomas, L (2018) Nike is about to give 7,000 employees raises, CNBC, 23 July. https://www.cnbc.com/2018/07/23/nike-to-adjust-salaries-bonuses-for-employees-to-address-pay-equity.html (archived at https://perma.cc/ YC4U-2XYN)

Thomas, L (2020) Read Nike CEO John Donahoe's note to employees on racism: We must 'get our own house in order', CNBC, 5 June. https://www.cnbc. com/2020/06/05/nike-ceo-note-to-workers-on-racism-must-get-our-own-house-in-order.html (archived at https://perma.cc/67HT-GWMH)

Tobin, B and Greenwood, M (2019) Wegmans ranks No. 1 for reputation as tech companies stumble in new poll, *USA Today*, 6 March. https://www.usatoday. com/story/news/2019/03/06/wegmans-harris-poll-reputation-survey/3078177002/ (archived at https://perma.cc/RTA5-LLEH)

Wegmans (2020) Feeding the Hungry. https://www.wegmans.com/about-us/ making-a-difference/feeding-the-hungry/ (archived at https://perma.cc/97C4-BFP3)

Zeno Group (2020) Unveiling the 2020 Zeno Strength of Purpose Study, Zeno Group. https://www.zenogroup.com/insights/2020-zeno-strength-purpose (archived at https://perma.cc/9LQ9-BQY2)

Zhang, H (2020) Dick's Sporting Goods will stop selling guns at 440 more stores, CNN.com, 10 March. https://www.cnn.com/2020/03/10/business/dicks-sporting-goods-remove-guns-from-440-stores/index.html (archived at https:// perma.cc/6ZDQ-UFX5)

08

How movement increases a merger's chances of success

There is cause for hope when you think about Abu Dhabi. The jewel of a city is the capital of the United Arab Emirates, set just off the mainland on an island in the Persian Gulf, and it wears its oil-export wealth and affinity for commerce on its sleeve. Towering glass-clad skyscrapers dot the skyline and shopping mega centres attract people with their luxury shops. The city's opulent structures, like the vast Sheikh Zayed Grand Mosque, are draped in white marble domes, Persian carpets and crystal chandeliers.

It is, quite simply, one of the most beautiful places to help the leaders of two of the country's largest banks bring meaning and coherence to a merger and, moreover, do something big and consequential.

That's what brought us to the city in 2017. StrawberryFrog was tasked with helping the UAE government and leadership of the National Bank of Abu Dhabi (NBAD) steward its merger with First Gulf Bank (FGB), a highly regarded, enterprise-driven financial institution, led by Abdulhamid Saeed, a brilliant thinker and visionary CEO. It was at the time the largest bank merger in the world.

Our assignment was to help the leadership cement the merger by creating a new unified brand experience: name, look, design, feel and purpose statement. But what this example will show is that igniting a movement for the new brand was extremely significant.

Merger and acquisition (M&A) deals make the world go round, and with time and deal values, complexities continue to increase. Mergers have been on the rise over the last decade, with 2015 yielding record levels of M&A activity – until a new record was set in 2018 when $2.5 trillion in mergers was announced in the first half of that year (Grocer, 2018). There may even be a new record by the time you're reading this. And as the business landscape endures seismic shifts following the COVID-19 pandemic, mergers and acquisitions will become even more likely as sectors contract and evolve.

That said, according to research reported in the *Harvard Business Review*, the failure rate for mergers and acquisitions sits between 70 and 90 per cent (Christensen *et al*, 2011), which at first blush seems remarkably high, but is not that surprising given how complex mergers and acquisitions are.

One of those complexities common in M&A is how peer-to-peer culture is redefining organizational culture. As we discussed in Chapter 4, it's increasingly more challenging for leaders to mandate culture, demand compliance and expect results. In a merger, not only are you asking two companies to integrate under one corporate mission, but you are bringing together two cultures, two personalities, two large groups with behaviours and rituals – and organizational stories and mythologies.

Movement Thinking creates the business operations process for the merger to defeat the odds and succeed, with everyone aligned to one single empowering, inspiring red thread.

Codifying the design of purpose, activating with Movement Thinking

Over the years, we have developed a framework that helps leaders increase the chances of a merger's success. When you put purpose in the centre of your merger strategy, you have the power of an animating idea that inspires every human. Aligning your strategy with that purpose and then activating it with a movement is the way to make meaningful and effective change.

It is human-led, not finance-led

A merger is not simply an initiative with a budget and a completion date. It requires a mindset that puts humans at the centre. A merger's momentum and focus aren't derived merely from a unified business plan, but rather on a clearly defined purpose that employees can be inspired by emotionally to believe and act on.

People within your organization will always build their own capabilities, aligned to the purpose of the new merger, to achieve their own ambitions and make an impact. But along with this can come friction and fear. Movement Thinking can avoid these issues and instead create hope and action.

People don't have relationships with new organization charts, but they do with a common purpose. Challenges are inevitable, but a cultural movement that activates purpose inside the company will ensure you have a deep cultural rudder to guide everyone from the top of the organization to the bottom. It will also provide much-needed inspiration and growth, as well as employee engagement programmes with consumer-grade communications.

That's why it was important for our team to be in Abu Dhabi. We knew that many of the colleagues who were with us on our flight from New York to UAE didn't exactly know where they were heading. The explanation of 'near Dubai' was only somewhat helpful. If people knew anything about the UAE – a nation less than 50 years old – it was likely that they'd heard something about the ski slope in a Dubai mall, or they knew of its airline Emirates, which StrawberryFrog helped build into a global icon by means of the now-famous 'Hello Tomorrow' marketing movement. We also knew that if we were going to help two prominent banks become one with a movement, we needed to deeply understand the cultures of each and the larger culture in which they operated.

Culture is king

Merging a company is hard to do. Yet it can be incredibly fulfilling and empowering for leaders and for employees. Mergers present both opportunity and anxiety. Possibilities are endless for leaders to transform both entities and use the new start to set a new direction with a performance culture. At the same time, change creates anxiety as many people are forced to think outside their default behaviour zone. Mergers put human behaviour on the front lines. That's why they can quickly spiral out of control if the leaders have not outlined their goals in an emotional way that breaks through.

Employees inside most companies have built up a wall of indifference to corporate messages. These communications typically lack emotional, meaningful, inspiring purpose, leading to a dearth of trust and understanding. What you can end up with is an unmotivated, tribalistic or even toxic culture that undermines a merged company's objectives. Just look at Amazon's $13.7 billion deal to buy Whole Foods.

When the online retail giant acquired the organic grocery chain in 2017, there was a high level of interest and intrigue. On the face of it, the marriage could yield some interesting results: organic groceries at scale and lower prices. To others, the coupling seemed like a case of strange bedfellows, with one company focused on logistics and relentless efficiency, the other on warm customer service and being *America's healthiest grocery store*. Though Whole Foods CEO John Mackey called the whirlwind courtship 'love at first sight' (Choi, 2017), others were wary. As Craig Crossland, associate professor of business at Notre Dame, wrote on CNBC.com at the time, 'As Whole Foods begins to rub up against the parent firm, there's likely to be a substantial culture clash' (Crossland, 2017).

And indeed there was.

By early 2019, Whole Foods employees were claiming they were being treated like robots (Sainato, 2018), that their dedication was being exploited (Clark, 2018), and scorecards to measure Whole Foods' compliance with Amazon's new inventory system were being used punitively (Peterson, 2018). Less than a year into the marriage, Whole Foods employees were taking steps to explore unionizing (Clark, 2018). Amazon responded with video coaching Whole Foods management on how to spot and discourage potential union behaviour (Sainato, 2018), and by April 2020 Amazon was reportedly using heat maps to track stores at risk of unionizing (Peters, 2020).

'The two companies may have seen the value in capitalizing on each other's strengths, but they failed to investigate their cultural compatibility beforehand,' wrote Michele Gelfand, professor at the University of Maryland and the author of *Rule Makers, Rule Breakers: How tight and loose cultures wire our world* (Gelfand *et al*, 2018).

Of course, we can't know for certain if these pains could have been avoided. Sometimes meeting in the middle is impossible and one partner simply dominates, shaping the other in its image. But we know from our experience that when employees are given a clear sense of purpose, crystallized by a movement inside the organization, the purpose becomes relatable in human terms versus business terms, and this helps the merger succeed.

By bringing employees together during a merger with a Movement Inside, you can:

- build a new culture focused on solving a bigger need in the world;
- drive a new customer/market/community-based understanding and focus;
- bring meaning to the work;
- unite two different cultures over a purpose activated.

Next, we'll look at how focusing on culture through an activated purpose has helped shepherd companies through corporate mergers of different stripes.

A powerhouse pairing: from NBAD and FGB to FAB

Getting back to Abu Dhabi, when we worked with the leadership of NewCo, the newly combined NBAD + FGB bank, the banking market remained fragmented, despite Abu Dhabi's increasing economic sophistication. The merger was a key signal to the market to consolidate and cut costs. According to Freshfields, the strategic advisory that worked on the deal, the Abu Dhabi government was also keen to create a banking champion to compete with other big regional banks (Freshfields, 2017).

StrawberryFrog led a wide range of activities on the merger that helped it succeed. First, we devised the purpose for NewCo. To move things forward, we held a FrogLogic session with leadership, working arm in arm to define success and look at examples of where StrawberryFrog had previously designed purpose. Moreover, we activated the purpose with a Movement Inside NewCo to establish a common culture, less about defining who this NewCo was and more to explain why it should exist.

To underpin our purpose recommendation, we had conducted stakeholder interviews with a wide range of employees from both groups as well as consumer and non-customer interviews. We conducted ethnographic research to understand where the consumer and popular culture were heading since the key to designing a movement is ensuring your purpose is relevant to the culture. We brought all these elements together for collaborative work sessions together with our new clients at NewCo. The outcome of this was the purpose *to help people grow stronger*.

Next, we had to develop a new name for the bank, a logo, and a fresh look and feel and design programme. Finding a new name is a laborious process, as many if not all of the best names have been registered somewhere in the world. Many nights we would wake up to a flash of genius only to see the flame of brilliance doused the next day when we would find the name being used in Turkey or South Africa. We eventually landed on First Abu Dhabi Bank and went from NBAD + FGB to FAB.

The 'Grow Stronger' movement

After vetting our purpose with stakeholders, our next task was creating a movement that would bring the purpose to life. As we set out to bring together the two different cultures of the legacy banks, we realized that we needed to do a number of things for the idea to deliver a clear and galvanizing idea.

First, it needed to explain why the merger was happening: *to grow stronger into one of the most powerful financial institutions in the world*. Second, it needed to provide a cause around which we could rally all employees: it was about helping Abu Dhabi and its citizens 'Grow Stronger' and understand financial literacy. And finally, it needed to inspire the employees in the combined company to grow as professionals in order to drive performance and better outcomes for the new bank and its clients.

The 'Grow Stronger' movement was launched internally among all the executives and among the employees. It was the base for training and for communications to the people that matter both inside and outside the bank. For executives and employees alike to feel included and part of the new company, we shared the story behind the name and the logo, providing clarity around the FAB brand. We created understanding and alignment around their new purpose – and the movement that was to activate the purpose. Employees at all levels rallied around the powerful idea of *grow stronger* on which to build their unique culture and impactful brand. They got excited about the merger and the future, replacing months of uncertainty and fear.

We developed a range of materials and tools to train and coach managers on the new brand and the movement, including an employee handbook, employee brand manual, employee engagement plan, and 'Grow Stronger' activations and giveaways. Immediately after, the name and branding were revealed with an impactful 'birth announcement' ad and traditional media campaign that drove people to the movement hub, growstronger.com, which was a destination for additional resources on financial literacy and strength. In addition, we trained external partners and consultants to the bank to become familiar with the new company and brand.

As Abdulhamid Saeed, the governor at the Central Bank of UAE and former group CEO of FAB, said about the movement:

> 'Grow Stronger' is more than just a slogan – it's a passionate movement.
> Helping our customers to achieve their goals and reach important milestones
> is at the heart of this movement, which will serve as a catalyst for growth and
> prosperity. Growth brings strength and strength brings growth – we want our
> customers to benefit from the movement and grow stronger with us. (FAB,
> 2017)

And grow stronger they did. Within the first year of operations, FAB achieved a net profit of Dh12 billion (roughly $3.2 billion), up 10 per cent from pre-merger; employee engagement rose by 8 per cent compared with the legacy banks' results; it was named World's Best Bank for Transformation by the

2019 Euromoney Awards for Excellence; and over 40,000 people joined the 'Grow Stronger' movement.

FAB CEO André Sayegh told *Euromoney* in 2019 that the merger 'proved to be correct, from a revenue angle, from a customer perspective, from an expense angle as well. The two banks as one became more efficient' (Euromoney, 2020).

Tim Burnell, who is now VP brand and marketing at Etihad Airlines, was the CMO who brought us in to do the work as well as our former client at Emirates Airlines. He told us:

> Despite the differences between private enterprise and society, leaders can learn much from how social movements engage and inspire people, applying the principles to create a powerful business operations and marketing process. I have seen this impact in my experience working with StrawberryFrog in CMO roles at FAB and Emirates Airlines.

The acquisition of a historic brand: T-Mobile and Sprint

In April 2020, when the merger of T-Mobile and Sprint was finalized, one of America's oldest brands was no more. Founded in 1899, Sprint began as a telegraph service that facilitated train dispatches, with thousands of miles of telegraph wire running along the track of Southern Pacific Railroad (the name itself was an acronym for the system: Southern Pacific Railroad Internal Networking Telecommunications). For decades it was a communications mainstay that kept the country connected. It pioneered long-distance calling for private customers in the 1970s and entered the wireless business in 1992 with the acquisition of Central, making it the country's only provider of wireless, long-distance and local calling (Duffy, 2019). While the company has suffered its share of troubles in the past, with suggestions that without a merger it would have struggled to stay afloat (Duffy, 2020), the loss of the storied company was still a blow to American corporate history.

Without a doubt the union was a shrewd business decision – together the new T-Mobile would become the second-largest wireless carrier in the US. As Brian Fung (2019) wrote in CNN, 'The merger could prove transformative for the US wireless industry.' Yet, it posed a potential cultural problem: half of the company's employees were from a company that no longer existed; they would be consumed by the dominant culture of T-Mobile.

As is the case in such acquisitions, the challenge becomes how to ensure that those on the 'takeover' side of a merger equation don't feel like the lesser partner in a union. How do you create a cohesive culture that is not fraught with tension or undermined by newcomers from the old Sprint? Would employees from the Sprint brand be enthusiastic to be part of T-Mobile, a previous competitor? Would the business objectives of merging T-Mobile's low-band and high-band spectrum with Sprint's mid-band spectrum holdings to build a best-in-class 5G network resonate with people in their day-to-day work? How would company leaders galvanize employees from both sides of the merger into one, strong new T-Mobile?

To bring the two cultures together, T-Mobile CEO Mike Sievert says the company focused on establishing a common purpose:

> The innovative culture of both companies motivates #TeamMagenta to disrupt with renewed enthusiasm. So, instead of looking at the cultures separately, we are taking the best from both companies. And in some cases, this could be crafting something entirely new.

Making moves with the 'Un-carrier' movement

This common culture with a common purpose was galvanized by the existing 'Un-carrier' movement. Established in 2013 by Sievert and then-CEO John Legere, 'Un-carrier' was T-Mobile's answer to what Sievert called 'a broken industry in desperate need of a customer advocate'. The 'Un-carrier' manifesto was to shake up the wireless industry, and by positioning itself as the antithesis to its competitors, T-Mobile set out on a mission to eliminate customer pain points.

The 'Un-carrier' movement is based on 'moves' to solve those pain points, and in its seven years T-Mobile has done 17 'Un-carrier' moves – things like ending annual service contracts, overages and domestic roaming fees, and offering better customer care.

This framework provided the perfect opportunity to inspire employees from both sides of the merger. The company now had a newfound scale and financial firepower to aggressively compete with AT&T and Verizon, backed by the new capacity of its merged network. Employees of the new T-Mobile were given the opportunity to find new ways to create industry-busting moves with the shared goal of becoming, as Sievert said, one of the most loved brands in the world, famous for putting customers first.

Sievert told us when discussing the merger:

We created a movement by shaking up a stupid, broken and arrogant industry. Through our 'Un-carrier' strategy and unrivalled customer-experience obsession, we are doubling down on what customers love about our brand – including a great value with a great network. But the truth is, there's unfinished business.

The next question, he said, was to continue to ask what more T-Mobile can do to show up for the customers and the communities they serve.

The 'Un-carrier' 2.0

The new T-Mobile is in essence a new company in an industry that is being remade by 5G technology, which is changing the world in ways even greater than 4G did. So, it's little surprise that Sievert said there was a lot to change. Naturally, there were efficiencies to be found between the two companies, which he said amounted to $43 billion and allowed the company to deliver better services at better prices with a dramatically lower cost structure. And the company's capacity increased 14 times over compared with standalone T-Mobile, which allowed it to leapfrog the competition in network capability and fuelled the company's goal to eliminate the digital divide by bringing 5G to 99 per cent of Americans within six years.

Those changes were being communicated internally and externally through the movement. In November 2019, the merged T-Mobile announced 'Un-carrier' Move 1.0, '5G for Good', which featured three bold initiatives that harnessed its new network capabilities to bring accessibility and connectivity to all Americans. Those initiatives included Connecting Heroes, which provided free talk, text and unlimited data to qualifying first responder agencies; T-Mobile Connect, which offered half-price monthly plans to help its most vulnerable clients remain connected; and Project 10Million, which worked to close the homework gap by giving school districts free internet access and mobile hotspots for 10 million eligible households. The first two were launched by summer 2020. In July 2020, T-Mobile also launched Scam Shield, a large set of free solutions to help protect customers from rampant scams and automated 'robocalls'.

The climate immediately around the finalization of the merger offered T-Mobile other opportunities to prove its commitment by showing up for customers and the communities it serves. Just as the merger of Sprint and T-Mobile was announced, the global COVID-19 pandemic hit. Seattle, which is very close to one of T-Mobile's headquarters, was one of the first epicentres of the disease in the US. It was terrible timing for the company (along with the rest of the world), but the crisis, and the company's ability to respond, crystallized a sense of purpose among the newly combined workforce.

In response to the pandemic, Sievert said T-Mobile was one of the first essential service providers to take bold steps to help mitigate the impacts of the lockdown orders across the United States. Anticipating increases in network demands and changes in usage patterns, the company took immediate steps to temporarily double its 600 LTE MHz capacity nationwide and significantly expand roaming for Sprint customers, who had different levels of service than T-Mobile customers.

T-Mobile was also a supporter of the FCC's 'Keep Americans Connected' pledge and waived late fees due to pandemic-related economic circumstances, ensuring that customers and small businesses would not have their service terminated during a critical period. Sievert said to us:

> I am proud to say that working with customers on flexible payment and plan options that support their needs is a muscle we started developing long ago as the 'Un-carrier'. Even before COVID-19, some customers had payment constraints, and we have thousands of care reps who work daily with them to create plans that keep people connected.

At the same time, the nation was also experiencing ongoing protests for greater racial justice and equity. The company responded by working to diversify its pipeline of talent, launching an apprenticeship programme for people of colour, and expanding development and training programmes. Through the company's memorandum of understanding with six national civil rights organizations, which was entered into in October 2019, T-Mobile committed to $25 million in community investment, including workforce recruitment and retention, procurement, entrepreneurship, and philanthropy and community investment.

Sievert said that because of the scale and technology gained by merging with Sprint, and the 'Un-carrier' ethos and culture built at T-Mobile, the merged company is poised for the technological and societal issues at play. 'We brought together the best of the best from both companies, and with that fortified culture, we are able to collectively overcome challenges and change.'

The merger of equals: unified by purpose, SunTrust and BB&T become Truist

We've discussed SunTrust at several points throughout this book and how the bank used both Movement Inside and Movement Outside to activate its purpose of *lighting the way to financial wellbeing.*

But the interesting layer to the SunTrust story is that as it was adding members to its 'onUp' Movement, which has crested at 6 million participants, Atlanta-based SunTrust was in the process of merging with rival regional lender BB&T of North Carolina for about $28 billion in stock (Reuters, 2019). It was the largest and most ambitious bank merger in over a decade; when the deal closed in December 2019, it made the combined entities the sixth largest bank in the United States, which became Truist.

The merger was considered by both parties as a combination of equals, as it united one's excellence in customer service with the other's innovative technology. But according to Truist President and COO Bill Rogers, they are equals in how they were driven by purpose. So, it's little surprise, then, that purpose was a guiding factor when coming together to become Truist.

Rogers, who is set to take the CEO mantle in 2021, told us when we spoke, 'We kept saying, this is why we merged. We merged because we both care about "why" in our businesses. The purpose that allowed our companies to outperform has also allowed us to merge.'

To roll out the merger, Truist executives did roadshows in 38 cities for employees (it would have been more had the COVID-19 pandemic not halted all in-person interactions). The presentation included no details on the merger integration, no updates on the business, no slides, graphs or charts. The entire conversation was around Truist's purpose, mission and values, which, Rogers said, resonated with teammates:

> We may have had different policies or execution strategies, but once everyone was aligned around purpose, it became a lot easier to make decisions for the house. It allows you to talk about your similarities and not your differences. So, purpose was a really key coalescing force in our merger.

Rogers said that while Truist was only eight months old at the time of writing, purpose was already driving decisions from its approach to philanthropy to its pandemic response to internal communications. 'Everything we do, we just start from this framework of purpose.'

Inspiring a new purpose

So, what is Truist's new purpose, its new guiding light? It's to *inspire and build better lives and communities*.

Just as the Truist visual identity draws on the strengths of each heritage company (the T monogram is made up of two Ts to represent Touch + Technology and the Truist purple is a combination of BB&T's burgundy brand colour and SunTrust's blue), its purpose is a blend of the purpose and mission of both the heritage BB&T and SunTrust brands. While the foundation of the mission and purpose that were instilled in heritage BB&T and SunTrust remained, the Truist purpose put intense focus on making things better for clients, teammates and communities, while respecting and honouring the two parts that made this new whole.

Dontá Wilson, Truist's chief digital and client experience officer, who also held the same role at BB&T, said to us that through the merger process leadership recognized that employees at the heritage companies were strongly aligned on the characteristics and cultural themes teammates found important. They also made it a priority to engage teammates and made sure they were part of the process. That meant when Truist shared its purpose, mission and values with employees, they were primed to receive the message; it was a natural transition for teammates to feel confident that they would be building on the strong foundations that already guided each heritage company, which is key to a successful culture. Wilson said:

> Our goal is that every teammate at Truist will live our purpose daily in all interactions in order to create a sustainable culture and business. So, not only do we want them to align to our purpose, we also want our purpose to resonate for them personally.

Inspiring agility

That Truist's shared purpose was developed and ready on what Rogers calls 'legal day one' of the merger helped the company quickly set course for a unified company culture. But it also meant the company was prepared for the tumultuous days that followed the unveiling of the new company.

He told us that to *inspire and build better lives and communities* was instrumental in how the company talked about social injustice and dealt with the pandemic. It also provided something of an imperative for the company to move quickly to activate that purpose.

FIGURE 8.1 When mission and purpose become one

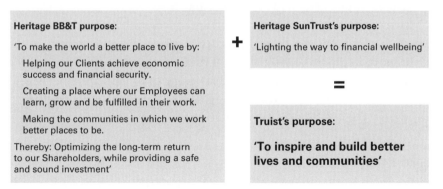

SOURCE StrawberryFrog

'The "inspire" part is forcing us to move a lot faster with more agility, because you can't really inspire unless you're first,' Rogers said. That approach led to Truist Cares, a programme launched on 17 March 2020, which committed $25 million to front-line needs and organizations to meet the immediate and long-term needs of the communities Truist serves and customers in need of financial relief.

Rather than waiting to get all of the details buttoned down, Rogers said the decision was made to launch it in a matter of days. 'We said, wait a minute, if we wait, we won't inspire. What if we just announced it on Monday morning? We set a whole new bar for what it means to inspire.'

The development of Truist Cares in the early days of the pandemic led quickly to a national marketing campaign introducing Truist Cares, and thereafter a second campaign featuring The United Way and Truist, and the first Youth Poet Laureate in the United States, Amanda Gorman.

Moving forward with purpose

With less than a year as a combined company at the time of writing, Truist was early in its journey when we examined how purpose helped guide the merger. Still, Wilson says the signs of success are clear. 'The Truist purpose communicates who we are and why we exist. It's facilitating our culture, driving teammate collaboration to serve clients and communities in new ways, and infusing pride for what Truist stands for.'

The company also established a 'best ideas win' ethos when deciding which purpose best practices to incorporate into Truist, and SunTrust's 'onUp' still lives on as the Truist Movement, with an even broader mandate of helping inspire and build better lives and communities.

Rogers also told us that the early experiences with Truist cemented his belief that being driven by higher-order purpose as a core strategy is the right move in a post-COVID world. 'I think companies that went into the pandemic that were purpose-oriented are going to be the substantial beneficiaries coming out. Right now, it's the glue. Tomorrow, it's the propellant.'

KEY TAKEAWAYS

- A merger unleashes the winds of change. When these winds are blowing behind you, momentum grows, but when they are blowing against you, change is challenging and mergers are susceptible to failure. When leading a merger, first design a purpose.

- Then, activate that purpose with Movement Thinking to create an inspiring, empowering and motivating culture within the new company to galvanize all employees, to help them feel the culture in their hearts, to thrive, giving you the best chance of bucking the merger trend.

- Use Movement Inside to create your best brand ambassadors.

- Once you've established the movement inside the organization, invite consumers and prospects to participate.

- Movement Thinking establishes a sustainably powerful force that imagines a new future for all and is significantly more engaging and motivating than tweaking the status quo. It is about abandoning old orthodoxies and seeing new possibilities, then building up to them in a step-by-step approach, activated by bold actions. Movement Thinking drives and accelerates purpose in a merger.

References

Choi, C (2017) Whole Foods CEO John Mackey talks Amazon: 'It was truly love at first sight', *Inc.*, 20 June. https://www.inc.com/associated-press/whole-foods-john-mackey-jeff-bezos-amazon-acquisition-deal-love-at-first-sight.html (archived at https://perma.cc/6XUS-R4TB)

Christensen, C, Alton, R, Rising, C and Waldeck, A (2011) The big idea: The new M&A playbook, *Harvard Business Review*, 1 March. https://hbr.org/2011/03/the-big-idea-the-new-ma-playbook (archived at https://perma.cc/J2TN-WBQ5)

Clark, K (2018) Whole Foods workers seek to unionize, say Amazon is 'exploiting our dedication', *Techcrunch*, 6 September. https://techcrunch.com/2018/09/06/whole-foods-workers-seek-to-unionize-says-amazon-is-exploiting-our-dedication/ (archived at https://perma.cc/KWH8-8RFM)

Crossland, C (2017) Here's the one glaring problem with the Amazon-Whole Foods deal, CNBC, 23 June. https://www.cnbc.com/2017/06/16/heres-the-one-glaring-problem-with-the-amazon-whole-foods-deal-commentary.html (archived at https://perma.cc/62CH-U6DS)

Duffy, C (2019) Sprint may soon be a dead brand... one way or another, CNN, 23 November. https://www.cnn.com/2019/11/23/tech/sprint-history-tmobile-merger/index.html (archived at https://perma.cc/ERM6-LB63)

Duffy, C (2020) One of America's most storied brands is no more, CNN, 3 August. https://www.cnn.com/2020/08/03/tech/sprint-tmobile-brand/index.html (archived at https://perma.cc/67U8-29AR)

Euromoney (2020) Class of 2019: First Abu Dhabi Bank, 9 January. https://www.euromoney.com/article/b1jsw8vf4kc6dw/class-of-2019-first-abu-dhabi-bank (archived at https://perma.cc/X5WL-NNMC)

FAB (2017) First Abu Dhabi Bank launches new brand identity, 1 May. https://www.bankfab.com/-/media/fabgroup/home/about-fab/corporate-governance/annual-reports/fab-launches-new-identity/fab_pressrelease_a4_2017-04-30-en_20170501082818.pdf?view=1 (archived at https://perma.cc/PTS6-FUYJ)

Freshfields (2017) First Gulf Bank-National Bank of Abu Dhabi: An unprecedented banking merger. https://www.freshfields.com/en-gb/what-we-do/case-studies/first-abu-dhabi-bank-case-study/ (archived at https://perma.cc/A6C6-ZGFR)

Fung, B (2019) FCC formally greenlights merger between T-Mobile and Sprint, CNN, 5 November. https://www.cnn.com/2019/11/05/tech/fcc-t-mobile-sprint-merger/index.html (archived at https://perma.cc/9HMP-2CWE)

Gelfand, M, Gordon, S, Li, C, Choi, V and Prokopowicz, P (2018) One reason mergers fail: The two cultures aren't compatible, *Harvard Business Review*, 2 October. https://hbr.org/2018/10/one-reason-mergers-fail-the-two-cultures-arent-compatible (archived at https://perma.cc/57ZA-MJGZ)

Grocer, S (2018) A record $2.5 trillion in mergers were announced in the first half of 2018, *The New York Times*, 30 June. https://www.nytimes.com/2018/07/03/business/dealbook/mergers-record-levels.html (archived at https://perma.cc/KD9V-JFP4)

Peters, J (2020) Whole Foods is reportedly using a heat map to track stores at risk of unionization, *The Verge*, 20 April. https://www.theverge.com/2020/4/20/21228324/amazon-whole-foods-unionization-heat-map-union (archived at https://perma.cc/64JL-UVF5)

Peterson, H (2018) 'Seeing someone cry at work is becoming normal': Employees say Whole Foods is using 'scorecards' to punish them, *Business Insider*, 1 February. https://www.businessinsider.com/how-whole-foods-uses-scorecards-to-punish-employees-2018-1 (archived at https://perma.cc/9HMS-SWBA)

Reuters (2019) BB&T to buy SunTrust in an all-stock deal worth $66 billion that will create the sixth-largest US bank, CNBC, 7 February. https://www.cnbc.com/2019/02/07/bbt-and-suntrust-to-combine-in-an-all-stock-merger-of-66-billion.html (archived at https://perma.cc/6AP3-FNYA)

Sainato, M (2018) Amazon training videos coach Whole Foods staff on how to discourage unions, *The Guardian*, 27 September. https://www.theguardian.com/business/2018/sep/27/amazon-whole-foods-training-video-union-busting-efforts-staff (archived at https://perma.cc/X7KC-4UHS)

09

How Movement Thinking
fosters collaboration

As buzzwords go, collaboration is a ubiquitous one. You'll find it everywhere, numerous articles are dedicated to the topic, the 'about' section on corporate websites wax eloquent about collaborative cultures, job candidates assert how collaborative they are on their CVs, and countless TED Talks hammer home the dogma that collaboration is essential to business. People in business are simply fascinated by collaboration.

That's because collaboration is an organizational multiplier that increases a leader's chance of success. As leaders face change coming at an increasing pace, collaboration can help give their organizations momentum and velocity. It means you can avoid being reliant on particular resources such as siloed budgets and instead pool resources and capabilities. When you align with other purpose-driven organizations with a common movement that share the same stand or enemy, you can explore what partners might be able to help and what your business could offer in return.

Incredible things can also happen when unexpected groups partner. In music and fashion, where the mutual brand-building benefit is well established, collaboration is a winning marketing play. In history, the ability of history's great leaders to form alliances and coalitions with others who shared their interests – from Genghis Khan to General Eisenhower to post-WWII European leaders Konrad Adenauer of Germany, Alcide De Gasperi of Italy and Robert Schuman of France, the fathers of the European Union – collaboration has proven to be a powerful strategic capability.

While so many business leaders say they want to be collaborative, the reality is, true collaboration in business is hard, and thus doesn't happen that often. Fostering collaboration in the C-suite, between the CMO and the CHRO as an example, and among executives throughout the organization, is a challenge for any leader. Too often aspirations fall prey to lip-service. But why? Why is it hard to share ideas and work together in a corporate setting? Why isn't the rallying cry 'let's create something awesome together' enough to actually get it done?

As you'll see below, significant barriers to meaningful collaboration are a lack of strategic focus, lack of leadership, as well as people-driven hurdles. To address these challenges, Movement Thinking can be essential. Because Movement Thinking provides a platform designed to bring different groups of people together around a shared cause, it can help leaders build a partnership strategy for growth that addresses business needs while clearly communicating to people why it matters to them and how they can contribute.

As you'll see in some examples that follow, Movement Thinking can enable collaboration to thrive inside a federation of companies and entities under one master brand, such as Mahindra Group or LifeBridge Health. It is how Christy Pambianchi, executive vice president and chief human resources officer of Verizon, helped form a group of CHROs to help talent during the pandemic, a group of leaders who historically would be fighting over talent (which we'll take a closer look at later in this chapter).

Why collaboration is challenging

Before we look at how some companies and business leaders have used collaboration to their advantage, let's examine some of the challenges they face.

A lack of leadership

Cross-functional collaboration is essential for businesses both in terms of growth and innovation but also in terms of workplace culture, which is even more important as more people work from home in the age of COVID-19. Yet, data shows that collaboration is not happening among members of the C-suite.

A 2019 Deloitte (O'Brien et al, 2019) survey of how collaborative executives are found that only 17 per cent of CMOs collaborate inside their company, let alone outside it. CEOs are even less collaborative internally, while other C-suite executives are only marginally more so, suggesting that collaboration is not baked into the way members of the C-suite think.

Similarly, the 2018 Global Human Capital Trends report, also from Deloitte, found that 85 per cent of those asked believed that a 'symphonic

C-suite', or a collaborative leadership, was important, yet only 46 per cent said they were ready for such collaboration (Deloitte, 2018).

A lack of clarity

So, if people want to be collaborative but aren't, according to research, what can leaders do to foster cross-functional cooperation?

In seeking to understand why so few brands and marketers use collaboration, Adam Morgan, partner of brand consultancy eatbigfish, found that 'partnership and collaboration is simply not baked into the way marketing currently thinks about how to scale its impact'. It's not enough to just say 'we're collaborative' because, given the choice, many workers will happily stick to their status quo. In order to engender it, you have to help people understand the why of collaboration.

Writing in *Admap Magazine*, Morgan outlines four strategic needs that benefit from collaboration – mutual survival, entrepreneurial impact (tapping into another brand's resources), navigating the rapids (working together at moments of great change) and hybrid vigour (for continual learning and renewal). These types of collaboration yield benefits such as survival, robust transition, ambitious growth and cultural renewal inside the corporation (Morgan, 2019).

FIGURE 9.1   CMOs have a vast opportunity to collaborate more

Who members of the C-suite say they collaborated with over the past 12 months

C-SUITE OVERALL

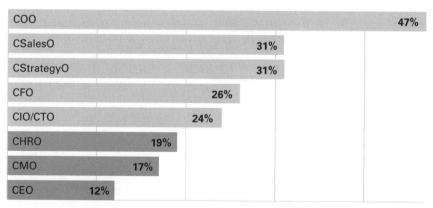

SOURCE Deloitte (2018)

Telling employees that collaboration is needed to ensure the future existence of a company is vastly different from looking for partners with whom to innovate and invent. Clearly communicating the purpose enables people to find the right conspirators to meet the task at hand.

The human hurdle

Another significant barrier to effective collaboration is the reality of people themselves. Whether they're focused on individual success, set in their ways, politicking for position or fiercely territorial, there are myriad reasons for people to give professional collaboration a pass. Whereas musicians are motivated by interesting ideas to elevate their music and build their audience, employees are often motivated by how their actions will make them look good to their boss. Work is not designed for collective input; it's oriented around individuals and their specific jobs.

As Krystal D'Costa wrote in *Scientific American* in an article on workplace anthropology, cooperation may be central to our social evolution, but Western cultural emphasis on individual successes – which is especially pronounced in America – creates a contradiction. Collaboration tends to be limited to overall business goals of the organization, whereas the day-to-day operations emphasize individual performance, even within departments that are organized around a shared principle.

The challenge, she says, begins with understanding the task itself. What are the collective goals and how can individual collaboration help that goal as well as the individual? Do the teams have the skills required for

FIGURE 9.2 A simple model for collaborative growth

	Four strategic needs	
	Enabling the Business Ambition	**Refreshing the Business and Category**
Existential Crisis	Mutual Survival	Navigating the Rapids
The Opportunity for Growth	Entrepreneurial Impact	Hybrid Vigour

SOURCE eatbigfish (courtesy of Adam Morgan)

collaboration? Is it clear who people should collaborate with? Process is the second piece of the puzzle. Are team leaders given flexibility to foster collaboration? Are individuals' cooperative efforts measured and valued? All of this is necessary to bring collaboration to life. As D'Costa (2018) wrote, 'We cooperate when we understand it will benefit us, and this is particularly true when it comes to questions of workplace success.'

Movement Thinking fosters collaboration

We've seen in previous chapters that Movement Thinking within your organization can beget clarity, motivation, trust. In the cases of the companies below, we'll show how Movement Thinking helped foster greater cooperation and collaboration.

An HR community response to COVID-19

Verizon's Christy Pambianchi was steeped in a movement mindset when the pandemic hit. The company was in the throes of its 'Forward Together' movement (as discussed in Chapter 4), which was moving towards making Verizon the *network that moves the world forward*. While great progress was being made under the visionary leadership of CEO Hans Vestberg, in her position as EVP and CHRO, Pambianchi was struck by the historic levels of unemployment, unseen since the Great Depression, and was driven to action.

After attending a forum on HR best practices during COVID-19, Pambianchi spearheaded a movement among CHROs from leading companies across multiple industries and formed People + Work Connect, an employer-to-employer movement. The point of the programme was to bring together companies that were forced to lay people off with those companies that, as a result of the crisis, were suddenly in urgent need of workers. Pambianchi recalls:

> I talked to a couple of my peers and said we can do better than just share best practices. What are we going to do to avoid 30 per cent unemployment and accelerate movement of talent between industries and companies right now so that the time people are unemployed is reduced? We looked beyond the borders of our companies and said we have a responsibility to the world at large and to the labour force. It's really bad for the world that there's 30 per cent unemployment, you know, and how can we help mitigate that?

Working together at a moment of great change, or navigating the rapids, Pambianchi, along with Lisa M. Buckingham (executive vice president and chief people, place and brand officer for Lincoln Financial Group), Pat Wadors (chief talent officer at ServiceNow) and Ellyn Shook (Accenture's chief leadership and human resources officer) sought to ignite a positive movement for a collaborative, inclusive community with a clear stand to help put people back to work quickly in areas of new opportunity.

At the time of writing, participating companies included ADM, Baxter, Blue Apron, Cargill, Frito-Lay, Lincoln Financial Group, Marriott, Mondelēz International, Nordstrom, ServiceNow, Walmart and Zenefits, plus 250 companies, including public sector jobs. Additionally, People + Work was able to quickly scale with the support and commitment to help put people back to work from Business Roundtable, Center for Advanced Human Resource Studies in the ILR School at Cornell University, Center for Executive Succession at the Darla Moore School of Business, Gallup and the CHRO Roundtable, HR Policy Association, Institute for Corporate Productivity, National Academy of Human Resources, Society for Human Resource Management and World 50.

Pambianchi said to us while reflecting on the launch of People + Work Connect:

> When you are wading into unknown or new terrain, as we are today,
> the companies that thrive have retired the word 'competitor' and instead
> build bridges to deliver at speed and scale. Collaboration is a core part of
> understanding and responding to your stakeholders' needs. By working together,
> you signal a readiness to put the challenge before your singular gain because
> solving the problem is the most important outcome.

Whereas these CHROs would in the past have been competing with each other for talent, with the pandemic in mind they locked arms and worked in concert to help save jobs and empower talent. This is by definition a movement ignited by four innovative CHRO leaders. And Pambianchi said she expects this type of collaboration to become the norm going forward:

> We should be competing with each other on products and services, but this is
> a call to action for the world. It's not good for anybody if there's 10 per cent,
> 20 per cent, 30 per cent unemployment. We should be above all else trying
> to get people gainfully employed. Now is the time to build a more resilient
> workforce – for today and tomorrow.

Mahindra: Rising to the occasion

Recalling the study from Deloitte that revealed that a scant 19 per cent of CHROs, 17 per cent of CMOs and 12 per cent of CEOs collaborate, it's remarkable how the Mahindra Group has been able to create an environment for collaboration to flourish in its matrix organization.

Historically, a company with a federation structure like Mahindra's would be mired in complexity. And companies with complexity will likely have the most problems collaborating. But when collaboration is rooted in the culture of the organization, it makes room for possibilities, more efficiencies, more alignment, and sharing of ideas and resources. When Anand Mahindra made autonomy and empowerment central to the company's culture, and activated it by bringing the company's purpose together with the 'Rise' movement, he was able to cut through the complexity and foster collaboration.

This collaborative culture is having financial payoffs. For example, investor Anupam Thareja, the founder of PI Capital and director at Royal Enfield, was wary of Mahindra's federation structure because of the complexity it creates. But his mind was changed when COVID-19 happened. He told us:

> That was the moment I told Anand Mahindra, your federation structure just might work. There was a sense of belongingness, the common culture established by 'Rise'. There was a trust because it was a small set, localized, people knew each other. He was responsible for them. [Each leader] was building that little bubble of himself within, of course, backed by the ethos of Mahindra.

The firm to beat collaborates across functions and up and down the hierarchy. Yet collaboration within companies is challenging and a cultural anathema, even though collaboration is a capability that lies at the heart of new forms of competitive advantage in today's business world – collaboration within the organization and even with organizations that share a common goal. One way to establish this common goal is to define a purpose, and moreover to ignite a movement within which you and your employees can drive positive change, both in centralized and decentralized companies. With Movement Thinking, we can train leaders to establish new strategic significance of internal collaboration and the operational realities of making it work.

KEY TAKEAWAYS

- Despite the intense interest in collaboration, truly working with others can be hard.

- In order to effectively collaborate, it's important to have strong leadership, which, in turn, provides clarity.

- It's also essential to understand that human nature is working against you; people are prone to work in ways they know and be territorial when it comes to working with others.

- A movement can bring a multidisciplinary group of executives together over a common stand or rallying around a cause.

- Movement takes you out of the day-to-day business and the functional aspects of operational work and into issues that live outside the organization. In doing so, differences melt away, commons are established, and a culture of collaboration is generated and rewarded.

References

D'Costa, K (2018) Why is cooperation so difficult in the workplace?, *Scientific American*, 29 April. https://blogs.scientificamerican.com/anthropology-in-practice/why-is-cooperation-so-difficult-in-the-workplace/ (archived at https://perma.cc/7XDS-XUGA)

Deloitte (2018) *Global Human Capital Trends 2018*. https://www2.deloitte.com/content/dam/Deloitte/at/Documents/human-capital/at-2018-deloitte-human-capital-trends.pdf (archived at https://perma.cc/XG8X-BEN5)

Morgan, A (2019) Finding our X: A strategic framework for collaboration, *Admap Magazine*, 1 November. https://www.warc.cn/content/paywall/article/admap/finding-our-x-a-strategic-framework-for-collaboration/129749 (archived at https://perma.cc/CGW5-NTKQ)

O'Brien, D, Veenstra, J and Murphy, T (2019) The makings of a more confident CMO, Deloitte, 18 September. https://www2.deloitte.com/us/en/insights/topics/leadership/redefined-cmo-role.html (archived at https://perma.cc/XGN7-93FP)

10

Mahindra Rise

A decade of movement

The night before lockdown orders were set to keep the citizens of India at home in an effort to curb the spread of COVID-19, engineers from Mahindra Automotive in Mumbai were up to something. Responding to the instant and urgent need for personal protective equipment, the employees were working with the co-founders of sanitary pad startup Saral Designs to make masks. As the pandemic tide swept across the globe, Saral co-founder Suhani Mohan knew her company could make a difference since the technologies behind sanitary napkins and medical masks were similar. The problem she encountered, however, was that no vendors were available for manufacturing.

Driven to help provide much-needed equipment for front-line workers, Mohan approached everyone she could think of and asked for help, including Shruti Agarwal, the executive assistant to Anand Mahindra, whom she'd met while studying at the Indian Institute of Technology Bombay. Within four hours, Mohan received a reply from Anand himself, who connected her with Mahindra Automotive. Together, the two companies had the new manufacturing unit up and running within 100 hours (Norzom, 2020).

Meanwhile, in Igatpuri, teams at Mahindra's automotive factory were trying their hand at rapid prototyping. The country's healthcare system was short on ventilators and they were devising a plan to make them. Within three days, the Igatpuri team had come up with a low-cost AMBU bag respirator that, at only 7,500 rupees (or about US$100), was significantly less than typical ventilators that cost upwards of 500,000 to 1 million rupees (Povaiah, 2020).

These initiatives were unfolding across the Mahindra Group, which employs 256,000 people across the world. Factories were being retooled to produce hand sanitizer, face shields and aerosol boxes – it was like the organization mounted a coordinated response to the health crisis. Except that it was totally spontaneous.

'Amazingly, there was no diktat from the top that all across the Mahindra Group they must do these activities. Instead, individuals made these decisions on their own,' Ruzbeh Irani, president, group human resources and communications of Mahindra Group, told us a few months after the pandemic started. He credits the three pillars of Mahindra's 'Rise' movement as the catalyst for their action: *accept no limits, think alternatively, drive positive change*. 'Because the philosophy of the company is so deeply rooted within the organization, the only question any of these individuals asked was, "How can I help?"'

Until now in our book, we've talked about Movement Thinking in pieces – as a leadership tool, as internal change management and a human resources tool to change employee habits, as marketing, as a framework to drive growth – but Mahindra offers a unique opportunity to look at how a movement can transform an organization over time – in this case over a decade – which we will do in this chapter. Within Mahindra, 'Rise' has been a sticky idea, as we see in its response to the pandemic. Moreover, it's been able to avoid decay. More than 10 years later, 'Rise' is still a powerful idea, if not more so than when it started, and one that is proving to be a guiding force as the company undergoes a change in leadership.

In a 2019 article in the *Harvard Business Review*, titled 'Put purpose at the core of your strategy', Mahindra Rise is held up as the gold standard (Dhanaraj *et al*, 2019). So, how did Mahindra get here? To understand the 'Rise' of today, we have to go back to New York, circa 2010.

The birth of a movement

As with many great ideas, 'Rise' started over dinner. Anand Mahindra, chairman of the Mahindra Group, met with Scott Goodson at Del Posto restaurant to break bread in New York's Chelsea district to discuss the Mahindra companies, where they were and where Anand wanted them to be.

Over the course of the evening, Anand recounted how he had been trying to institutionalize a culture of innovation inside the group to drive growth and positive ESG impact, but that this was challenging with his federation of companies and that the CEOs of those individual companies couldn't align on 'who' they were as a group.

An Indian multinational conglomerate headquartered in Mumbai, with operations in over 100 countries, Mahindra's businesses cover aerospace, agribusiness, automotive, construction equipment, defence, energy, finance and insurance, information technology, leisure and hospitality, logistics, real estate, retail and two-wheelers. With over 150 individual companies operating in 20 industries, it is considered one of the most reputable Indian industrial corporations. At the time of Scott and Anand's meeting, decision-making at Mahindra was convoluted and misaligned, and progress was slowed down by layers of procedures.

It's no wonder Anand Mahindra was grappling with how to align the branches of the organization.

The problem, as Scott saw it, was that Anand was solving for the wrong problem. Trying to unify a matrixed structure based on what Mahindra does was a losing proposition. When the company's holdings are so vast, explaining what Mahindra does as a conglomerate to the world with clarity was an impossibility.

This is something we see often – a federation of companies or matrix organizations gets stuck trying to develop a brand, especially when those companies meet the needs of different consumers. For instance, how do you build a corporate culture without a corporate brand? And moreover, how do you do this for a conglomerate that manufactures tractors and runs a retail chain of baby products? The mistake these companies make is they try to explain to consumers what they do and use the traditional brand-building model to achieve this when they should be focused on telling people who they are. Federations make it especially challenging because many of the companies have nothing in common. That's where a defined purpose comes in, one that galvanizes the employees by activating the purpose with a Movement Inside, then out.

Once you do that, you stop trying to explain *what you do* (because, to be honest, it's too complicated to describe) and instead focus on *what you stand for*. This becomes stronger when the idea you stand for is relevant to people in their daily lives because it can unite a multidisciplined, multicultural organization. And that's why Scott recommended that Mahindra define a purpose that lives well above the companies and their mission and vision that is then brought to life by a movement, aligning with what people aspire for and who they think they are.

At the same time, Anand's ambition was to systematize the company's culture into one that was innovative and customer-centred, and he knew establishing a common culture in the organization with all employees would achieve this transformation.

Scott said at that meeting, 'You don't know what kind of company you have here.' True, it was a multi-headed hydra led by strong-willed CEOs. But it also had a strong legacy of turning expectation on its head and leading with ingenuity in a resource-strapped country. This was the company that took a tractor engine and put it on a Second World War Willys Jeep to beat the oil crunch in the 1970s. Then in the 1990s, Mahindra had the vision to put the equivalent of three years' profit into research and development to create the Scorpio, an urban SUV, in only five years and at a fraction of the development cost invested in Detroit, Stuttgart or Toyota City to bring a new car to market.

Reflecting on that conversation, Anand said to us that he remembers how Scott told him that movements were the new way in which people will build brands and company culture and that those movements have to come from within while also recognizing what is happening in the world around them.

When discussing 10 years of 'Rise', Anand said to Scott:

> You told me that people didn't trust large corporations anymore. You said there was a huge trust deficit and that for a company to be worthy of consumers' trust, they would have to demonstrate a higher-order purpose. And I always tell people that this was a year before the Occupy Wall Street movement began.

FIGURE 10.1 Mahindra 'Rise' launch campaign ad

SOURCE StrawberryFrog

Discovering purpose within

This conversation gave birth to a purpose project. Mahindra hired StrawberryFrog to research the company culture and history, interview key stakeholders across the federation, and visit several factories. But the team also interviewed Mahindra consumers and customers across India and in eight key markets for the company. After a dinner with a farmer and his family in the Indian state of Uttar Pradesh, Scott found that similar conversations played out over the following weeks with farmers and automobile owners and technology buyers around the world. The stories gathered along the way were remarkably similar: families on farms in India, Chile, South Africa and the US all talked about how the new generation was moving off the land and into larger cities. They talked about the challenges daughters face taking over farms instead of sons. In South Africa, India and Turkey, as a larger number of people are educated and the economies continue to rise, more people are rising into the middle class, with new hopes and aspirations and opportunities. These are the kinds of people we identified as Mahindra automotive and tractor buyers.

But more, we were able to identify university towns in the US and in other countries as key opportunities for our movement, because university towns tend to have research centres with people who demand reliable cars and are open to cars from other countries, even India. Within Mahindra, we found that stakeholders inside the global federation of companies in all the eight markets had a universal desire to drive positive change in their communities, a powerful insight that helped us define the pillar of *driving positive change* as one of the key foundations for the 'Rise' purpose and movement. In addition to gathering insight from within the company, StrawberryFrog spoke with non-consumers and cultural and technological thought leaders, futurists and visionaries into the research, topping it all off with behavioural economists and ethnographers, in order to gain a genuine picture of how culture was being reshaped on a global scale. If you speak with your consumers, you end up with a picture of where you are, but when you speak to non-customers, especially in new sectors, you can envision where the brand can be.

Once the data and insights were woven together into a clear universal picture, StrawberryFrog assembled Anand Mahindra, Pawan Goenka, president of the automotive and farm sectors, Ruzbeh Irani, the strategic lead of the company, plus the heads of key companies. FrogLogic sessions (which we detailed in Chapter 6) were held over the course of several days and the insights were shared to the amazement of the participants – mostly because these insights showed a universal story relevant to people across India, across sectors, across the globe. Exercises were conducted to inspire leaders to identify orthodoxies that limited the company from becoming the innovation cultural phenomenon Anand envisioned for the group.

After this meeting, and with all the inputs and feedback received, StrawberryFrog returned from India to its offices in New York to develop the 'Rise' purpose and its three pillars (described in Figure 10.2) and activated with the 'Rise' movement, enabling the company to change the culture to one driven by innovation.

Ruzbeh Irani said that what set 'Rise' apart was that it was not simply a marketing exercise; it put purpose at the core of strategy; it was born from within. The pillars of *accept no limits*, *alternative thinking*, and *driving positive change* coalesced from the interviews within Mahindra. The concepts of shaping our own destiny and challenger spirit resonated uniquely with Mahindra customers across the globe. Irani said:

> All of this meant that 'Rise' as a philosophy was already deeply embedded within our people, and it simply remained for it to be articulated. It is for this reason that the 'Rise' philosophy was championed by all businesses because, even though unnamed, it was a philosophy they already lived by.

A serendipitous series of events

In hindsight, Anand attributes the fact that Mahindra started the 'Rise' movement to two serendipitous events. The first was that meeting in New York, where a casual dinner conversation turned into the launch pad for a company-changing movement.

The second came early in the discovery process. As StrawberryFrog was helping Mahindra understand and articulate 'Rise', Karthik Balakrishnan, who at the time was head of corporate brand marketing, said to Anand that they were faced with a choice: to put 'Rise' out there as a slogan or campaign, or embrace it as a movement. 'He told me it's a nice tagline and it might be a good campaign, but if we wanted to be transformational it was going to take years,' Anand recalled.

Looking back at the two key interventions, Anand told us in conversation that the commonality was that he listened to the ideas of others. He said:

> It wasn't clear to me that I was at a fork in the road. I think leaders have to be able to listen to anyone, particularly someone who comes in and tells you that you're standing in front of something but you're not seeing it.

FIGURE 10.2 Mahindra 'Rise' philosophy

CORE PURPOSE

We will challenge conventional thinking and innovatively use all our resources to drive positive change in the lives of our stakeholders and communities across the world to enable them to Rise

Accepting No Limits

- Think big, think global
- Challenge conventional thinking
- Agility with discipline
- Take well-reasoned risks
- Seek breakthrough solutions

**RISE by
Daring to Disturb the Universe**

Alternative Thinking

- Pursue new approaches
- Celebrate diversity
- Focus innovation on customer needs
- Invent your way to growth

**RISE with
Your Ingenuity**

Driving Positive Change

- Step into your customer's shoes
- Build quality to delight customers
- Forge strong relationships
- Work hard, have fun

**RISE by
Shaping Destinies**

CORE VALUES

Good Corporate Citizenship • Professionalism • Customer First • Quality Focus • Dignity of the Individual

SOURCE Mahindra company information (courtesy of Charles Dhanaraj)

That's when he decided that with 'Rise' he could institutionalize serendipity, that by creating a movement that motivated people to think alternatively and accept no limits, people within Mahindra might be able to spot and act on their own forks in the road they might face. Anand said:

> 'Rise' is about empowering our employees to do good things that bring in profits but also benefit the communities in which we operate. We take on challenges. And constantly look at things differently, looking at problems differently. Most important, 'Rise' is about having a strong social conscience and being driven by the desire to make a positive difference to people's lives.

Institutionalizing a movement

Building on these pillars, the 'Rise' movement had a powerful tagline: 'There are those who accept things as they are. And those who rise to change them.' It had buy-in from the uppermost echelons of the company, and it was responding to an idea on the rise in culture – that large corporations were untrustworthy.

That, in a way, was the easy part. In order for a movement to take hold, people have to understand it and buy into it. To methodically proliferate 'Rise' as a cultural anchor across the Mahindra Group, a structured action and communication plan was developed and rolled out to all employees at all levels of the organization, because, as Figure 10.3 illustrates, the purpose and movement have to be understood by everyone, from stakeholders to employees, investors and the public.

FIGURE 10.3 Movement Thinking versus Movement Think

SOURCE StrawberryFrog

C-suite executives worked together to unify communication and ensure that the message was coherent at all platforms and by every leader. A series of workshops, involving the top 300 leaders of the group, was held to socialize the concept and conceptualize the focus areas for executing the change agenda. These leaders were then tasked with rolling it out to their teams all the way down, as Irani put it, 'until the last mechanic at the most remote dealership in rural India was also familiarized with the "Rise" philosophy'.

Irani told us that five projects were created in the first year to standardize and bring 'Rise' behaviours into human resources processes such as communications, leadership competencies, change management capabilities and recruitment. Similarly, four projects covering reward and recognition, performance management systems, talent management, and learning and development were initiated in the second year. The movement also established a cohesive standard and design guide for all marketing across the Mahindra Group.

As a part of communicating the change agenda, each business trained and nominated 'Rise' champions – a team of 100 change agents named 'Risators' – and engaged its ecosystem of dealers and suppliers to onboard them into the concept.

To kick off the cultural implementation of 'Rise', StrawberryFrog organized and executed training of the top 200 executives in the company. The goal of the sessions held in Mumbai was to present the 'Rise' movement and then role-play with these executives to help them problem-solve through the lens of 'Rise'. StrawberryFrog brought in a dozen coaches and trainers to India and worked through a series of sessions with the executives.

Galvanizing a culture

Once 'Rise' was effectively communicated across all levels of the business, it was time to create tools to internalize the culture in the hearts and minds of Mahindra employees. There were several elements that came into play.

'RISE' PORTAL

An internal 'Rise' portal reinforced the spirit of 'Rise' by finding and disseminating metaphors and stories that showcased behaviour associated with the 'Rise' pillars. The portal contained selected stories, a brand book, videos, games, merchandise, a 'Rise' anthem and an internal e-learning programme named iRise. Over the years, it has acted as a singular and holistic platform to connect employees.

FIGURE 10.4 Brand culture hinges on a compelling brand movement

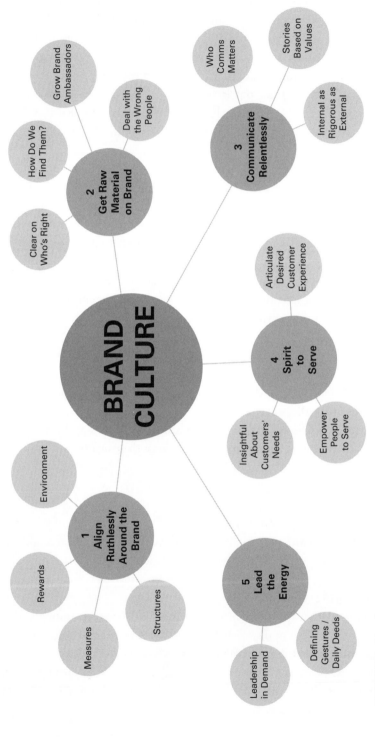

SOURCE StrawberryFrog

'RISE' STORIES

Features like 'Rise' stories encourage people to exchange stories that demonstrate 'Rise' behaviours in the workplace, and a contest was held to share those stories at the department level, the business level, the sector level and finally at the group level, which revealed how people lived 'Rise' in their everyday moments. The stories create awareness around the concept of living the 'Rise' movement and educate employees on how the 'Rise' philosophy connects to their role within the business.

'RISE' AWARDS

Rewarding the desired behaviour is one of the best ways of reinforcing it. Following the same philosophy, 'Rise' Awards are institutionalized to recognize employees who have truly lived 'Rise' behaviour. They are categorized into 'Rise' Awards for white-collar employees and 'Rise' Awards for front-end transformers or blue-collar employees. This recognition for individuals and teams displaying 'Rise' philosophy leads to a uniform understanding of what behaviours are rewarded and reinforced in Mahindra.

Rise inside

As we discussed in Chapter 5, movements can be used internally to change, evaluate and reward the action and attitudes of employees. At Mahindra, 'Rise' was integrated throughout its internal processes, business goals, training practices and performance management conversations, and served to motivate its leadership and workforce to find areas where they could live 'Rise' daily.

For instance, when Mahindra employees progress in their career to a new level, their leadership competencies are assessed and re-engineered to integrate the behaviours in the three pillars of 'Rise'. According to Irani, over the course of a career, it is more likely that successful employees 'demonstrate competencies linked to "Rise" and behaviours that are fundamental to living the three pillars'.

'Rise' is also integrated into its 360-degree employee feedback, feeding into career conversations and those on performance improvement. The belief is that if an employee is assessed on parameters linked to 'Rise' behaviours, they are more likely to focus on enhancing their behaviours to show how they're living 'Rise'.

The movement is also key to Mahindra's recruitment process. Citing 'Rise' as an important factor in recruiting the best talent, Irani says:

It has always been a part of Mahindra's HR culture to empower people and give them early real responsibility. The empowering force of the 'Rise' philosophy gave life to this. Not only would young and dynamic professionals be attracted by the purpose, they would experience others living the purpose as they join.

Rise outside

When it came to igniting the 'Rise' Movement Outside, StrawberryFrog worked with Mahindra to create and launch a multimedia campaign called Spark the Rise, an online platform designed to connect change-makers across India with one another, which was anchored by an uplifting anthem commercial encouraging people from all walks of Indian life to rise up to make a change.

A keystone of that effort was the Spark the Rise Competition, which sought to help people experience the brand idea expressed in the word 'Rise'. The initiative provided grants to innovators, entrepreneurs and regular citizens looking to drive change, supported them through mentorship and workshops and generally helped communicate the ethos of 'Rise'. As Karthik Balakrishnan told Next Billion in 2013:

> When we were thinking about different ideas to take 'Rise' to the outside world, we asked ourselves if doing something unconventional was the best way forward. We looked at one of the key principles of 'Rise' – the principle of 'empowerment' – and asked if we could empower those who are already making a difference. How could we multiply their impact? What could we do to help others 'spark' positive change? (Gutta, 2013)

Ideas submitted were related to technology, infrastructure and transportation, energy, agriculture and development, and social entrepreneurship, and yielded innovative ideas such as a hydraulic wheel lock, a system that can lock any wheel on a car, preventing it from rotating, allowing the driver to get out from wherever they're stuck – useful on India's rural roads – and a rainwater harvester that diverts rain underground, allowing it to seep into existing groundwater, thereby contributing to sources of clean drinking water (Schwartz, 2011).

Spark the Rise wasn't just advertising, it was a big idea that helped establish Mahindra as a champion of innovation. It prompted action and had a galvanizing impact.

The 'Rise' pillars in action

If Anand was hoping to breed a culture of innovation with 'Rise', a look back over the last decade reveals the fruits of that labour. Whether innovation in technology, in how it serves its communities, or how it balances business needs with those of the planet, mapping ideas to the three pillars of 'Rise' has led Mahindra into new territory.

Accept no limits

Mahindra's ambitions to become a global innovation powerhouse driven by technology are summed up in its FUTURise framework, which focuses on advancements in mobility, urbanization, farm tech and IT. This has led to many industry firsts, including the Arjun NOVO, a first-of-its-kind tractor that maximizes productivity and provides the best fuel efficiency, and Blazo, India's first smart truck. Here are some of the ways in which Mahindra's innovation has moved the needle.

Mahindra & Mahindra, the Mahindra Group's vehicle manufacturing corporation, is the world's largest maker of tractors (The Economist, 2020). As such, much of conglomerate's automotive innovation is dedicated to the agribusiness sector. But that doesn't mean there isn't an inherent need for speed among its engineers. When it comes to making vehicles with wheels, Mahindra has broken barriers with super-fast machines that prove that speed can also be ultra-energy efficient.

- **Formula E Racing**
  Mahindra is one of 11 founding teams of the ABB Formula E all-electric street racing championship, and the 2020/21 season marked its seventh in the sport. The team's breakthrough win on the circuit came in the 2016/17 season, and Swedish driver Felix Rosenqvist brought the Mahindra teams two more victories in the 2017/18 season. For the 2020/21 season, Mahindra Racing unveiled an all-British drivers' lineup with Alexander Sims and Alex Lynn behind the wheel (Chaudhury, 2020), and in late 2020 was in talks with Formula E to bring a race to India (Kew, 2020). Mahindra Racing's purpose goes well beyond the realm of thrill-seeking and bragging rights; its racing vehicles are a proving ground for new technologies and production practices. As stated on its website, Mahindra Racing uses the spectacle of

sport to send a powerful and meaningful message to help alter perceptions and accelerate the adoption of electric vehicles in a bid to counteract the climate crisis (Mahindra, 2020).

- **Pininfarina Battista**

  If the 'Rise' movement is about innovation culture, about accepting no limits, about using ingenuity to drive positive change, it's best summed up by its pinnacle innovation: the Pininfarina Battista, the fastest road-legal car ever designed and built in Italy (Mahindra, 2019). The world's first electric super-luxury vehicle, the Pininfarina Battista is the result of a partnership with world-renowned Italian design house Pininfarina, designer of Ferraris, in which the Mahindra Group gained a 76.06 per cent stake for €25.3 million in 2015. With a price tag of $2.6 million and top speeds of 217 miles per hour, the 1,900-horsepower vehicle was one of the fastest electric vehicles on the planet when it launched in 2020 and produces zero emissions. The car blends classic Italian innovative technology that demonstrates the potential of electric mobility in a perfect combination of what Anand Mahindra in Chapter 4 called 'things of meaning and beauty'.

Accept no limits, but not at all costs

This vehicle is what Irani refers to as one of Mahindra's BHAGs – Big Hairy Audacious Goals. He counts the Scorpio and Mahindra's ascendency to become the world's largest manufacturer of tractors among them. But, he points out, while BHAGs can lead to innovations, they're not made at all costs.

One can look to the 70 per cent investment by automotive company Mahindra & Mahindra in South Korean automaker SsangYong for evidence of this balance. Mahindra acquired a stake in the SUV company in 2010 in order to expand its portfolio and technology. 'Apart from sharing products, we also plan to share engine, technology and connectivity solutions, including the hybrid solution,' Pawan Goenka, then managing director at Mahindra & Mahindra, said at the time (Chaliawala, 2018). Indeed, this relationship with SsangYong allowed Mahindra to create the breakthrough technology that powered its first-ever carbon-neutral engine factory (more on that in a bit).

By 2020, however, Mahindra was looking for a new investor so that it might divest itself of its holdings in SsangYong (Reuters, 2020).

Irani says that when looking to stretch beyond known limits in search of those BHAGs, 'it isn't to say that business decisions don't have their place'.

Instead, when business decisions are made through the lens of 'Rise' and its pillars, it serves to help others understand them:

> Being the first Indian company to set an internal carbon price does take away from short-term profitability, but also works towards driving long-term positive change. If a new leader inherits this decision, she will not question why it was done, but instead, understand it derives directly from the core purpose of 'Rise'. As long as the guide to her decisions is also 'Rise', there is continuity within Mahindra to do the right thing.

Alternative thinking

Most banks don't strive to serve the unbankworthy. But that's what Mahindra Finance did when it formed a company called Mahindra Rural Housing Finance, a non-banking financial company (NBFC) that offered vehicle financing and financial services to underserved parts of the country. Most people in rural India were poor and illiterate with no collateral, no identity documents, and inconsistent cash flow that was largely dependent on the season's harvest, not to mention at the mercy of the impact of monsoons. To meet these people and offer them a viable financial option, Mahindra Finance needed to completely rethink basic processes like repayment terms, customer approval and branch location (Dhanaraj *et al*, 2019). The outreach strategy involved recruiting workers who spoke the local dialect to go village to village to reach rural customers (Dhanaraj and Malnight, 2019).

In 2015, those efforts were expanded when it helped rural customers rise above their circumstances with housing finance loans with interest rates of 14 per cent for undocumented rural residents – a marked improvement compared with the 40 per cent other moneylenders offered those same customers. As Charles Dhanaraj, the Temple University professor we spoke to earlier, wrote in *Harvard Business Review*, Mahindra Finance recognized an opportunity and provided a middle-ground option that appealed to its growing base of customers, many of whom would come to Mahindra Finance when they could grow their wealth to start small agribusinesses (Dhanaraj *et al*, 2019).

'Throughout its expansion, Mahindra Finance was guided by its goal of helping rural citizens improve their lives. The company identified and committed itself to value propositions that allowed it to deepen its relationship with its customers, which in turn created additional streams of revenue and profits,' Dhanaraj wrote in *HBR*, adding that Mahindra Finance had grown to become India's largest rural non-banking financial company, serving 50 per cent of villages and 6.9 million customers.

Drive positive change

When Anand attended the World Economic Forum at Davos in April 2019, sitting on stage with Al Gore he reaffirmed his pledge that Mahindra would be carbon-neutral in 2030, 10 years before the 2040 deadline outlined by the Paris Climate Accord (Mahindra Group, 2019). His claim was not an empty one. In November of the previous year, just five months earlier, Mahindra's engine manufacturing plant in Igatpuri had become India's first carbon-neutral – the third in the world – facility.

As Vijay Kalra (who was then CEO, Mahindra Vehicle Manufacturers and Chief of Manufacturing Operations at Mahindra & Mahindra) said at the time:

> We have been able to achieve this great milestone through our continual drive on energy efficiency projects, a sharp focus on the use of renewable energy, leveraging technology for energy management and planting of trees inside the plant periphery to absorb the residual carbon.

One of the initiatives that helped the Igatpuri plant to achieve carbon-neutrality was the implementation of cold testing of engines instead of hot load testing – a process benchmark from its synergy with SsangYong Motors (Nair, 2018).

This is just one of the many initiatives that fall under Mahindra's Rise for Good banner. Much more than philanthropy or corporate social responsibility, Rise for Good is a guide for conducting business that drives positive change for all stakeholders of the Mahindra Group – including communities and the planet, as well as its businesses. Some other examples are shown below.

- **#CutTheCrap**
  As part of using the Rise for Good platform to bring about environmental awareness and social change, Mahindra's #CutTheCrap campaign pledges to establish sustainable waste management practices. Most significant in this effort was the transition of its engine-making plant in Igatpuri into a certified Zero-Waste-To-Landfill facility. Since then, 20 more facilities have followed suit, Ruzbeh Irani told us, leading Mahindra to recycle, reuse and compost over 140,000 tonnes of waste across its companies in 2018 alone. Not only that, he said, but Mahindra factory workers regularly help train other facilities through the process. 'They're mavens to the cause. Having a lodestar that includes thinking alternatively and accepting no limits to drive positive change is an enabler of combatting orthodoxies and getting to a better place.'

- **Nanhi Kali**

  The education of girls is a cause that is near and dear to Anand Mahindra's heart. That's why in 1996 he founded Nanhi Kali, an organization that supports education for underprivileged girls in India. While it was already a successful and noble initiative by the time 'Rise' was launched, it benefited from the movement and is a core component of Mahindra's community focus. Since 'Rise' began, there have been a number of initiatives to sustain the support of the education of girls through Nanhi Kali. A provocative 2014 initiative called The Girl Store helped raise awareness around child sex slavery. Through a website made to mimic online shopping, the project allowed people to donate funds to help buy a girl's education, thus empowering them and helping them break the cycle of exploitation. In 2018, *A Girl Story* was an innovative donation-based film series in which a young girl's future was determined by whether or not there were enough donations to help her go to school. Proceeds of both went to Nanhi Kali.

- **Business for Good**

  Following the mantra that 'doing good makes good business sense', many of the Mahindra Group's businesses have goodness as a core proposition. Take, for instance, Mahindra Susten, a leader in India's solar power sector. In late 2019, the company unveiled Kadapa Ultra Mega Solar Park, a 25-square-kilometre solar facility that was completed in only six months and generates 250MW annually, displacing approximately 275.6 million metric tonnes of CO_2 every year (Pradesh, 2019). And its Project Suryamitra is giving women from various socio-economic backgrounds opportunities in the engineering industry. Overall, the Mahindra Group generates US$600 million revenue from green products, generates 1590MW from solar, and serves rural clients in over 300,000 villages with Mahindra Finance, which, as we mentioned earlier, was born out of the quest to create businesses that help people rise above their current station in life.

- **The Rise Fund**

  Beyond ensuring that Mahindra's own businesses are guided by a higher purpose, Anand Mahindra is a member of the Founders Board of The Rise Fund, along with conscientious capitalists like Jeff Skoll, Richard Branson, Pierre Omidyar, Mellody Hobson, Jim Coulter, Mo Ibrahim, Reid Hoffman, Laurene Powell Jobs and Bono. The mandate of the $4 billion funds differs from other philanthropic ventures in that it includes generating financial returns for all stakeholders as a core objective, in addition to bringing positive socio-economic change (Barman, 2018). Not simply a do-good exercise, the goal of the fund is to help new generations of entrepreneurs develop businesses that are profitable while also delivering positive and sustainable impact.

Rise to the future

When Anand Mahindra launched 'Rise' within his federation of companies, he was the man behind the wheel, the one who was steering his many ships in the direction of helping people rise. Ten years later, however, Anand is stepping down from his role as executive chairman and is handing the reins of the Mahindra Group to his successor, Anish Shah, who takes the role of managing director and CEO as of April 2021.

That begs the question, without its founder, how will 'Rise' evolve in the future? How valuable is the movement as power transitions from one leader to another? How ingrained has 'Rise' become and where does it go from here?

When we spoke to Anish Shah, he told us that 'Rise' is a guiding force during the transition. As leadership evaluates key trends, strategic directions and what initiatives could come on the basis of that, he said 'Rise' has helped shape the thought process. 'We're seeing "Rise" as timeless right now,' he said.

Shah's view of 'Rise' was shaped by what he saw coming in from the outside. Before joining Mahindra, he was president and CEO at GE Capital, a job he was very happy with. In conversations with Anand, Shah says he was very focused on the company's culture:

> That was my biggest question. Will I be happy here? The role, the
> compensation, the career path, that was all secondary. I did not want to move
> unless it was a place where I would love working and I could see myself being
> there for the next 20 years.

That the company's values and culture were evident from the outside because of 'Rise' was enough to convince him to join the company.

Now at the helm, Shah told us that 'Rise' is more important than ever. The pandemic has caused the Mahindra Group, as with businesses everywhere, to evaluate how the world is changing around them. It's also presenting new opportunities for its companies, like producing masks and ventilators and face shields. Regardless of how long term those businesses become, Shah said it's caused the company to look at how Mahindra's businesses can function in a broader capacity.

> We will have to look at transforming many of our businesses to go from
> a traditional play to either a scale or a platform plan, which is a modern
> ecosystem-based play. That is where the 'Rise' philosophy comes in, helping
> people think beyond the limits, because if we are looking at playing in only one
> part of the ecosystem that may not be enough.

This signals that 'Rise' will likely undergo a pivot to address the new landscape.

This thinking aligns with where Anand himself sees business changing in the years to come. As evidenced in his role in The Rise Fund, he's a driving force for community capitalism, which places a priority on the wellbeing and sustainability of a community. As he wrote in *The Telegraph* in June 2020, the pandemic revealed how inextricably interrelated the world is and that community capitalism is the next step for business in the post-COVID-19 world – that purpose will truly come first when it is aligned with the assumption that people act out of enlightened self-interest (Mahindra, 2020). He wrote:

> Even in our 'Rise' philosophy, there is an underlying assumption that it is in our own interest to enable others to rise, bringing us with them. That does not detract from the idealism of the purpose, but exhorts and enables it. Purpose-led capitalism, where enlightened self-interest aligns with community interests, is the future for business.

Being a proponent for this bold vision also syncs with what he hopes his impact will have been while leading Mahindra. He told us, 'When I'm asked about my legacy, my hope is that anyone who worked here, whether for a short duration or their entire career, will say, "I was the best that I could be while I was at Mahindra".' His hope, in short, is that employees were able to rise while at Mahindra, and helped others do the same.

References

Barman, A (2018) Anand Mahindra 'rises' for a good cause, *Economic Times*, 22 January. https://economictimes.indiatimes.com/news/company/corporate-trends/anand-mahindra-rises-for-a-good-cause/articleshow/62598076.cms?utm_source=contentofinterest&utm_medium=text&utm_campaign=cppst (archived at https://perma.cc/4VQH-BPTB)

Chaliawala, T (2018) Mahindra and Mahindra to use SsangYong brand to expand portfolio, *Economic Times*, 26 November. https://economictimes.indiatimes.com/industry/auto/auto-news/mahindra-and-mahindra-to-use-ssangyong-brand-to-expand-portfolio/articleshow/66803047.cms?utm_source=contentofinterest&utm_medium=text&utm_campaign=cppst (archived at https://perma.cc/2YT4-J55F)

Chaudhury, S (2020) Mahindra Racing announces big changes for 2020–21 Formula E season, 26 November. https://www.evoindia.com/motorsport/motorsport-news/big-changes-for-mahindra-racing-in-formula-e-season-7 (archived at https://perma.cc/435J-BW9S)

Dhanaraj, C and Malnight, T (2019) Mahindra Finance: Accelerating growth, Case IMD-7-1700, 9 March.

Dhanaraj, C, Malnight, T and Buche, I (2019) Put purpose at the core of your strategy, *Harvard Business Review*. https://hbr.org/2019/09/put-purpose-at-the-core-of-your-strategy (archived at https://perma.cc/WDJ5-DU7V)

The Economist (2020) The pull of India's tractor-makers, *The Economist*, 15 October. https://www.economist.com/business/2020/10/15/the-pull-of-indias-tractor-makers (archived at https://perma.cc/7GNA-XRAZ)

Gutta, S (2013) How Mahindra's 'Spark the Rise' is igniting impact, *Next Billion*. https://nextbillion.net/spark-the-rise-is-igniting-impact/ (archived at https://perma.cc/TT34-GABZ)

Kew, M (2020) Formula E and Mahindra working towards India race, Autosport, 29 November. https://www.autosport.com/fe/news/153835/formula-e-and-mahindra-working-towards-india-race (archived at https://perma.cc/7CQU-S67D)

Mahindra (2019) Pininfarina Battista – the world's first pure electric luxury hyper GT revealed, 4 March. https://www.mahindra.com/news-room/press-release/pininfarina-battista-the-worlds-first-pure-electric-luxury-hyper-gt-revealed (archived at https://perma.cc/NQ44-EVC6)

Mahindra (2020) About Formula E. https://www.mahindraracing.com/formula-e/ (archived at https://perma.cc/7SFQ-WZPS)

Mahindra, A (2020) Post-Covid capitalism should care for people and the planet, *The Telegraph*, 12 June. https://www.telegraph.co.uk/business/how-to-be-green/post-covid-capitalism/ (archived at https://perma.cc/4YA7-27BE)

Mahindra Group (2019) YouTube, 4 April. https://www.youtube.com/watch?v=-l3niECpwl8 (archived at https://perma.cc/AR8K-4HPE)

Nair, U (2018) Mahindra's Igatpuri plant becomes India's first carbon-neutral facility, *Autocar Pro*, 20 November. https://www.autocarpro.in/news-national/mahindra-igatpuri-plant-becomes-india-first-carbonneutral-facility-41459 (archived at https://perma.cc/UY56-54V8)

Norzom, T (2020) COVID-19: An email to Anand Mahindra led entrepreneur Suhani Mohan to produce 3-ply masks with Mahindra engineers, Yourstory.com, 3 April. https://yourstory.com/herstory/2020/04/covid-19-anand-mahindra-entrepreneur-startup (archived at https://perma.cc/SJ92-PSUX)

Povaiah, R (2020) Covid 19: Mahindra gets ventilator prototype ready in 48 hours, thequint.com, 26 March. https://www.thequint.com/tech-and-auto/car-and-bike/mahindra-creates-ventilator-prototype-in-48-hours (archived at https://perma.cc/S926-ZYEL)

Pradesh, A (2019) Solar plant for the Kadappa Ultra Mega Solar Park by Mahindra Susten, Susten Blog, 19 November. https://www.mahindrasusten.com/blog/solar-plant-for-the-kadappa-ultra-mega-solar-park-by-mahindra-susten/ (archived at https://perma.cc/9U64-AJSR)

Reuters (2020) Mahindra to give up control of struggling South Korean unit amid Covid-19, *Business Standard*, 12 June. https://www.business-standard.com/article/companies/mahindra-to-give-up-control-of-struggling-south-korean-unit-amid-covid-19-120061201323_1.html (archived at https://perma.cc/J968-9PW4)

Schwartz, A (2011) Mahindra wants to 'spark the Rise' in India, *Fast Company*, 13 October. https://www.fastcompany.com/1678634/mahindra-wants-to-spark-the-rise-in-india (archived at https://perma.cc/RQG2-6WLC)

11

How to be a galvanizer

So what do you call a company, brand or individual who has activated purpose via a movement? We've settled on the term 'galvanizer', which is defined as 'a leader who stimulates and excites people to action'.

When we think of the consummate brands that exemplify our philosophy – activating purpose through movements – we can't help but notice that they share not just a common penchant for great business results, but also a common spirit. Think about Patagonia, Pampers, Seventh Generation; think about Method, REI and Mahindra. They wear their values and aspirations on their sleeves and invite those of us who believe similarly to join their mission. They rouse us, they energize us. In short, they galvanize us.

Being a galvanizer is not about convincing, coercing, fooling, incentivizing, or even bribing someone to act. A galvanizer gets people to act because they want to, because they agree with the cause and mission that the brand is on. It identifies a shared burning motivation that unites consumers and brands in the same quest. It is a brand or a leader who has identified a disconnect between the way things are and the way they should be and seeks to close the gap between the two.

We set out to write a book that dispelled some myths about purpose and put forth our philosophy. But where we felt other books fell short was on real-world advice about actually doing something with purpose. And as movement-makers for over 20 years, we felt we were in a unique position to offer that kind of 'from the trenches' guidance. In this closing chapter, we wanted to sum up our best advice to organizations seeking to be galvanizers and transform their business through an activated purpose.

We've offered some pretty detailed 'how-to' advice throughout the previous 10 chapters. So in closing, here are seven principles to live by if you want to think and act like a galvanizer. We'll use examples from our previous

FIGURE 11.1 How to be a galvanizer

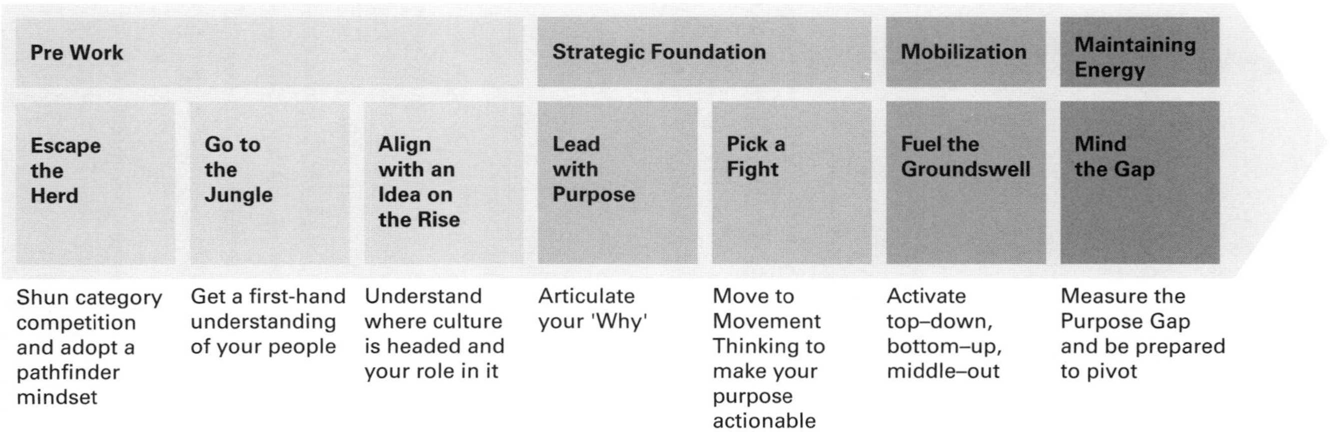

Pre Work			Strategic Foundation		Mobilization	Maintaining Energy
Escape the Herd	Go to the Jungle	Align with an Idea on the Rise	Lead with Purpose	Pick a Fight	Fuel the Groundswell	Mind the Gap
Shun category competition and adopt a pathfinder mindset	Get a first-hand understanding of your people	Understand where culture is headed and your role in it	Articulate your 'Why'	Move to Movement Thinking to make your purpose actionable	Activate top-down, bottom-up, middle-out	Measure the Purpose Gap and be prepared to pivot

SOURCE StrawberryFrog

chapters to illustrate each point and as reminders of the brands and companies that are getting it right (and sometimes wrong.)

Escape the herd

Flee the confines of category competition and adopt a pathfinder mindset

Before even thinking about purpose strategy or a movement to activate it, there's important mental preparation to be done for you and your team. You need to adopt a mindset that breaks out of 'category think' and shuns warfare with industry rivals. This matters because, to be a true galvanizer, you have to break the mould rather than play by the rules of your industry or category. Competing head to head with competitors actually makes you seem more like them than truly different.

Consider how for years luxury cars have been in a game of one-upmanship on the same set of competitive drivers. If one added a safety feature, another tried to outdo them. If BMW made technological innovations, Cadillac was sure to counter-punch with its own version. This ongoing street fight meant cars in the luxury space, which were once highly individual, were becoming commoditized. The differences between the brands were simply getting smaller and smaller.

Then along came galvanizer brand Tesla in 2008. It didn't fit on a traditional luxury car positioning map because it was playing by a different set of rules. It combined two things nobody thought were possible – being a performance vehicle *and* being eco-friendly. It gave people a combination of benefits they didn't even realize they wanted. It was seen as visionary, opening up a whole new way to think about a vehicle. It was true to its purpose of *speeding mankind towards sustainable energy*. Even if Tesla never sold another vehicle again, it has reformed the luxury car category. Next to its innovative and purpose-driven technology, it makes all others seem traditional, inside-the-box thinkers that resemble each other more than they do Tesla.

So the first step in becoming a galvanizer is to realize that when we compete on the same category parameters as our direct competitors, the best we can hope for is to become a somewhat different version of them. A galvanizer is never captive to category competition but rather breaks free from it altogether.

Once you've got out of a 'category think' mindset, you need to replace it with thinking like a pioneer and a pathfinder, pushing beyond the boundaries of what's supposedly possible in your industry or category. For example, the Always brand, referenced in Chapter 3, ignored the category conventions in feminine hygiene and took on the issues of girls' self-esteem – a bold and controversial stance in a highly functional and staid category. The TrueNorth snack brand, referenced in Chapter 1, broke from the repetitive marketing of the snack category and encouraged Baby Boomer self-actualization. REI went beyond thinking of itself as a conventional retailer, took up the cause of greater time in the outdoors and closed its stores on Black Friday. These were mould-breaking moves which helped rally people to the brand's stand. And that's what being a galvanizer is all about.

Align with an idea on the rise in culture

Understand where the culture is headed and your role in it

If you don't compete in a category, in which arena do you compete? For most galvanizers, that realm is culture. They understand their place not just in the industry but in both popular culture and overall society. As such they are current and talked about. They are part of issues that are in the news, and they often make news themselves. Patagonia, for example, is frequently mentioned in coverage of climate change, and Ben & Jerry's on issues of social justice. Understanding and then aligning with ideas on the rise in culture is the way to make that happen.

Competing in culture comes with potential pitfalls, however. That's why some brands never attempt it. This is true, for example, in much of packaged goods, where companies and brands tend towards competing on functional attributes. Think about the seemingly infinite number of skincare brands touting new ingredients or the food brands with new flavours or improved taste, devoid of any reference as to their larger role in the culture. Other brands try competing in the cultural realm and miss, as we discussed in Chapter 1 with the example of Pepsi's Kendall Jenner fiasco. Still others hit on a relevant idea on the rise in culture, but lack the credibility to pull it off – think Gillette and toxic masculinity that we discussed in Chapter 1, or possibly even Nike and racial injustice discussed in Chapter 7.

Galvanizer brand Smart Car put itself on the map by aligning with the rising backlash against overconsumption with its ongoing 'Against Dumb' movement. Jim Beam began moving towards galvanizer territory and became relevant to a new generation when it aligned itself with the female empowerment trend. Spokesperson Mila Kunis helped the brand be seen as fighting the patriarchy and in the process grew the brand at levels not seen in decades. Orexo (Chapter 6) aligned with and helped fuel the trend towards putting the taboo subject of opioid addiction out in the open.

In Chapter 6 we also discussed some of the ways we go about identifying and digging into cultural trends, including secondary trends analysis and semiotics. This work can help potential galvanizers understand not simply where culture is but where both culture and society seem to be headed. Doing this kind of cultural analysis is a necessary early step in the purpose journey because it helps you understand your role in the world.

Finally, aligning with an idea on the rise can ultimately also give you a jumpstart on activation. That's because when you do so, your brand can quickly become part of conversations that are already happening out in the world.

Go to the jungle

Get a hands-on understanding of your people

Sandy Thompson, head of marketing consultancy Fixt, has said about consumer research, 'If you want to understand how the lion hunts, go to the jungle, not the zoo' (Thompson, 2006). By this she means seeking to understand people from behind your desk or a focus group mirror doesn't give you a realistic picture of who they are or how they view you and may leave you misinformed about what really motivates them. When we seek to understand people outside their natural habitats, it changes how they respond.

While we believe that brands should be more purpose-centric than consumer-centric, that doesn't mean we don't put huge value on consumer insight. But we feel strongly there's a wrong and right way to go about gathering that insight. Specifically, to get to your higher purpose, you need to understand not so much people's opinions, but the meaningful role you can serve in their world. To get people to care, act and join your movement, you need to learn not what they *say* they do but observe how they live and what they do. Galvanizers have a deep, intuitive understanding of what people *will* do, and things they don't yet know that they want, that you can't get just by doing traditional market research. Less-used techniques like ethnographic research, discussed in Chapter 6, are a much better alternative.

Too few companies and brand leaders make the effort to get out from behind their desks and observe their customers, prospects and employees directly. A spirits brand came to us a few years ago asking for help with strategic direction for the brand, and they shared with us extensive focus group and survey research among their primary audience – 20-somethings – indicating they felt technology was too omnipresent in their lives. Based on this, the client's hypothesis was their role in 20-somethings' lives was to get them to put away their technology and have more human interactions. Over cocktails made with the client's products, of course.

Realizing that what people say and what they do are two different things, we had a hunch there might be more to the story. Sure enough, when we went out to spend time on college campuses, at frat parties and in 20-something bars, it became clear that the clients' research was misleading. That despite whatever these consumers said in focus groups, when you observed their behaviour, you saw that mobile phones were actually at the very centre of socializing and real-life human interaction (especially 'hooking up'), and that they'd never willingly give them up. The brand needed to work with technology, not against it, to find a meaningful role in their lives.

The same principle applies inside companies with employees. The Japanese have a phrase for direct observation as a management tool called 'genchi genbutsu', which roughly translated means 'go and see'. It's based on the idea that indirect information such as research reports is not the best way to get insight. Rather, actually going and seeing the situation first-hand is more likely to get you beyond the obvious to a real 'a-ha'.

To practise 'go and see' means that leaders don't spend all their time in offices and meeting rooms, and don't receive all their information via emails or reports, but rather go and see for themselves. One advocate for 'go and see', Toyota's chief engineer Taiichi Ohno, has been quoted as saying: 'Don't look with your eyes, look with your feet… people who only look at the numbers are the worst of all' (Miller, 2017).

Galvanizing leaders don't just sit behind a desk – they get out and understand people in the real world. Before embarking on finding or activating your purpose, ask yourself how recently you sat down face to face with customers, prospects or employees and asked them about their lives. Doing so will give you an understanding of your role in their world you can't get any other way.

Lead with purpose

Articulate your 'why'

Armed with a pathfinder mindset and an understanding – or at least some hypotheses – about your role in culture and people's lives, you're ready to articulate your higher purpose. As we stated in the first chapter, this book is *not* intended as a primer on 'finding your purpose', as there is an overabundance of books and articles on that topic. That said, as we saw in Chapter 7, our Purpose Power Index research indicates there are four questions proven to identify brands with a true higher purpose. Asking them of yourself may help you 'land' your own purpose:

- What is your higher purpose that's bigger than just making money?
- What is your role in improving the lives of people and their communities?
- In what ways are you committed to changing the world for the better?
- What are you doing that doesn't just benefit shareholders, employees or customers, but society as a whole?

In this process of articulating their purpose, we've observed that some companies and brands don't aim high enough. They land on a purpose that's either highly functional or emotional but doesn't really state their greater role in the world. This includes purpose statements you've probably seen before, like *We exist to delight customers* and *To make the highest quality products*. Other purpose statements are full of meaningless corporate-speak that leave you scratching your head. For example, *To empower the creation of scalable, bleeding edge solutions and expand core competencies*. Still others just don't ring true. For example, Monsanto, often criticized for causing health and environmental problems, has this as its purpose: *To deliver products and solutions, to meet the world's growing food needs, conserve natural resources and protect the environment.*

Contrast these with the purpose statements of some of the galvanizers we've discussed in this book. For example, Mahindra is *A federation of companies, bound by one purpose – to rise*. Smart Car's purpose is about finding unconventional transportation solutions to urban congestion and environmental issues. Verizon exists to *create the networks that move the world forward*. LifeBridge Health exists to *care bravely*. Walmart exists to help families *save money so they can live better.*

Galvanizers have purpose statements that are clear, meaningful and inspiring. Warby Parker, for example: *To offer designer eyewear at a revolutionary price, while leading the way for socially conscious businesses.* Or The Body Shop: *To become the world's most ethical and truly sustainable business.* Or Patagonia: *Patagonia is in business to save our home planet.* Or Crayola: *To unleash the originality in every child.*

Galvanizers manage to define their role in a way that shows not just what they are good at, but what value they bring to the world at large. If you can do that, you'll attract not only customers and prospects but fellow believers in the higher mission you serve.

Pick a fight

Move to Movement Thinking to make your purpose actionable

Activating purpose with a movement is the defining characteristic of a galvanizer. We stated it before, but it bears repeating: nobody joins a purpose. They join a movement inspired by a purpose. That's why you need to reframe your purpose statement in Movement Thinking to make it actionable. Purpose is by definition often a lofty statement, and it's sometimes hard to know exactly what to do with it – even a great one. A movement can fix that. Furthermore, while purpose points to what is important about your company or brand, it doesn't necessarily point to what is different about your brand – a movement can help you not only activate your purpose but also make it more distinctive and ownable.

The soap brand Lifebuoy is a great example of this. It has sparked a global movement to help reduce child death rates by promoting handwashing. Earlier in this book, we illustrated a range of other good examples, including:

- **Pampers 'For Baby Development'**
  The brand, working with StrawberryFrog, decided to take a stand for baby development rather than just create a poop catcher, and in the process we developed and launched the world's first performance-enhancing nappy that was two times thinner than competitors', allowing for more movement. It led to a collaboration with Pampers, the NFL and Drew Brees, and Olympian parents in the US, the UK, Canada and around the world.

- **Always 'Like A Girl'**
  The brand took a stand against a deeply ingrained insult and sought to rewrite what it means to play 'like a girl'.

- **American Express Stand for Small**
  Amex took a stand against the dominance of big-box and online shopping and stood up for bricks-and-mortar entrepreneurs and community-based businesses.

- **Bombas Socks**
  In starting a movement for dry, comfortable feet for all, Bombas has donated over 5 million socks to places like homeless shelters that desperately need them.

Verizon's purpose of *creating the networks that move the world forward* was reframed in movement terms to become the 'Forward Together' Movement Inside, which is about moving the world forward together, one good deed at a time.

SunTrust's purpose of *lighting the way to financial wellbeing* was reframed to become SunTrust: the 'onUp' movement, which seeks to take people from financial stress to financial confidence. By identifying the enemy of pervasive financial stress in people's lives, and the quest of bringing an end to it, SunTrust gave its purpose a sense of urgency that motivated both employees and customers.

But there are some major pitfalls we've observed when brands move to Movement Thinking. These include failing to define the change they want to see in the world, choosing the wrong enemy (hint: it's not your competitor), or, more frequently, taking a stand that's really just an ad campaign.

Ultimately, a galvanizer is about action and changing important things. Brands like Seventh Generation, Patagonia and REI have a real dissatisfaction with something important in the world and seek to enlist people in transforming it. Sparking a movement is the secret weapon for unleashing your purpose out in the world.

Fuel the groundswell

Activate top–down, bottom–up and middle–out

Internally, galvanizers activate on three levels: top–down, bottom–up and middle–out. And as we saw in Chapter 2, research has shown that the middle layer of management is the key to successfully cascading the cause through-out the organization. Externally, galvanizers inspire mass participation and small group buy-in among 'believers'. Movements activate people rather than just advertising to them.

LifeBridge Health, as we showed in Chapter 5, had successfully created a groundswell in its various divisions by rolling out an ambassador programme for its 'Care Bravely' Movement Inside. Busy and often sceptical physicians actually requested to be included in the training. Verizon's 'Forward Together' Movement Inside is symbolized by a purpose coin, a physical coin given to the top 300 leaders to bestow on members of their teams who were leading by example and inspiring those around them to put purpose at the centre of what they do. After two weeks, recipients pass it on to someone else living the brand purpose.

As we saw in Chapter 5, the enemy of a successful Movement Inside is only having a top–down mandate coming from the C-suite. Employees have to want to participate. It can't be an order. When this happens, energy and enthu-siasm for the underlying movement are either non-existent or quickly fade. A big watch-out for Movement Outside is that some companies have a tendency to turn them into advertising campaigns. There's nothing to join or participate in; there's only a message about the company and its so-called stand.

Without mobilization, a movement is meaningless. By activating top–down, bottom–up and middle–out, you can ensure yours doesn't die on the vine.

Mind the gap

Measure the Purpose Gap and be prepared to pivot

Galvanizers know that energy and enthusiasm can easily wane over time. So they measure energy and enthusiasm. Is purpose still your rudder 18 months later? You need to measure the Purpose Gap.

The Purpose Gap essentially describes the distance over time and down through the organization between a purpose being announced and its continued understanding and use at the bottom of the organization 18 months later. So the test of a purpose is, obviously, not whether it is met rapturously when it is unveiled by the leadership team, but whether it is still being used by front-line staff a year and a half later (or three years later).

If it's still vibrant and alive, that's the sign that it's healthy. If not, it's a sign that something's amiss and it might be time to pivot.

We measure the Purpose Gap by actually asking people some key questions, usually through an employee survey. The things we measure include:

- understanding of the company purpose and movement;
- feeling like they are living the purpose;
- degree of participation in the movement;
- level of energy and enthusiasm they have for the purpose.

Too often, by the time the vision from top management trickles down to the rank and file, it's lost clarity, energy and passion. A movement can help purpose gain energy as it cascades throughout the organization. But galvanizers know that without paying attention to the Purpose Gap, they won't know if their team is losing energy and passion.

How you can be a galvanizer in your own organization

A galvanizer isn't just a brand or organization leading change in the world – it can also be an individual, a leader that is seeking to drive that same kind of change. For instance, if you're the CEO of a company aiming to transform and grow, the language you choose can affect the outcome. When seeking a new chief marketing officer or chief human resources officer, the job description should say: play a big, important role, leading the company's efforts to boost revenues and profits by *galvanizing* the people who matter to the brand/company inside and out.

While being a galvanizing leader is probably the subject of its own book, we wanted to close by sharing some advice we gathered over the course of writing this book from people who've done it. But first, some advice of our own: if a picture is worth a thousand words, a movement is worth a million.

Lean on your personal purpose

'I'm crystal clear on my personal purpose – to have the biggest impact on as many lives as possible by helping people become their best. I have this urgency to make a difference. That urgency drives me to keep the message fresh, exciting and interesting so that people connect. Because the only way you're actually going to have change is if people find your movement interesting and fun.' (Susan Somersille Johnson, CMO, Prudential, and former CMO of SunTrust)

Share your purpose with prospective hires

'The key to getting a movement started and driving real change is connecting your company purpose with people's personal purpose. You have to focus on telling people the why. Why are we doing something? Is this something that you connect with? Is this something that you're passionate about? Because if it is, then let's do it together.' (Christy Pambianchi, EVP and CHRO, Verizon)

Approach purpose with passion

'If you're going to lead a purpose-driven company, you really better care about it, because at the first sign of a challenge in your business, or a new investor coming in with a different set of perspectives, if you don't deeply, deeply care, you'll fall. And that passion is what's going to drive people to want to join your company and be a part of it.' (Scott Tannen, CEO, Boll & Branch)

Be clear about your purpose

'Deep in our bones, we all want to be part of something bigger than ourselves. When a company is clear about its purpose, it becomes incredibly aligning and unleashing. It creates a level of connective tissue and mutual understanding that is an undeniable forced multiplier. When given a bit of oxygen to breathe, purpose comes alive as a movement that propels an organization to become an even more compelling expression of its reason for being.' (Stacey Tank, Chief Transformation Officer, Heineken)

Listen to your people

'What are your major stakeholders, beyond your shareholders, telling you about the purpose you fulfil in the world? Go listen to your employees about where they feel unfulfilled, where are they disengaged? Are your accountability systems dehumanizing them? Because if your people don't feel seen and heard and regarded, and they feel undignified in how you treat them, you've got a lot of work to do. If every day they feel like another cog in the wheel, then you have not activated their souls to care about what they're doing because you've demonstrated that you don't care about them as human beings and their own growth and development. You've got to start there.' (Ron Carucci, Co-founder and Managing Partner, Navalent)

Start small, then scale

'Creating a movement often starts small. But as a big company, we have the potential to scale and create a meaningful difference. It is clear to me that a positive vision can begin with a passionate individual or a group of T-Mobile employees – I've seen it happen. I've also seen it gain force and result in real, meaningful change as other partners and influencers join the effort.' (Mike Sievert, President and CEO, T-Mobile)

Acknowledge it's not a fad

'Some agencies and brands jump on purpose and treat it like a fad or something that could be used to add a layer to your marketing. But they don't understand quite how fundamental a shift is going on in the world. You have to really see that this isn't an ephemeral thing. That something really substantive and tectonic is happening and this is going to be around for a long time.' (Afdhel Aziz, Co-founder, Conspiracy of Love)

Anyone can be a purposeful leader

'If I were to say that I was the kind of leader that was born to be leading people with purpose, that would be a white lie. Being a purposeful leader doesn't have to be in your DNA. But what does have to be in your DNA is the ability to listen to people who tell you that you're being either short-sighted or blind and that you can't see what's going on out there.' (Anand Mahindra, Chairman, Mahindra Group)

Are you ready to be a galvanizer?

We started this book with a story of how StrawberryFrog evolved from a creative-driven advertising agency to a Movement Marketing agency, into a company helping leaders galvanize people and organizations around shared purpose via Movement Thinking to achieve competitive advantage. We have done it for Google, Emirates Airlines, P&G, SunTrust and Mercedes, and in so doing, set out a new competitive advantage with Movement Thinking. This idea will galvanize you while challenging your habits and the formulas of the past, providing new ways to think about insight, sources of growth and sources of meaning for modern businesses and the people who run them.

All of this emanates from how we ourselves were seeing how the world was changing, that people were expecting companies to be better corporate citizens, they were demanding that brands actually give a damn about people and the planet. Movement Thinking is a tried and tested business process to galvanize human beings – to turn on the switch in people's minds that leads to action instead of turning it off.

Being a leader today means being a galvanizer. What you do, in many ways, is as simple as that: being ready and willing to ignite and empower people to be part of the solution. As much as we've spent this book recounting stories of those who've successfully activated their purpose with a movement, and as much as we've outlined a framework for activation, both inside and out, the truth is, there is no definitive map. There is, however, a caseload of movements that we have designed and stewarded, and through all those experiences, we can add value to those wishing to spark and grow a movement that delivers measurable results. When you are galvanizing thousands, millions of people, you can recognize and appreciate the power of movements to move people, with a business goal in mind. It requires the humility to know that your audience – whether employees or consumers – will be the carriers and translators of your message. It demands deference to the amount of time, money and effort required to authentically activate purpose. And oh how difficult it is to galvanize people with a blank sheet of paper.

As we hope you've come to realize through reading this book, there are excellent strategies that really work to get leaders from A to B. Purpose is not a novelty; it's a business necessity. How you activate it depends on people being champions of the cause. It requires galvanizers. Just like you.

References

Miller, J (2017) Toyota's top engineer on how to develop thinking people, Gemba Academy, 15 May. https://blog.gembaacademy.com/2008/08/04/toyotas_top_engineer_on_how_to_develop_thinking_pe/ (archived at https://perma.cc/N25E-79F6)

Thompson, S (2006) *One in a Billion*, powerHouse Books, New York

INDEX

Note: page numbers in italic indicate figures or tables